Rise Again

Nova Scotia's NDP on the Rocks

Howard Epstein

Empty Mirrors Press
Halifax • Nova Scotia • Canada

Copyright © 2015 by Howard Epstein

Editor/Publisher: Christopher G. Majka
Layout/Design: Christopher G. Majka
Cover Illustration: Wave Washed Shore (1993), watercolour by Alice Reed.
Published in 2015 by Empty Mirrors Press

Dear Sara!
I hope you find elements of interest
in this book.
with much love!

ISBN 978-0-9695104-5-1

Library and Archives Canada Cataloguing in Publication

Epstein, Howard M., 1949-, author
    Rise Again: Nova Scotia's NDP on the Rocks / Howard Epstein.

Includes bibliographical references and index.
ISBN 978-0-9695104-5-1 (pbk.)

1. Nova Scotia New Democratic Party. 2. Nova Scotia--Politics and government--2009-. I. Title.

JL229.A8N69 2015   324.271607   C2014-908316-5

Empty Mirrors Press
6252 Jubilee Road
Halifax, Nova Scotia
Canada B3H 2G5

Printed and bound in Canada by etc. Press Ltd.

Contents

Appendices: Available online at *www.howardepstein.ca*

For decades, Howard has been a collector of lost mittens, which, to add cheerful colour, he displays during the winter on his clothesline. A fan of these, he was sponsor of legislation that made it illegal for municipalities to ban clotheslines.

1

Foreword

T his is not an autobiography. And for that my family and friends are no doubt truly thankful. It is no more than a political memoir, covering at best less than half of my working life, and much less than my whole life. Which maybe even has a bit left to go. I have omitted as much of my personal life as I could. I have written this account mostly for my own interest. Or, as an exercise in memory, now that I have drifted off into the obscurity of retirement. (I am told it is useful to find something to stimulate the brain.) And to ruminate over how I have spent the last fifteen years in active politics. And to try to consider if what has happened has had much of an upside. In politics it is difficult to measure success. This is because often even the simplest looking issue takes an enormous amount of time to deal with. Plus, success sometimes means doing nothing, or could mean just partial success, or heading off something that is not so good. In fact, what I do conclude is that the efforts have been enormous and the results mixed.

In some ways I regret that it has fallen to me to write this account. Although now that Graham Steele has published his book on the NDP government,[1] I have decided to publish this memoir, which was originally just a personal exercise, not wanting only one account to be on the record. I hope other accounts will follow.

One of the many suggestions I have made to the NDP leadership, but that has been ignored, is we retain the services of an official historian. I made this suggestion when we were still the Opposition. I had in mind someone who would have been granted access to records, meetings, staff, and caucus sessions – all on a confidential basis – so that an account such as this could come from a professional historian. But it was not to be. So it goes. Thus, this is not an official history, just my own rambling and unstructured notes.

I am aware of omitting or not dealing at enough length with some important topics. Grade school education policy, arts and culture, the graduate retention tax rebate programme, immigration, the problems the party had with Elections Nova Scotia over certain contributions resulting in a fine, biomass, the termination of a nurse-practitioner working in Digby Neck: these are all examples. Unfortunately, this memoir is already lengthy. I have written about what I knew best, and could best attest to.

Like all authors, I wonder about my potential readers. Those who are looking for references to themselves can check the index. To the extent I do hope for readers, I hope for my children to have a look, and beyond that for party members curious about how things have seemed to one active participant, and for planners of future political undertakings, especially of the NDP brand, to take note. While this is a local Nova Scotia story, our history has been all too typical of progressive politics throughout Canada – indeed elsewhere as well. There are lessons to be learned from this account. Perhaps not the ones I point to, but lessons nonetheless. Here is undoubtedly the place to quote P. J. O'Rourke: "We journalists [and memoir writers] don't have to step on roaches. All we have to do is turn on the kitchen light and watch the critters scurry."[2] In politics as in the rest of life, it is not always clear who is who in such analogies. There is always a lot of scurrying, the light is always weak, and what sort of critters we all are is not easy to discern.

I know that many of the residents of Halifax Chebucto, the constituency that elected me five times, have wondered what I have been up to the last few years. Before my retirement from electoral politics, the comment was sometimes made that they did not hear so much of me in the news. This is true. The position of a backbencher in a majority govern-

Retiring as the MLA for Halifax-Chebucto.

ment is mostly a low profile one. The publicity, authority, and decision-making are all left to the members of Cabinet. The rest of us have more limited functions. Still, we do serve on committees, we do participate in full caucus meetings, we do get the opportunity to raise issues inside the government, and we do speak in the House. As I hope this account will show, I have been busy all of the time I have served as MLA, even though it has not always been visible to the public. Not having been in the Cabinet does, however, limit the information I have.

Life does not offer what we expect. Or maybe hope for. Or even plan and train for. It offers lessons. And though it is not always immediately clear what those lessons are, they are always there to be found.

My own life plans have varied. At one point I studied literature and thought of teaching it at university. Work has taken me away from Nova Scotia, first to Ottawa, and later twice to Toronto. I have practiced law on my own; have worked for the largest law firm in the nation (the Federal Department of Justice); have taught at five universities; been executive director of a variety of organizations, most notably the Ecology Action Centre; have represented unions; have specialized in the legal aspects of psychiatry, and then of land use planning, a subject I taught at the Dalhousie Law School for almost twenty years. And I have been a politician, elected seven times in central Halifax first to city council and then to the Legislature. On the face of it, this has been a peripatetic career. But at the same time it has not been directionless.

In all of the work I have done, I have sought to find ways to effect positive change in the world at large. Many people would probably say the same of their lives. My focus, however, has been politics – broadly understood. To me politics means public policy. We could say, in an Orwellian variation, that all actions are political, only some are more political than others. Along those lines, a lot of my life has been a sort of training for political life. I have always read economics, have offered volunteer services to or served on the boards of community agencies (Canadian Civil Liberties Association, St Joseph's Children's Centre, the North End Community Health Centre, Harbour City Homes, Heritage Trust of Nova Scotia, Ecology Action Centre, Greenpeace Canada, Canadian Centre for Policy Alternatives), and most of my work has involved advocacy over public policy such as environmental sustainability, post-secondary education, and land use planning. As early as age seventeen I thought someday to be a cabinet minister in Nova Scotia: in the Education or Justice portfolios, I then thought.

It was to be more than forty years after those first uninformed and imprecise thoughts, that the actual chance to be in a Cabinet occurred. As is well known, Darrell Dexter did not put me in his Cabinet, not in 2009 after the election, and not on the two subsequent occasions when there were either vacancies or expansion in the size of Cabinet. Of the small group of six NDP MLAs first elected together in 1998 and then re-elected in each subsequent election (Dexter, Corbett, MacDonell, MacDonald, Estabrooks, and Epstein) I was the only one not given a portfolio. Naturally, I have not been happy with this exclusion. But it has not been my life's focus, and I have long since reconciled myself to this frustration of a hope. On election night 2013, as we were about to be thumped at the polls, I was interviewed on TV and bluntly said what I thought accounted for this dramatic ouster. I ascribed the loss to a contrast between lavish funding of big businesses with cuts to important government services like education. Graham Steele, also retired from politics, and a CBC com-

During the 2003 election campaign: John MacDonell, Jerry Pye, Darrell Dexter, Dave A. Wilson, Howard Epstein, Joan Massey, and Peter Delefes.

mentator for the evening, said I had just never gotten over not being appointed to Cabinet. This was simply not the case. I am a truth-teller. If someone asks me what I think, I tell them. Being forthright on election night had nothing to do with not having been in Cabinet. By the time of the 2013 election I had decided a year earlier not to run again, and had also internally processed my backbencher status (see Appendix 9, my farewell speech to the Legislature on April 29, 2013 for my parting observations). In pointing to the contrast between how our Government had handed out money to very profitable corporations while at the same time cutting important services' budgets such as in education, I was not sniping but just stating the obvious. As the votes came in that night, it was clear that Nova Scotians thought as I did.

Still, I have heard myself described as "the fellow who lost all the debates" or in a generally meaningless bout of name-calling, "not a team-player," and these memoirs – which without a doubt are critical – as overly negative. It is certainly the case that I have been unhappy with my Government. I was profoundly disappointed. But this has had nothing to do with my own fate, and everything to do with the policy decisions made. At one point Frank Corbett was moved to say at caucus that no one had gotten less of what they wanted than me. In the context, it was clear he was talking policy, not the absence of a Cabinet appointment

It is certainly true that I do not like losing debates. At Law School, my partner Geoff Fulton and I won the debating championship three years in a row. I know how to debate, but in politics what has been obvious is that the debates have for the most part not been about the facts, or about what is the best policy for Nova Scotians, or about being articulate. Politics in our caucus has, more often than not, been about the best strategy to get re-elected. And major policy decisions were either never brought to caucus (e.g., Muskrat Falls, or the amount of money to go to Irving for the shipbuilding contract), or were brought only after the decision had been announced or a commitment made. It emerged over the first year that the Premier's Office was the locus of decision-making; the opportunity for caucus to influence events diminished rapidly.

After the 2009 election victory, Darrell quickly invited anyone in caucus who was interested in Cabinet to come individually for an interview. I remember our chat well. He and Susan Dodd (a professor at the University of King's College and a long-time NDP election planner) were the others present. Darrell quickly moved to the question of whether I would resign from Cabinet if decisions I did not agree with were taken. My reply was that if there were open and transparent decision-making, and honest debates held, then losing a debate would not be an occasion for resignation.

I have frequently been asked why I was not appointed to Cabinet. The question is really one for Darrell. My own thoughts are and cannot be other than speculation. But this point of a concern over a potential resignation is as close as I can come to any explanation that Darrell might offer. I have never heard him say anything else.

It is an interesting point. At its core it is flawed, of course. Whether in or out of Cabinet, any MLA could always resign from their party's caucus. To have a cabinet member resign might be more embarrassing, but in either situation a resignation is a problem for a Government. I tend to think something else was at work, and that the talk of resignation was a proxy. Darrell knew full well that he was going to be pursuing policies I would not like. Not having me in Cabinet achieved two things. One was that he did not have to listen to critical opinions more than necessary, or encounter a minister who would go slow on implementing disliked policies, or be in a position to bring forward agenda items that he was not interested in. The other is that a signal was sent to the progressive wing of the party, and to progressives in community organizations, that their views were not going to have any voice in the Cabinet. This was particularly read in that way inside the province's environmental movement.

There may have been another consideration. Cabinet ministers have some automatic profile and a potential power base inside any party. Darrell may have considered me as a potential rival for party leadership. This was never actually the case. My hopes had always been to be in a progressive NDP cabinet. I was never interested in the party leadership. The rituals of formal occasions have never interested me. I never needed the ego stroking of being the 'chief.' I never ran for leadership on the occasions when there was a vacancy, or even took steps to organize a leadership campaign. When asked I was always clear that I was not interested. I am a worker, a policy person, someone who wants to get things done.

What is noteworthy is that over the four years of our Government, I did not resign. The resignation that did come was by Graham Steele, our Minister of Finance, precisely, he now tells us, because he disagreed with an important policy decision. Given Graham's administrative competence, this was a serious loss. I was often sorely provoked, and did seriously consider sitting as an independent on a couple of occasions, but I did not leave. My staying was not determined by loyalty to Darrell, but to the basic ideals of the party, and a faith that we can and will do better.

Elizabeth May has been a friend for many decades. I admire her work. She has raised with me – as have others – the possibility of joining the Green Party. Federally, the Greens are starting to move. And in New Brunswick, David Coon, the party leader has just been elected as an MLA in Fredericton. Here, though, the provincial party is virtually non-existent. In the absence of a system of proportional representation, moving to a Nova Scotia Green Party, or starting another party, is a doubtful undertaking. Not impossible, and if the NDP continues to fail to adhere to progressive policies then this may well be an enterprise worth exploring.

There is certainly talk out there. But for now, at least until the question of new leadership for the NDP has been resolved, most progressives are either staying with the NDP, or putting their efforts into NGOs, or are waiting – but not yet starting a movement for a new party.

At every turn, there were viable alternatives for the NDP in power. However, the NDP has been corrupted through an internal takeover by those who see themselves as professional career politicians and their staff whose main consideration is their own jobs. They have decided that the way forward for the NDP is to be in the "middle." To be "mature" as Ontario NDP leader Andrea Horwath has said, a term Maureen MacDonald as our interim leader also uses. In the 2014 Ontario campaign Horwath's NDP flopped; they were rightly skewered by *The Globe and Mail's* Jeffrey Simpson for their platform:

> "This is conservative talk. [...] Apart from the generalized bankruptcy of the NDP's platform, what is striking about the party's approach is the strange mixture of traditional nostrums with conservative populism. [...] Here is a province that ... has a poverty challenge, something that used to be a staple of New Democratic discourse. Yet the provincial NDP all but ignores this challenge. It won't touch income inequality or have much to offer about trying to lift up the disadvantaged. Instead it frets about gas prices ... presumably because, like the other parties, it is now fixated on the ill-defined 'middle-class.'"[3]

This is exactly where Darrell was and the party leadership remains. There is, "no DNA test for belonging to the NDP," said Darrell on various occasions. In fact, this is not quite the case. There are core traditional worldviews that have characterized the NDP. The NDP is the party of labour more than of big business. It believes in the efficacy of the state as an instrument of economic power to achieve a more equal society. It is open to public ownership. It looks nationally and internationally to connect with other progressives. It promotes peace. It values and supports social infrastructure. It has a strong environmental tradition. There is a set of party policies that have been adopted by policy conventions over the decades. There are the indicators of party thinking conveyed by speeches or bills introduced in the Legislature while the party was in

Opposition. All of these position the NDP at an identifiable place on the political spectrum.

To achieve transformation of our society, the core problem is not absence of knowledge of what a better way of life would look like. The barriers to change are something else. In virtually any aspect of life – energy, fishery, forestry, agriculture, mining, manufacturing, land use planning, delivery of core services, economic development, taxation – we know better ways of how to go about doing things. This is not to say that all scientific or technical problems have been solved, far from it. But absence of knowledge is not what leads to no or slow change. The true barriers to change are the absence of political will, and adherence to the *status quo* because the *status quo* is already profitable, or because the process of change is dislocating. But transformation is essential. Our government was not a transformational government.

In Opposition times we had signaled something quite different. For the most part we had brought forward sensible policy suggestions in line with traditional party values. At the same time, there are other factors in the Canadian NDP record. There have been provincial governments in British Columbia, Saskatchewan, Manitoba, and Ontario. To some extent these have been centrist governments, though not completely. The NDP in British Columbia under Dave Barrett was ever mindful of core NDP values. Bob Rae's government in Ontario struggled with a difficult recession, and did some good work, even though it abandoned its promise of a public automobile insurance scheme, and reopened public sector contracts to impose cuts. York University scholar James Laxer nailed it in 1996:

"Within a few years it became apparent that the NDP provincial victories were merely Pyrrhic. So compromised were the New Democratic provincial governments by the policies they adopted and by the times in which they governed that social democrats descended to a level of despair unparalleled in their history. [...] Instead of changing the country in ways their constituency had hoped for, NDP provincial governments jettisoned most of what they had long espoused, adopting instead the new and alien politics of restraint, cutbacks and adaptation to globalization. The lesson learned from this turn of events was a devastating one: social democrats do not deliver on their promises. They talk a good game, but in the end, their policies differ little from those of other parties."[4]

In Nova Scotia we had hoped for more. It was not to be. To explore recent history is not to ignore the future. It is to ensure there is some chance that the future might be different. It is never easy to look back and to admit to having gone astray. It is painful. It is uncomfortable. It is embarrassing. And it is necessary.

Our party's current leadership, despite the language they are using, do not "get it." The party's April 2014 Convention showed a serious disconnect. On the opening night Darrell was honoured and spoke about the party's record of accomplishment in office: "I'm pleased with what we did and in what we accomplished...." In other words, we have nothing to apologize for. Much the same message came from party president, lawyer David Wallbridge: the Government did a lot of good things but, "unfortunately we did not bring the public along with us." The next day, Maureen as acting leader, did apologize. Sort of.

"We made some mistakes in government. The disappointment was made perfectly clear to me at the door. Our hard work was not enough. For the mistakes we made I am deeply sorry. I can assure you, we get it. The NDP gets it. And we've been given a time out."

This statement would have been promising, and uniting inside the party, except that the specifics were not there. As examples of lessons learned, she said that the government did not act quickly enough to deal with the Great Recession; internally it, "tried to do too much, too quickly;" and then there was the perpetual fallback, "a failure to communicate." After her speech, elaborating on the nature of the economic "mistakes" she explained it took too much time to start getting infrastructure projects out the door, giving the example of the new Convention Centre, the new Halifax Central Library (not an NDP-initiated project), and the shipbuilding contract. This was bad enough, since it is the Convention Centre and the big money for the Irvings that were the focus of a lot of anger from long-time party supporters. She went on to scold critics saying, "we are now a mature party," that is, "in a new stage, with new conversations not old debates," and we should, "not be out of the mainstream," and should, "not become a debating club for the comfortable." That, "we need practical solutions."

Comment among delegates was highly critical of Maureen's speech. It was seen as perpetuating exactly what had been problematic with the Dexter government. It restated exactly what long-time party supporters did not like and what voters at large rejected. In no conceivable way is this "getting it."

The Nova Scotia NDP is at a critical point in its history. We have been reduced to third-party status. We are virtually bankrupt. Membership has declined to an unsustainably low level. Leadership is preoccupied with defending its record and is resistant to serious change. None of this augurs well for our chances to form government again or to achieve status as an inspiring source of ideas. The drift to the middle has not served the NDP well in British Columbia or in Ontario, nor did it here, nor will it federally come the 2015 election. The examples could not be clearer.

For the most part, this account covers the period 1998 through 2013, and was mostly written in May–June 2013, then supplemented after the October 2013 election, with some tinkering since then. I initially found it somewhat therapeutic to get thoughts down on paper, but then just plain painful and sometimes enraging to revisit topics. Thus it became the opposite of therapeutic and took somewhat longer to complete than planned. But necessary.

In this account I have explored topics or events that I witnessed personally or that became part of the public record. As I have continued to chat with Dippers or members of the general public, I have heard stories of encounters that confirm that our government's interactions were even worse than I knew. This is profoundly depressing.

I am painfully aware that much of this account may sound like an extended, "I told you so." And although in many instances I did tell my colleagues so, I do know that no-one's political judgment is perfect. Here is a good example of one of my own failings from 1998 our first year as Official Opposition:

This memorable cartoon of me holding a shotgun, with rounds fired off in all directions, and saying, "Now we ask questions," was in *The Chron-*

Republished with permission from The Chronicle Herald.

icle Herald, June 5, 1998. Shoot first, ask questions later. Funny, and apt, and in some way the whole event shaped much of my career inside the party. Here is what it was about.

The minority Liberals were about to bring in their budget. As Finance critic reporters asked me whether the NDP would be supporting it. I said no, that a budget vote was not so much about its contents and more about whether you had faith in the government – it was a confidence vote. Since we had no confidence in the Liberals to govern, we should not support their budget, but attempt to bring them down. Indeed, that was the whole point of the reporter's question, which after all was being asked about an unseen budget.

My points made sense to me. But they were a novice's thoughts. As was brought home to me in a swift meeting with Robert Chisholm and Chief of Staff, Dan O'Connor. First, important positions on policy were not for individual MLAs to determine; caucus as a whole should discuss these things. If any one person in the party could unilaterally commit it, it was the leader, not a critic. Second, with a statement made on the record, public attention would shift away from the NDP and move to the Tories, thus offering them some extra publicity: would they support the budget or not? It was clear Robert thought I wanted to be party leader and was acting independently so as to establish an internal constituency of support, and begin to move in that direction. In fact, as mentioned previously, this has never been my interest. What I always hoped for our leaders was that they would be better leaders, not that I would ever take the job myself. But ever since that time, leaders have regarded me as not a team player, as too independent, and as a potential rival to be sidelined.

It is certainly the case that from time to time I have found myself in disagreement with some of my colleagues. In this I have not been alone. Kevin Deveaux for example dissented from the caucus position on property tax subsidies for the Ultramar oil refinery and said so in the Legislature. Graham Steele disagreed with caucus on supporting some of John Hamm's proposed changes to the expenses system, and voted against them. Later, Sterling Belliveau disagreed with the elimination of Shelburne as a stand-alone seat as a result of the electoral boundaries process, and he said so. This example was particularly unusual in that Sterling was then in Cabinet and there is a long parliamentary tradition that a cabinet member who wants to publicly disagree with his government's policy on something should give up their cabinet position. When we were in opposition, I disagreed with giving support for changes the PC government was proposing to the *HRM Charter* so as to change the legal tools for land use planning in the Halifax downtown. The speeches about Bill 181 from November 2008 make clear the differences.[5]

How do caucuses adopt positions? In ours, the process has not been entirely successful. Most of my colleagues expect use of consensus. Consensus means that everyone agrees, or if some disagree they do not so strongly disagree that they do not want to live with the decision. Our experience was that this is not always how it works. Over time there was drift towards most serious decision-making being in the hands of the leadership, with caucus being informed later, not seriously consulted in advance.

The fifteen years 1998–2013 have been a busy time at large in the world. With the end of the Cold War, Russia underwent internal restructuring that has left it corrupt but still powerful. Nations such as China and India have enormous populations and are well along in developing their economies, though both have enormous internal problems of poverty, pollution, and ignorance. The USA, our neighbor and main business partner, suffered a traumatizing attack in 2001. It responded by undertaking wars in Iraq and Afghanistan that are not over yet, and which seem to have been virtually pointless. There is serious and widespread upheaval throughout the Middle East, with what future it is impossible to predict. Africa is beset by wars and other afflictions as it continues its long post-colonial struggle. The world economy took a big dive after 2007 and has not yet solidly recovered. Europe was especially hard hit, and its financial system seems weaker than expected. The globe experienced the hottest several decades since a thousand years ago, and global climate change occasioned by human activity is a well-accepted fact among scientists. The oceans are in trouble from this, from overfishing, and from pollution. We still rely on carbon as the main energy source. The price of oil went over $100 per barrell, then recently fluctuated wildly, and has seriously affected economic activity. Parts of the world suffer drought and continue to live in poverty. The move to living in urban areas has accelerated enormously, resulting in many people accommodating themselves precariously in slums, with what health and social consequences no one knows. Pandemics spread from new diseases. The connectedness of the world through new technologies had advanced at an astonishing rate, allowing the creativity of the contemprary generation to be displayed beautifully. In the meantime we here in Nova Scotia have been paddling our little boat in the midst of this enormous stormy turmoil.

My thanks to all those who read the manuscript prior to its publication; also to Ray Larkin and Cliff White for their ongoing friendship, and especially for their support this past couple of years; to the Canadian Centre for Policy Alternatives which continues to do inspiring work; and to the wonderful staff at the Legislative Library. I am hugely grateful.

2

Why We Lost in 2013

Every day is a gift. It is a fresh opportunity to tackle what you've left undone previously. It is a fresh opportunity to do better what you had tried to do before, but had not done well enough. It is a fresh opportunity, but one that always comes with its own history.

On the morning of March 25, 1998 I rose early and walked downtown heading to City Hall and my day's work as a councillor. The day after any election always has a small but distinct feeling of change. Certainly that is apparent on the streets. The candidate signs, which had been a colourful feature of the streetscape (and for some, a bit of an aesthetic nuisance), have been mostly removed, crews having collected them overnight. Minds have moved on. For those heavily involved, the immediate pressure of a campaign has dissipated. Winners and losers have had a small amount of time to adjust and to think about what comes next. And so it was. In the previous day's election, the NDP had jumped forward, winning nineteen seats in the Nova Scotia Legislature, a tie with the incumbent Liberals, and the first time so many Dippers had been elected in the province. I was among them. The news was dominated by the results. The air of change was aided by some early spring mildness.

As I strolled along Spring Garden Road, thinking it over, I passed restaurants and coffee shops, with big windows facing the street. The same thing happened at two of them: as I passed by, people got up from their seats and applauded. This was completely stunning. Wonderful, but stunning. It was a moment that has stayed with me as one of the most remarkable in many years of political experience.

I waved. Probably I beamed. But I did not view this as a personal compliment. It was the result of history. It had to do with the long years Alexa McDonough had spent leading the Party and building its credibility. It had to do with the hard work of NDP MLAs like John Holm. It had to do with the attractiveness of Robert Chisholm as an enthusiastic young leader. Clearly it expressed something critical. People had voted for significant change. They were looking for it. They were looking for politics to be done differently in our province. They had hopes. And they had chosen the NDP as the vehicle of those hopes. In crucial respects, since finally becoming Government in 2009, we let them down. I apologize.

Apologies are complex matters. I can apologize on my own behalf, though indeed, as I hope will emerge, I have done my best over time to speak up at the caucus table for core progressive principles and measures. So for myself, I apologize for problems with the results, not so much for my efforts. An apology is a very personal undertaking. Thus it is not possible to apologize on behalf of others. They have their own thoughts to think, and their own conclusions to reach. Apologies imply a hope for some forgiveness. And they have to be assessed as to sincerity, coupled with actual solid indications of change in behaviour.

Being interviewed by the media.

At the NDP convention in 2014, interim leader Maureen MacDonald started her speech with what sounded like an apology, but turned out not to be. It has been depressingly clear that the party leadership remains blind to what led to the 2013 defeat. Maureen claimed, "We get it." Very few in the room were convinced. For her examples of errors she cited the economy, being too ambitious, and communications. What the government did wrong about the economy, she said, was fail to get enough jobs in place soon enough. In her press conference afterwards, she specified the Halifax Convention Centre as an instance; apparently the only problem she saw is that the Centre is not being built fast enough. Traditional party supporters – virtually all opposed to this boondoggle project – have been outraged. This was no apology, not to party members, not to the public. We have a long way to go.

Fundamental to understanding why we lost in 2013 is a correct understanding of why we won in 2009. The party leadership was and remains convinced that the win came through centrism. But that is not so. A strong part of the win came from having held out the promise of being different. The failure to act as a Government in the ways suggested when we were the Opposition proved fatal.

The newspaper headlines in 2009 read, "Orange Crush," a triple ambiguity: the orange team had crushed its opponents; a baffling reference to the popular sweet drink (Attractive but with limited nourishing qualities?); and the voters had a crush on the orange team (Momentarily intense but destined not to last?). All prophetic, as it turned out.

A cynical political aphorism runs as follows: "No matter who you vote for, they turn out to be the government." Such an attitude can be simply humor, mild cynicism, or even bitter disappointment. Higher expectations for government is something the NDP promoted while in Opposition, benefited from in 2009, and then suffered from in 2013 as voters slumped in their support through disappointment. "As ye sow, so shall ye reap." (*Job* 4:8) Or as is said in more secular circles, "What goes around, comes around."

And yet, it has to be made clear just what people were disappointed in. In fact, the NDP Government suffered no major scandal of its own, certainly nothing in terms of corruption (the MLA Expenses Scandal was all-party). A reasonably honest government was, in and of itself a serious accomplishment. Long-time *Globe and Mail* columnist Jeffrey Simpson wrote a book in 1988, called *Spoils of Power,*[1] which dealt with political patronage in Canada. "Patronage," he said, "Is the pornography of politics, enticing to some, repulsive to others." (p. 6) The chapter on Nova Scotia makes for embarrassing reading. He noted, "the strong current of political patronage that runs through the history of Nova Scotia." (p. 171) Divvying up the spoils – of paving, of jobs, of contracts, even toll-gating to be allowed to place product with the Liquor Corporation – was just "politics Nova Scotia style." (p. 171) Moving decisively away from that has been one of the significant accomplishments of the NDP in power. No longer is Nova Scotia the worst performer, certainly compared with Quebec and its construction-industry ties to government, or to Ontario and the scandal around its Ornge air ambulance services. Not only was there no NDP corruption scandal, there was legislation to wind up the old Liberals trust fund, widely seen to have originated with kickbacks from companies seeking to do business with the Liquor Corporation. We also adopted other measures to strengthen the electoral process. For roads, the Department of Transportation issued its first five-year paving plan based on criteria of needed repairs for new construction. Thus, we directly addressed the two main topics that had been historic cesspools. An honest government, or one more or less honest, is a major change for the better in Nova Scotia political life. And yet at the same time, adherence to the medical maxim of, "first, do no harm," is not necessarily much of an accomplishment. No one has to feel like slinking home each night, but still, is this all there is?

The Party itself has claimed further accomplishments. The budget was balanced, in the face of a serious recession and a severe decline in royalty revenues from the offshore. Unemployment declined. Gross Domestic Product (GDP) grew. And not all of this was concentrated in the Halifax Regional Municipality (HRM). An effort was made to support industry, and thus jobs, in all parts of the province. The Health portfolio's many troubled topics such as ERs (Emergency Rooms), access to a GP (General Practitioner), long wait times for access to some specialists, cost of medications, and mental health, were all grappled with, and with distinctly more success than had been accomplished for years. Long-term energy costs were addressed through the Muskrat Falls deal with Newfoundland to secure hydroelectric power. And a shift to more renewables in electricity generation, along with serious caps on greenhouse gas (GHG) emissions, occurred. Land was purchased and set aside for either outright protection or for some level of limited use; a longtime target of 12 per cent of the landmass for protected areas was exceeded. Steps were taken to better support those at the low end of the income scale, through the Affordable Living Tax Credit, through the Poverty Reduction Tax Credit, and through improvements to the minimum wage and the Income Assistance system.

The Party also pointed to better internal administration. It pointed to better relations with public sector unions, even with tough negotiations, something to be contrasted with the one-time NDP government of Bob Rae in Ontario in the early 1990s, and in a similar period of recession. And it pointed to plans being articulated for the future: an economic development plan (*jobsHere*), a natural resources plan, one for agricultural lands, one for affordable housing, one for roads, one for renewable electricity, and one for aquaculture.

So why was there a big turnaround in election results in 2013 compared with that initial victory in 2009?

The answer is complicated. And at the same time it is simple. Citizens, I believe, want both vision and competence from their governments. So far as competence, our government was an average government. We behaved pretty much as any Nova Scotia government of the Liberal or Progressive Conservative variety had behaved in the past. We dealt with problems as they arose. We tinkered with departments. We worried about money. We worried about electricity affordability. We hesitated about changing taxes. We talked as if we had a long-term vision but really it was all about getting through to the next election. And that was the problem. After decades of being in the Opposition and promising something different, it was simply not there. And Nova Scotians resented it. And so Nova Scotians turfed us.

Much of the story of our government has to do with jettisoning NDP policy in favour of the drive to bring the budget into balance. During the first year, some work was done on policy priorities. Caucus was canvassed for ideas, and there was some back-and-forth with the Premier's Office before the whole exercise disappeared. What resulted was a group of slogans that then appeared in all press releases: "providing better care sooner;" "creating good jobs;" "making life more affordable;" and "living within our means;" all of which were also meant to drive the overall agenda. The overall preoccupation with getting the budget into balance became a highly problematic dynamic. It was problematic because it led to some unfortunate policy choices such as reductions in funding throughout the education system. It was problematic because it tended to preclude new spending, i.e., spending on new programmes. And it was problematic because the issue of how to get through a recession was being addressed more through public sector expenditure restraint than a mix of other options.

The entire scenario can be put down to Darrell Dexter. In his drive to win the 2009 election he went to a position that had no basis in reality, and that was completely unnecessary since we were likely to win without it. He declared that the NDP would balance the budget within the first year and do so without raising taxes or reducing services. What a ridiculous thing to say.

Although he and the Minister of Finance said that the state of the province's books could not have been known, this is simply not the case. Anyone reading the PC budget from the spring of 2009 would know immediately that the province was headed into a deep fiscal hole. This was apparent from the extent to which the Tory government was relying on revenues from the offshore to fund core expenditures. The royalties were not being put into a "rainy day" fund, or used to pay down the debt. The spring 2009 budget that Rodney MacDonald adopted showed $450 million coming in from offshore royalties, a huge amount. But it was also publicly known that these royalties were about to dramatically decrease, because the Sable Offshore Energy Project (SOEP) was winding down. So no one could possibly have expected to balance the next provincial budget with no tax increases unless they were also about to cut spending irresponsibly. It was just not on. Later, the suggestion was made internally that, entirely apart from the offshore royalties, the province was headed for a big fiscal hole in any event, because of unrestrained spending. This is not what the studies said.

Finance Minister, Graham Steele.

Nonetheless, the fiscal hole that the province "discovered" in 2009 was treated as a major crisis.

It became necessary, therefore, to raise revenues. The strategy the government adopted was to set out a plan to balance the budget in four years through a combination of measures: increased taxes, reduced expenditures, plus growth in the economy. This was the strategy adopted following a formal study by Deloitte that documented the fiscal problem, and then a study by four leading economists suggesting how to deal with the problem.[2] The Finance Minister then set out to hold wide public consultations about which taxes to raise, and by how much, as well as the relative weight of tax increases versus spending cuts. The extended consultations gave Graham Steele as Finance Minister the chance to speak publicly nonstop for many months. Were it possible to dwell excessively upon so improving a topic, one might be tempted to say that Graham had done so.

The core political peril of this scenario is that it allowed the opposition parties to talk unceasingly about how the NDP broke its promises right off the bat – promises that should never have been made. It also focused public attention on the seeming virtue of low taxes.

The result was a promised temporary increase in the HST of 2 per cent. This increased Nova Scotia's HST from 13 per cent to 15 per cent. With each percentage point of HST representing about $175 million in revenues, this change was significant. And later, the proposal to reduce the HST back down to 13 per cent was also significant, because the lost revenues would be virtually impossible to replace. So determined were the leaders of the party to try to exhibit financial mastery that the 2012 Budget promised to reduce the HST by 1 per cent by July 1, 2014 and then a further 1 per cent a year later, or earlier if so directed by Cabinet.

This was a complete delusion.

In terms of specific themes leading to the marked turnaround, I tend to think of them as:

• The burden of incumbency. This means not having the advantage of being able to criticize a government, especially an unpopular one. It also means limited ability to blame previous administrations for having left messes needing cleaning up. After four years in power this point, though with some validity to it, was weak.

• Worldwide economic pressures. This means taking office at a time when the most serious recession since the 1930s Depression was in full force. Recovery has been exceedingly slow. The result has been serious unemployment rates especially outside of HRM, decreased business being done, and thus inadequate revenues for government compared with increasing expenditure costs. Crucially, it has meant voter uncertainty about their jobs and financial futures.

• Disappointment of long-term supporters. This means that the core supporters the Party could usually rely on for votes, money, and work at election time, came to see the government as drifting away from their traditional concerns and priorities. Support for the Convention Centre in downtown HRM, being seen as an uncritical supporter of big business, not being sufficiently focused on anti-poverty measures, and being tepid about some environmental issues, are all examples of this.

• Unfortunate election basics. This means failure to build the Party organization. It also means a bungled redrawing of electoral boundaries. And it extends to the resignation of the Premier's Principal Secretary, Matt Hebb, the Party's most experienced election organizer, to take another job, just months before the 2013 election.

• Cumulative alienation of communities and communities of interest. At a minimum, this means progressive general alienation from the political process: the voter turnout in 2009 was 58 per cent, the lowest ever, and in the 2013 election it stayed at that low level, up slightly and insignificantly to 59 per cent. More specific to the NDP, this means the precipitate decision to cease subsidization of the Yarmouth ferry, with no alternative in place. It means the mishandling of relations with the Acadian community over electoral boundaries. It means virtually uncritical support for aquaculture, which did not go down well in Guysborough and in some areas along the south shore. It means offending parents of school children by being more interested in cutting spending than in improving quality. It means tackling the universities in a ham-handed way. It means clashes with the municipalities over changes to the operating Memorandum of Understanding (MOU). It means public fights with some school boards. It means clashes with the environmental community over weak forestry policies. It means making new economy urban taxpayers feel ripped off through big financial support for what is probably a sunset industry, pulp and paper. It means a peculiar fight with Talbot House. It means resisting a formal inquiry into the Nova Scotia Home for Coloured Children.

• Entanglement in energy issues. This means forgetting the important role electricity rates have played in provincial elections. It means being seen as too close to Emera and Nova Scotia Power Inc. It means boosterism of the complex Muskrat Falls/Maritime Link project.

• Abandoning the brand. This means being seen as not sufficiently committed to creating a more egalitarian society. It means a slow start on Income Assistance reform, and on affordable housing. It means accepting the tax system that the old-line parties had structured. It means being tied to the interests of big businesses after years of campaigning on a theme that said, "It's time to elect a government that's on the side of ordinary Nova Scotians."

• Breaking promises. This means the quick backing away from the one-year-to-a-balanced-budget promise as well as backing away from the promise to keep rural emergency rooms open. Both were unrealistic commitments, and poor policy. The commitments were made for cynical electoral advantage, and later required supplementary reports to "justify" the changes. All of this was so blatant, however, that it immediately undermined confidence in the government.

• Too much centrism. This means believing that the NDP came to power by trying to look like the other parties, and overlooking the change element. It means regular support for business, and avoiding serious steps to support labour. It means marginalizing the progressives inside the Party, the very people who could have been relied on to work hard for the Party in elections and to speak in support of it in between.

• Poor communications. This means to some extent the absence of vision documents, and to some extent being slow to get the Party's message out. This was a regular complaint privately and at caucus meetings. The planning documents for the future were widely seen as vacuous (e.g., housing) or not being followed (e.g., natural resources).

• Stubbornness of the leader. This means his fateful promise to balance the budget in the first year of a mandate and to do it without raising taxes. This means his attachment to his inner circle of staff (an exclusively male bunch – always a big mistake). It means his determination to demand loyalty and to see differing views as disloyalty.

The role of the leader in an election requires a special focus. It is possible for voters to take a different and more positive view of a leader than of their party as a whole, but generally in Nova Scotia provincial politics that is not how it works. A leader carries their party's message. The press follows the leader as a way to focus attention, and bring out party platforms. The leaders debate is televised and parties advertise using the image of their leader. Certainly some individual MLAs who have established their own reputations and base of support can run somewhat independently of a leader, although that is always risky. A leader is chosen to embody the image a party wants to project, and then over time takes on the burden of what a government has chosen to do. This happens because the leader is the main person in the press on important issues, and even when not, it is simply the case that the leader is the embodiment of the party and the focus of whatever attitude the public has formed about the totality of party policies and choices and performance.

There was no doubt that Darrell Dexter had lost public affection. He had been relentlessly promoted as a regular fellow, the affable uncle you would be keen to have over to the BBQ or sit down with for a beer. A regular guy, but still educated and talented. He started in the Opposition as a frumpy guy that *Frank Magazine* made fun of as, 'sartorially challenged,' a bit overweight, but modest. ("NDP fashion police continue manhunt for Dartmouth man ... a Dartmouth-Cole Harbour lawyer who party officials believe to be completely harmless but highly unsightly.")[3] As time went on he campaigned in a blue blazer and open neck shirt (no tie) in imitation of the John Hamm style, and began to link the party

NDP FASHION POLICE CONTINUE
MANHUNT FOR DARTMOUTH MAN

The **New Democratic Fashion Police** are continuing their manhunt for a **Dartmouth-Cole Harbour** lawyer who party officials believe to be completely harmless but highly unsightly. **Mr. Darrell Dexter** was last seen in the **Westphal** area where he was protesting the closure of the Tacoma Drive **K-Mart**. Party officials refuse to say just what Mr. Cardin was attired in at the time of his ~~arrest~~ election to the **House of Assembly**. However, speculation has intensified that Mr. Dexter may have left the K-Mart area altogether and moved on to the **Westphal Laundromat** where the warm water isn't expected to affect his rayons, acrylics, or polyesters.

"There may be some shrinkage but I feel we can still get Mr. Dexter poured into something suitable," **General-Secretary Robert Chisholm** told **Gentleman's Quartley.**

Meanwhile, **Ms. Rosemary Godin** of Sackville-Beaver Bank denied dressing Mr. Dexter but did however admit to, on occasion, attempting to dress former **CBC-TV** reporter, **Mr. Phil Forgeron.**

Atlantic Canada Frank April 21, 1998   29

to his name and image. His name was featured on posters. A billboard above the entry to the Halifax-Dartmouth bridge featured his face and name for months. Literature featured him. The 2009 platform was, "Darrell Dexter's plan for today's families." In logo we became Dexter's NDP. In the 2009 election party-designed lawn signs for each candidate also had Darrell's picture. When the expenses scandal hit, Darrell was shown to have spent money for an expensive camera and to have had his Barristers' Society fees paid by the government for a decade. This did not go down well. And as Premier he appeared in tailored pinstripe suits, cufflinks, and designer glasses.

In the John LeCarré novel, *Tinker Tailor Soldier Spy,* the retired MI5 investigator George Smiley is brought back into service to look for a Russian mole. At one point, hot on the trail, he rhetorically asks a senior member of the service, "Ever bought a fake picture?" Smiley's point is that in those circumstances, and especially if you have paid a lot of money for it, you really want the picture to be genuine – you want it, to the point where you will be blind to the evidence. So it is with hired staff, with elected officials, and so it is especially with leaders.

The Election

"It was invisible, as always," is the famous beginning to Theodore White's account of the USA presidential election that brought John Fitzgerald Kennedy to the White House, *The Making of the President, 1960*. For elections involving millions of voters, and based upon an arcane system of Electoral College votes, results may well be invisible in many presidential elections. (Although the science of influencing voters has become quite sophisticated, and polling likewise.) It is generally quite otherwise in a small place like Nova Scotia. It is not unusual for experienced campaigners to have an accurate feel for the results in their particular constituency. Or for the parties to have a good idea of overall results because of the rolling daily polling they usually do during the election. At the same time, many elections here are hard to call. It is not always the case that a general public sentiment emerges and is palpable. And with three parties competing, the splits in votes can allow winners (both individuals and parties) to emerge with percentages of the vote that do not directly relate to overall level of support.

From the very beginning in 2009, it was hard to miss that change was in the air. John Hamm had been something of a popular Premier. His successor, Rodney MacDonald, however, was widely seen as a failed choice. And the PC party had been in government for a decade.

Proportional representation (PR) is the main alternative to our first-past-the-post (FPTP) voting system. But no party here has ever put this forward seriously, nor did the NDP when in government, although as the longtime third party it had often looked to PR as a way to improve its numbers in the Legislature. In 2009, the NDP benefited from the first-past-the-post system, in that our achievement of 45 per cent of the vote won 60 per cent of the seats. One lesson, if indeed any immediate example were needed, should have been that PR is a system whose time has come, even though at its core PR is a system that relies on tolerance for minority governments.[4] In 2013 there was a reversion to the norm and the NDP took fewer seats than our overall percentage of the votes might have warranted, 7 seats or 14 per cent but with 27 per cent of the popular vote; a serious mismatch. The difference in results had to do with the splits, constituency by constituency.

Early in 2013, the likelihood of a minority government was in the air. Whether it would be an NDP minority or one led by the Liberals was, however, far from certain. What did seem likely was that the voter turn-out would not be high, and that for those who did trouble to vote, their age would tend more towards being over 50 or 55 than between 18 and 30. Seniors tend to vote. But the overall trend of voter participation has been in a long decline. In the 1960 election the rate was 80 per cent; by 2013 it had dwindled to below 60 per cent.

This is an amazing change. However, it is not unique to Nova Scotia. All over Canada, and in western democracies, the pattern is similar. A lot of thought, but not many practical steps, have gone into this problem. Paying people to vote or fining them for not voting are often mentioned as possibilities, though neither seems really an attractive option. Education about the importance of participation is probably the best approach, but likely to be a slow process. Better performance by our elected officials would probably be best of all: demonstrating that electoral politics does matter, and that participation in choosing elected representatives therefore makes sense. It is not that people are not interested in the crucial issues, I think; it is more that many have a deeply cynical view of the undertaking. They choose then either to tune it all out, or to put their energies into civil society, meaning they tackle issues themselves directly rather than look to governments. Strong non-governmental organizations (NGOs) abound. But so does cynicism.

In the campaign, all parties were using fear and hope. The Opposition parties were intensely focused on holding the government to account for every item dealt with in its term that had an adverse element. In Yarmouth and the southwest of the province, it was the cancellation of the CAT ferry link to the USA and its impacts on tourism. In the seats with significant Acadian populations, it was the terms of reference for the Electoral Boundaries Commission that meant dilution of their voting influence. In Cape Breton, it was the persistent high unemployment numbers. In the HRM suburbs, it was pressure on the schools. Everywhere it was the rise in power rates, the general increase in cost of living, and fears about jobs and the economy. But the NDP was intensely focused on the future. The essential preliminary work had been accomplished, it said – the budget had been balanced, the worst of the recession was through, organizational and policy plans were in place, big projects were in the works – the province was about to turn the corner the Premier regularly said, using a phrase with its unfortunate echoes of Depression-era politics ("Prosperity is just around the corner," said Herbert Hoover in 1929 in the face of the stock market crash).

Not only was the NDP inviting the public to look forward, it was able to remind voters of every misstep of previous Liberal and Tory governments, thus warning of the dangers of reversion to the failed past. The Liberals had cut back on child dental care, had laid off nurses, had tried to hide a $600 million deficit as an off book special health fund. The Tories fought nurses and paramedics over their collective agreements.

Still, the hard reality for Dipper MLAs elected for the first time in 2009 was that they entered their second election with no coattails to drag them along. In 2009 Darrell Dexter was popular, Rodney was unpopular, and being on Darrell's team was a big plus. Not so in 2013. In the months leading up to that election, the word coming back from door-to-door preliminary canvassing was that voters liked their MLA but did not much like Darrell anymore. The shine had worn off. For some, it was reminiscent of the 1999 election in which the other parties were successful in portraying Robert Chisholm as power hungry; this dragged down the party more than any unpopularity of individual NDP MLAs.

When, in late 2012 and early 2013, I looked at the seats one by one, I thought the odds favored a minority. A popular vote level in the 36 per cent to 42 per cent range usually results in a minority government, although in our Legislature that could mean anywhere from 19 to 25 seats. To win a majority, it usually requires at least 45 per cent of the vote, and then the range of seats could be from 26 on up depending on splits. In 2013, the Liberals took 48 per cent of the vote and took 65 per cent of the seats. This mismatch between popular vote and resultant seats is fairly typical of the first-past-the-post system and illustrates vividly what a mistake it was for the NDP to ignore proportional representation when we had the chance to engage with it. The PCs and the NDP both took 27 per cent of the vote in 2013. The PCs elected eleven to our seven. On a PR basis, both opposition parties should have taken 13 seats. That would have left the Liberals with 25 seats, just under a majority.

Internally, especially as 2013 advanced and the polling results were not very good, the talk was of how to come from behind in light of the polls which had been regularly showing the Liberals ahead. Comfort was taken from the recent elections in BC and Alberta, as well as Ontario and to some extent Quebec. The lessons being drawn were that incumbent governments can be hard to beat, that the polls can be misleading about what voters will actually do on Election Day, that the campaign itself matters a lot, and that negative advertising tends to work. This last was not happily accepted at caucus. To deal with the criticism, the leadership started avoiding using the term, and spoke of ads that "defined" the opponents, that "drew contrasts" that portrayed the opposition as risky, and reminded caucus that what we were calling negative advertising was nothing so bad or personal as the way Stephen Harper went after Michael Ignatieff and Stéphane Dion or how negative ads were used in the USA.

Part of the problem we faced can be illustrated by looking at a poll that came out in June 2013 that focused on young voters. The Springtide Collective interviewed 693 people between the ages of 18 and 30, most of them students. Their preferences (the Liberals slightly ahead of the NDP with the PCs and Greens well back) were more or less in line with the general population. What was particularly interesting about the poll, though, was the satisfaction question, which was matched with level of interest in politics. There were two problems for us. The first was that the higher the levels of interest in politics, the greater the level of dissatisfaction with the government. The other was that for everyone else, those not at all interested or not very interested, the best they offered was "somewhat satisfied." Indifference prevailed among most voters. And irritation among those most engaged. A big problem.

But the leadership did stop talking about gaining seats. It would be a very easy slide from a majority to 25 seats or below as a minority. And even if the party did win, either a slight majority or a minority entitled to try to govern if it had the most seats, I regularly thought of the joke about the understudy tenor at *La Scala Opera*. One day the famous lead is taken ill and the understudy is called to sing in his place. The opera is *Tosca*. He sings the Act I aria of *Cavaradossi, Recondita armonia*. The audience cries out, "Encore. Encore." He sings it again. Again the audience cries out, "Encore. Encore." So he does. But again they cry out for an encore. Amazed, he steps to the front of the stage and addresses the audience and thanks them but explains that really they do have to get on with the full opera. "Encore," they shout, "Encore; sing it again. Sing it until you get it right." At its most optimistic, that is what this election result is for the NDP. The voters are not terribly impressed, but neither are they so put out that they want nothing to do with the party. The message from holding 27 per cent of the vote is that they want to give the NDP the opportunity not to do it again, but to do it better – to get it right.

Our Campaign

Campaigns are always full of surprises. The objective of a campaigning political party is to play out a thirty-day script in which daily activities have been planned, in which a set message board is repeated and repeated (stay on script), in which mistakes are avoided, in which every misstep of opponents is to be pounced on. Photo-ops. Cheery ads featuring the leader. Hints at the riskiness of voting for the opposition. This is all planned but cannot be absolutely controlled. Something untoward is bound to happen. Maybe a poor performance in the leaders' debate, like Russell MacLellan giving dead air for seven seconds against Dr. Hamm in 1999. Maybe a candidate turning out to be a liability, like the unfortunate Julia Skipper, the NDP candidate in Colchester South in the 1988 election whose husband was charged with growing marijuana in the midst of the campaign. In 2013 it turned out to be an allegation of homophobia made by a staffer in the Ramona Jennex campaign, resulting in the fellow's dismissal and an apology to the defamed Liberal.

Still, voters will often, for a first time government, be somewhat forgiving. That has been the record in other provinces, although in Nova Scotia it had been twenty years since back-to-back majority governments. If there was any pattern here it was of a majority followed by a minority: thus 1993 and 1998 for the Liberals; 1999 and 2003 for the Tories.

The 2013 election was just full of surprises. It was a classic case of a government defeating itself. For the first time in 130 years, Nova Scotians did not offer a government a second chance, even as a minority. The first NDP government in the eastern Canadian five provinces was gone. Darrell Dexter lost his own seat in Cole Harbour. The traditional election night gathering at the Lord Nelson Hotel was completely glum and attended mostly by staffers and party officials, while small gatherings of NDP supporters sat home and moaned and fumed.

The Liberals and PCs did not offer platforms of much substance. Most of what they said was very poor policy, or outright nonsense. There was nothing to attract a thoughtful voter. The "Red Tide" was mostly discontent with the NDP.[5] And disappointment. One main lesson for the Liberals has to be that they too can be unceremoniously turfed in four years' time if they fail to deliver solid government. Indeed that must be the PC hope and plan, to move from their new status as Official Opposition to government in 2017.

Both the Liberals and the PCs had promised to alter the administrative system for health care by reducing the number of boards. The theory is that as the District Health Authorities are reduced in numbers, some 130 administrators would be eliminated and the money would be redirected into front line services. It is far from clear that this plan makes any sense; the amount of dollar savings is tiny within the health bud-

Darrell Dexter conceding defeat in the 2013 provincial election at the Lord Nelson Hotel.

get, the problems in the system have relatively little to do with formal administrative structure, and local areas outside of HRM may well come to resent loss of input and control. So, too, for electrical power rates promises. The PC's claim to be able to freeze rates for five years would only have postponed any legitimate increases to arrive later in a punishing cluster. Likewise, their refrain that there is fat to be cut from government is completely bogus, and did not cut much ice with voters. Even more ridiculous was Jamie Baillie's comparison of Nova Scotia's debt to that of Greece and the city of Detroit, which went bankrupt: our province is nowhere near being in those ranks, and to suggest that we are abandoned all the credibility Mr. Baillie should have brought to his position given his background in finance. The Liberals promises to "open up competition" by allowing direct sales of electricity by independent power producers to customers or reducing bills by shifting the cost of Efficiency Nova Scotia to Emera shareholders, was simply irrelevant. Any small amount of "independent" power will have no effect on rates. And making the utility bear the cost of Efficiency Nova Scotia might be morally satisfying but because every dollar of Nova Scotia Power money comes from customer billings, shifting which column that particular item comes from will again have no effect upon rates.

Where this will leave the Liberals in terms of an agenda that will appeal to people is far from obvious. One point that is worth noting about their platform is that they won without promising to lower taxes. Specifically, they said that there was no point in promising a timetable for lowering the HST since they would need a chance to assess provincial finances from the inside. This is a completely sensible point, but one the PCs would not adopt because their core beliefs are anti-tax and, basically, anti-government. Nor would the Dexter NDP government dare speak of retaining some higher taxes since it had convinced itself that its tax policy should be Tory tax policy, that on fiscal and economic matters traditional progressive and social NDP policies should just be ignored as electorally counterproductive.

One of the main problems for the NDP with the 2013 result is not just the huge loss of seats, not just the humiliating ouster of the leader in his home seat, and not just the weakness of the particular grouping of

Launching the 2013 election campaign with Sid Prest, Tanis Crosby, Abad Khan, Darrell Dexter, Mary Vingoe, and Gregor Ash.

seven MLAs left (two urban, five rural), but the missed opportunity to elect a new generation of MLAs. Talented candidates like Tanis Crosby, Abad Khan, André Cain, Drew Moore, and Gregor Ash all failed to win seats. As a group they are distinctly younger than the previous caucus, and certainly than the resultant caucus; more importantly they are the future of the party. They failed not on their merits, but as representatives of the Dexter NDP.

Where there were no NDP incumbents, all the seats were lost: Halifax Fairview (Graham Steele), Halifax Chebucto (myself), Timberlea-Prospect (Bill Estabrooks), Halifax Atlantic (Michèle Raymond), and Dartmouth South (Marilyn More). Not one new person was elected to the NDP caucus. And the two most progressive caucus members to re-offer, Jim Morton and Gary Burrill, both were defeated. Not one Dartmouth seat went to the NDP, nor did anything on that side of the harbour. On the Halifax side of the harbour only Maureen MacDonald held on, and just by the skin of her teeth in a constituency in which there should be no doubt of NDP victory. Metro, once an NDP base, went overwhelmingly to the Liberals, Maureen and Dave A. Wilson, in suburban Sackville, being the only two exceptions. Disgracefully, the Metro voter turnout at a low 50 per cent was even lower than the low provincial turnout of 59 per cent. The disgrace is not that of the voters so much as it is that of a failed party organizational effort and a failed campaign. In the end, some longtime NDP voters probably did indeed stay home, though that is not the story of the defeat, and certainly not the place to lay blame.

The NDP campaign was not well done. Given the accumulated discontents, it had to be brilliant, but it was pedestrian. The essence of the problem was a need to set out a clear vision for the future, a grand scheme. Instead, the platform was cobbled together as a list of small specifics – this would not do. The basic justification for the first term, that it required the fiscal discipline of balancing the budget, that it tackled the basics of job creation, and that due to all of this a course was set for transformation to an overall better life, was in the end not made clear. There was no vision of an overall better life. The stated strategy was to have voters focus on the future rather than to have the party's campaign spend time defending the past. That instinct was correct, but there was no execution, and there was no execution because there was no true vision for the future.

This can be illustrated by looking at the health portfolio. As Minister of Health, Maureen MacDonald had demonstrated high competence in tackling wait times for some specialties, access to a family physician, some aspects of mental health, cost of pharmaceuticals, and emergency resources in rural areas. These are longstanding problems of the system that both PC and Liberal governments had wrestled with. We did it better. And it needed to be done. But improved basic competence in administering a system is not enough of an NDP agenda. In Health, that should have extended to a significant emphasis on poverty (a major cause of ill-health[6]); to a network of community health clinics on the model of Halifax's North End Community Health Centre; to more reliance on nurse-practitioners, pharmacists, and midwives; to severe limitation on privatization of the system; to more physicians being on a different payment model than fee-for-service; to standing up publicly for a national Pharmacare programme. To some extent each of these saw very small advances, but at no time was there any statement of an overall comprehensive direction. The preference, as in all portfolios, was for dealing with small, discrete items and problems as they popped up, and if there was an overall vision it was not stated. In the end, it was the absence of an articulated future vision that undermined the faith in positive change that had been the NDP brand in Opposition.

On election night, Darrell gave a gracious speech, as journalist-blogger Parker Donham[7] noted, in which he said, "The people have spoken. And as democrats we respect their decision." He then went on to say the party could be proud of its accomplishments in office, listing advances in health, electrical renewables, and economic development, then adding, "And most importantly to me, we have reduced the number of people living in poverty." While the accomplishment is to some extent real, the pride is hard to credit. This remark of Darrell's has to be seen as having been addressed to party members, where anti-poverty is a priority; it was not an articulated priority of the Dexter government, where anti-poverty was seen not only as low priority but also as an electoral liability.

Stephen McNeil campaigned on an implied message of, "I am not Darrell Dexter." It worked. Though what it did demonstrate is not just that governments defeat themselves, but the serious volatility of voters. In the series of elections leading up to 2009, NDP candidates – in seeking to convince voters to elect the first NDP government – would sometimes say, "If it turns out you don't like us, you could always vote us out," and this is just what happened. And this is exactly what could happen to the Liberals in a few years. On this point, Jamie Baillie got it quite right: "If you didn't like the NDP," he said, "You won't like the Liberals either." There is every prospect that the Liberals will be a dissapointment. Their big advantage will be that the next few years may be ones of mildly improving

economic performance. And with no commitment to reduce the HST on any fixed timetable, or against running deficits, revenues to government should allow for some flexibility and more spending. Still – and entirely irrespective of the minimalist platform the Liberals ran on – people will have high expectations, and will vote next time based on resentments as much as anything else.

Another way of seeing the 2013 election – besides that it was simply boring – is to wonder why the Liberals got such an easy ride from the media. The Nova Scotia public was truly poorly served by our journalists (with a few sporadic exceptions) during this election. No one grilled the Liberals, to probe for details, to question assumptions. One small exception came from *Chronicle Herald* columnist Claire McIlveen a few days before the election, but her specific examples of Liberal "messaging" were weak. She did call their platform, "thin (creative use of white space, we call it in the newspaper business). When it comes to politics, negative spin obscures reality,"[8] which was very much to the point. Still, her main focus was on the NDP, wondering why Dexter made the "mistake" of failing, "to stand up for himself and his government until the last week or so – too little, too late." This was an interesting comment from the generally Tory-and-big-business-friendly *Chronicle Herald* newspaper. It, along with much of the business press and business organizations, was quite supportive of Dexter's approach to government, approving of the way he flowed money to support the attraction or retention of industry or to build the Convention Centre. What is telling is that no matter how much they were fans of Dexter's brand of NDP, when the moment came they were quite happy to stand aside for a return to an old-line party, the Liberals as it happened to be.

The Tories made themselves largely irrelevant. The strong emphasis Baillie put on paying for any new programmes through cutting "unnecessary, wasteful" expenditures in the public sector was simply not believed by anyone. It is well past the decade when a politician can convincingly campaign on "cutting the fat." No one believes there is any fat remaining. Here and there an example might be found, but voters have long since realized that "cutting fat" means loss of services. It was a pointless basis for a campaign, and was clearly trying to retain the support of the core

Tory vote, especially in their traditional stronghold territory (Pictou, Colchester, and Cumberland counties). This was unfortunate, because Jaimie Baillie is actually a smart and articulate fellow with a lot to offer to public life.

To many of us, the problem was not that Darrell failed to stand up for his pro-business record, but that he failed to apologize for it. Or, for other failings. In a letter sent out by the party over his signature late in the campaign, and designed to get out the core vote so as to stem losses, he said, "I made some mistakes and I learned from them." In fact, the only decision he ever admitted publicly or at caucus that was a mistake was the Yarmouth ferry. Nothing else. Was it a mistake to legislate the paramedics into binding arbitration? Was it a mistake to give money to Cooke Aquaculture? Was is a mistake to beat up on Talbot House? Was is a mistake not to hold a full public inquiry into the Nova Scotia Home for Coloured Children? Was it a mistake to pump money into the pulp and paper industry? Was it a mistake not to push Ottawa aggressively for upgrades to the Canada Pension Plan (CPP)? Was it a mistake to push housing way down the public agenda? Was it a mistake to approach education as another expenditure rather than as an essential service where we would do everything to seek quality? Was it a mistake to be a big booster of Emera/Nova Scotia Power? Was it a mistake to go negative big time as a central campaign tactic? Not according to Darrell.

If there ever was a slight chance of winning the 2013 election after it became apparent early in the year that there was drift to the Liberals and that Darrell was a liability, it would have been if he had apologized for mistakes, offered some solid policy choices that headed in a new direction, and then resigned.

I have suggested this possibility to political colleagues. The part they question is the leader's resignation. But when they reflect, the conclusion they come to is not that it is a bad idea, just that it was not in the cards. A resignation of this particular sort is not in Darrell's personality and for the central planners in the party, too much effort over many years had been put into melding his name with the party's. As George Smiley says, "Have you ever bought a fake picture?"

There was some useful commentary from Parker Donham in his online *Contrarian* column.[9] Brian Flinn in his *AllNovaScotia.com*[10] items kept a useful accounting of the business statistics. But when it came to an overall summary, the best came from Tim Bousquet at *The Coast.* Published just before the election, "The politics of bullshit,"[11] nailed the dilemma:

> The next premier of Nova Scotia will be ... a white man. He'll take a centrist approach to all issues, developed after extensive consultation with focus groups and party pollsters.
>
> The next premier will continue Nova Scotia's long history of millions of dollars in subsidies and tax rebates for corporations from away. He'll be good friends with the new president of Nova Scotia Business, Inc., who will be hired soon after the election. The two will be the featured guests at Chamber of Commerce breakfasts, where all the be-suited guests will gush about Halifax becoming a global financial services centre – "the next Singapore," the newest version of, "the next Celtic Tiger" – thanks to the miracle of government "investments" in private companies. [...]
>
> The next premier of Nova Scotia will talk a lot about jobs, especially when he announces big "investments" in corporations from away. He won't lower tuition rates, and so the increasing student loan debt burden will cause more graduates to move out of province to get better-paying jobs. [...]
>
> Without any discernible differences between the parties on the large issues before voters – not to mention the complete avoidance of lots of large issues that should be before voters – it doesn't much matter who wins the election. [...]
>
> All three parties propose nickel-and-dime changes in expenditures, and put all hope on the fairy tale idea that we'll see a big increase in provincial income by luring mega corporations into the province, which will hire lots of workers and pay lots of taxes. [...]
>
> When the NDP formed its first provincial government in 2009, the expectation in some circles was that the party would put an end to corporate welfare, but the exact opposite happened: they doubled down on it. Under Darrell Dexter, the NDP has completely abandoned its socialist roots, and has dumped hundreds of millions of dollars into corporations in the name of economic development.

Basic points about the Liberal platform were left unquestioned by the press until after the election. Thus, the CBC radio held interviews with noted health consultants Mary Jane Hampton and Dr. John Ross about the question of the merger of health boards, not during the campaign but after. Both agreed that although some merger might help a bit, the dollar savings, if any, would be minuscule, and that the number of health boards was a complete side issue in the panoply of health issues.

On the Liberals' energy proposals, *AllNovaScotia.com*[12] ran a highly critical item by energy expert and Dalhousie University electrical engineering professor Larry Hughes a week after the election. "Breaking the monopoly," for the benefit of independent power producers, he wrote, would not be very practical since all providers need a reliable source of backup power, and would not lead to stable or low costs for customers. As for moving the costs for Efficiency Nova Scotia to the books of Nova Scotia Power, it might be good politics but it is questionable policy and offers no savings. (Hughes has excellent ideas about our electrical energy system, and should not be understood to be suggesting that nothing can be done. Year in and year out he has set out his very sensible and well-researched proposals, largely to have them ignored.)

With a majority, the Liberals will have at least four years before needing to look at another election. The Constitutional upper limit is five years, but it is not usual for governments to go the full term. During that time the PCs will be working to take the government away from the Liberals, certainly working not to lose their status as Official Opposition and fall again into third place. But they are having a tough time of it; the desertion of MLA Chuck Porter to sit as an independent being the outward sign of serious internal discontent. For the NDP, the same dynamic of seeking recognition will be at work, though in a much tougher circumstance.

Having been so thoroughly thumped, assessment, analysis, blame and rebuilding will all be on the agenda. As will leadership. Closely connected to the selection of the next leader will be policy.

This is a time for the rescue of the NDP enterprise. It has gone seriously wrong. Abandoning the established policies was always justified inside the party as a necessary step in winning elections. The last four years have shown how mistaken that was. The 2009 election was not won by trying so hard to look like the other parties, but by a combination of the PCs defeating themselves, and the hope for change in a positive way that attached to the NDP through years of building credibility and setting out an alternative agenda while in opposition. The four years of government systematically undermined that, with the serious negative result that we now see. The central players in this fundamentally flawed version of the enterprise will have to stand aside (not just from their jobs, which has happened, but from trying to control the party): Darrell, his Chief of Staff Dan O'Connor, Principal Secretary Paul Black, and Director of Communications Shawn Fuller. There has to be frank admission that the direction was wrong from start to finish. If the net result was that the Fraser Institute gave the NDP government top marks for our governance, we hardly need more indicators that we went seriously astray.

Darrell and Dan worked as a team to skew NDP politics for over a decade. Unfortunately, many party members allowed this to happen. In looking back over the last few elections, the trend has been all too apparent. It is easy to forget from election to election just what the problems were. A decade ago, in 2003, the party undertook its usual formal post-election analysis. At the time, I wrote a lengthy analysis of the problems with the 2003 campaign (Appendix 3). Its main points were that the party had for too long ignored the basic work of building solid constituencey associations, even where we had incumbent MLAs; that the campaign was not an "NDP campaign" in that Tory-style slogans were adopted and we didn't campaign on poverty, homelessness, labour, the environment, arts and culture, job creation, small business, or women's issues; and that in the end we missed an opportunity to win government. Exactly these points had been made by the party membership at length following the 1999 election.

Much of this decade-old critique continued to characterize what happened in the 2013 campaign. The Liberals campaigned in 2013 on a theme of "trust." A lot was packed up in that. First, it implied that the Dexter NDP couldn't be trusted. Without having to say it, the word reminded voters of Darrell's promise to balance the budget within the first year and to do so without raising taxes – a broken promise. Without having to say it, the word reminded voters of the stark difference between Darrell as Premier (friend of big business) and the NDP in Opposition (friend of "working families.") Without having to say it, it reminded voters of Darrell's involvement in the expenses mess. Second, though, there is a sense in which elections are always about trust. No matter what else the ballot box question might be, trust is always a part of what determines votes. In this, politics is the same as the dynamics in families, in religious institutions, and in the stock market. Anyone in any position of power, no matter how modest, can only go forward if those they deal with have faith in their probity, their skills, and their good intentions. And while I strongly emphasize the importance of traditional NDP policies as crucial to how the party must reposition itself in order to go forward, trust is bound up with that. Voters must be able to trust us to follow through.

The stark differences between the "old NDP" and the "new Dexterite NDP," differences that were apparent to long-time party members and supporters as well as to the public at large, include:

Old NDP	New Dexterite NDP
Social Democrat	Neo-Liberal
Promotes local self-reliance	Accepts free trade
Peace-oriented	Uncritical of militarism
Environmentalists	Environment subordinate to businesses
Small business, farmers	Friend of big businesses
Friend of labour	Not a big priority
Managers	Managers
Deficits if necessary	Balanced budgets
Progressive taxation	Low taxes
Anti-poverty	Tepid on this
Class conscious	Not
Prepared to wait	Hungry for power as a government

How the Nova Scotia NDP arrived at this point requires a look back at the party's history. Our many years of Opposition showed real strengths of principle, along with some significant mis-steps. Looking back will allow us to look forward.

Clockwise from upper left: Jim Aitchson, Helen MacDonald, Alexa McDonough, John Holm, Darrell Dexter, Maureen MacDonald, Robert Chisholm, Jeremy Akerman.

3

Seems Like Old Times

I n the caucus meeting room hang photos of all of the provincial leaders, going back to Micki MacDonald in 1953. Then there is Jim Aitchison in 1962, Jeremy Akerman in 1968, Buddy MacEachern in 1980, Alexa McDonough in 1980, John Holm in 1994, Robert Chisholm in 1996, Helen MacDonald in 2000, and then Darrell Dexter in 2001. It has been a long run. While my focus here is on the period I know best, i.e., since 1998, the electoral leap forward that year came with specific antecedents, decades of hard work, and many struggles.

Gauche caviar is the French phrase; in English, it is "champagne socialist." The Americans have "limousine liberal." In other countries and languages there are equivalent terms. To some extent it implies hypocrisy, though not always. What it points to is a well-recognized phenomenon that those with ample education are often likely to favour an egalitarian society, even when they benefit themselves from positions of advantage and comfort in the *status quo*. There has always been something of a division inside the party in Nova Scotia between the university-based membership and the mostly Cape Breton working-class unionized membership. This certainly has evolved over the years, but for a long time was a fact of life for the dynamics of the party. Nor is it confined to Nova Scotia. It is a characteristic of the NDP throughout Canada, and of left parties throughout the world. It is far from obvious why even these distinctly different educational backgrounds should lead to tensions, though it is easy to see the focus of dispute when it comes to environmental matters. In Nova Scotia this has evolved around coal mining primarily, though its most modern manifestation has been around forestry and hence industrial policy in general.

One of my favourite MLAs was Paul MacEwan, one of the longest serving MLAs ever with 33 years in the Legislature. MacEwan started as an NDP MLA but later ran as an independent, as a representative of the Cape Breton Labour Party, and finally – when our times in the Legislature overlapped – as a Liberal. He was a scholar, and his book on the NDP in Nova Scotia during the time Jeremy Akerman was the leader, is a fine, detailed account of those years. It includes this retrospective, going back to the Farmer-Labour party.

> The Co-operative Commonwealth Federation, or CCF, was set up in Nova Scotia in 1938 by the coal miners of District 26, United Mine Workers of America. It never really succeeded at breaking out beyond the steel and coal areas of industrial Cape Breton, although there it managed to have some representatives elected federally or provincially at all times between 1939 and 1963. The most noteworthy figure in the CCF successes in Cape Breton was Clarence Gillis, MP for Cape Breton South from 1940 to 1957. Provincially, the CCF elected one MLA in a 1939 by-election, three MLAs in 1941, two in 1945 and 1949 and one in 1956 and 1960. The members who served were Douglas MacDonald, Donald MacDonald, D. N. Brodie, Russell Cunningham and Michael MacDonald.
>
> The CCF was badly mauled in the 1958 federal election and was reorganized into the New Democratic Party in 1961, under the national leadership of T. C. "Tommy" Douglas. In the federal election of 1962, the voters of Cape Breton South elected an NDP MP, Malcolm "Vic" MacInnis, but he was defeated in the 1963 election nine months later. This was the sum total of CCF and NDP successes in Nova Scotia until Jeremy Akerman came along.
>
> Under Akerman, the NDP elected two MLAs in 1970, three in 1974 and four in 1978 to the Nova Scotia Legislature. Federally in 1974 and 1979 it elected Rev. Andy Hogan as MP for Cape Breton East Richmond, so that in 1978 and 1979, it had out-done anything electorally ever done under the CCF banner in terms of winning seats.

Beyond that, under Akerman, the NDP for the first time in Nova Scotian history put up a third-party candidate in every provincial riding in the province, on two occasions, first in 1974 and again in 1978. Statistics could be quoted to show percentage growth by riding, but without that it can be said that he built his party up a great deal.[1]

Included in Appendix 1 are the Labour, CCF, and NDP votes and seats back to those years and for every election since then. MacEwan's overview appears to be correct. Progress has been slow, including very barren years. Where MacEwan is also acute is on the nature of internal disputes in the NDP. He is inclined to emphasize a split between Cape Breton working-class oriented pragmatists and Halifax pipe-smoking academics more interested in ideological purity than in winning elections. Some of his figures are sobering: at one point, in the late 1960s, party membership was decidedly based in Cape Breton (713) compared with 259 for the rest of the province, only 94 of whom were in Halifax County and 100 in Pictou County. In recent decades the shift has been decidedly to Halifax both in terms of memberships and as a source of monetary support for the party, with the three Halifax Peninsula constituencies regularly and emphatically leading.

The time between the barren 1960s through to 1980 or so was largely a time of internal bickering. MacEwan describes it in painful detail. Still, MacEwan and Akerman were successful in being elected in 1970 and there followed a burst of NDP activity both in the Legislature and in terms of organization and publicity. Buddy MacEachern was to join the other two in the election of 1974, and then Len Arsenault in 1978. Dalhousie political scientist, J. Murray Beck sums up Akerman's time as NDP leader thus:

Jeremy Akerman

> Generally Akerman's approach was pragmatic rather than doctrinaire. Declaring that the old parties were tied hand and foot to big corpora-

tions, he made a special appeal to small business. Because much of the old radical left had departed, he had been able to broaden the party membership, helped by his outstanding performance and moderate course in the legislature.[2]

One of the points MacEwan makes is to draw attention to the role of the provincial secretary. This is the chief staff person of the party. In those days, the position was held by Peggy Prowse and then by Serena Renner. MacEwan resents their roles as partisan activists inside the party, rather than just as administrators. There is a varied history on this. It is not surprising that a leader will want a provincial secretary who is supportive, and certainly will not want one who is working against them. We have had a long list. It includes Nancy Doull (married to former Halifax mayor, Allan O'Brien, and still a party stalwart), Mary Morison (who later worked for Bob Rae when he was Ontario Premier), Dennis Theman (a lawyer active with Crown Attorneys' Association as its president, respected to the point that the Canadian Association of Crown Counsel named an award for him) Bruce Cox (later Executive Director of Greenpeace Canada), Ed Wark (originally Darrell Dexter's campaign director and later a lobbyist), Matt Hebb (later Darrell's Principal Secretary), Mike MacSween (a solid Cape Bretoner, and a possible future candidate), Jill Marzetti (an efficient Ontario native, now returned there), and now Mike Poworoznyk. For the most part, the issue with the official party office in recent decades has not been about internal factionalism so much as basic competence in building membership numbers, raising money, making sure constituency associations are functioning, and complying with provincial elections laws.

In the 1981 election, all of the Cape Breton NDP MLAs lost their seats. By that time, MacEwan had left the NDP, which he referred to as the New Plutocratic Party[3] having been expelled in June 1980 not long after Akerman resigned as leader. MacEwan had formed the Cape Breton Labour Party for which he was elected, his fourth straight success at the polls.

The 1981 election brought Alexa McDonough to the Legislature, as MLA for Halifax Chebucto, and as leader of the Nova Scotia NDP.

At a caucus retreat in 2010, Graham Steele told the story of how he went door to door the first time he was trying to get elected, in the company of Alexa McDonough. They would meet people, and Alexa, who was then no longer the provincial leader and had moved on to federal politics, would try to introduce him. Graham would come forward to chat, but to no avail. All that would happen is that the person would call out to others in the house: "Honey, it's Alexa. Come see Alexa. Hello, Alexa." Graham would say: "Hi. I am Graham Steele, the NDP candidate in Fairview. How are you? What have you been thinking about as the issues?" No luck. They would stare right through him, and go back to calling out: "Honey, it's Alexa, come meet Alexa."

The core of the story was completely true. Alexa shines like the sun in Nova Scotia politics. She is completely beloved, and deservedly so. She slogged it out for the party, and more importantly for her constituents, for long years in the Legislature. She built the credibility of the party by speaking common sense, by being accessible, by being honest, by being on the side of regular folks, by taking on the government on issue after issue. She was exactly what the NDP has claimed to be. She must be sorely disappointed.

Alexa comes from wealth and prominence. Her family are the Shaws of Shaw Brick, later the Shaw Group, a company dating from 1861 and started in Hantsport. It deals in construction materials, and in construction itself, in wood pellets, as well as in major building projects through Clayton Developments. According to the company's website[4] it, "developed residential communities housing over 50,000 people in the Halifax Regional Municipality," making it a major presence in the local business world. Alexa's brother Robbie had a longtime alliance with the Liberals, acting as chief of staff to Premier Gerald Regan, later moving to be a vice president at Dal-

Alexa McDonough

housie University. Her cousin Allan C. Shaw was for years on the board of directors of the Bank of Nova Scotia, where public disclosures show him as owning upwards of $5 million in their shares. She was married to Peter McDonough, QC, a corporate lawyer and senior partner at McInnes Cooper. Alexa's dad, Lloyd, was active in progressive causes, including the CCF (Co-operative Commonwealth Federation) where he was the first research director. Both Allan and Robbie are noted as community-spirited people, stalwarts of local charities and of think tanks. The family mores they exhibit are held in common with Alexa. Hers is a remarkable local family.

Educated as a social worker, Alexa had a very early awareness of social injustice, including a focus on Africville. As Alexa Shaw, she had a stint as a reporter for *The Chronicle Herald*, where she wrote articles about Africville. An early Liberal, she moved away from the party to join the NDP, and ran unsuccessfully federally in 1979 and 1980 in Halifax before turning to provincial politics.

After Jeremy Akerman resigned, Alexa was chosen as leader quite decisively in July 1980. It was a stormy time. Paul MacEwan had just been expelled from the party, essentially for his public attacks on other members. She was to spend some eight months following events from the gallery of the House before getting the opportunity to run in the 1981 election. It was a triumph for her in some real ways. She ran on a modest platform that included establishing a provincial energy corporation, and repealing the *Michelin Bill*. She won her Halifax Chebucto seat, and became the sole NDP MLA since the other NDP MLAs in Cape Breton lost their seats. (MacEwan, as the Cape Breton Labour Party, kept his seat.) What was triumphal was not just winning a mainland Nova Scotia seat for the NDP for the first time, but that the percentage of the overall vote for the party reached 18 per cent, and in Halifax County it was 25 per cent – an amazing number.

Alexa is smart, hardworking, affable, attentive to detail, sympathetic, friendly, determined, a good speaker, and charismatic. People like being around her. She naturally attracts loyalists: it is not that she pushes for it; people just enjoy being on her team. And all of this comes across to voters. She was a tremendous success as our provincial leader.

Looking at her performance in the House, it is clear that her grasp of how to deal with the government improved by leaps and bounds over time. During her first year, her questions to Ministers and her resolutions tended to lack focus. As the only member for the NDP her entitlement to ask questions was limited, so those limited opportunities could have been better used. Her introductory speech was good, though. She noted her "triple jeopardy" in the House: she was the only Dipper, the only woman, and a rookie. She then canvassed a host of issues ranging from seniors' needs for home care, to income assistance for single parents, to housing affordability, to the treatment of former Speaker Paddy Fitzgerald (who had been convicted of rape and had been disbarred) to education, to the offshore and forestry and the Economic Investment Fund. It was a good start. [Amazingly, Alexa was only the third woman to be elected as an MLA. She had been preceded by Gladys Porter (PC, Kings North) and Melinda MacLean (Liberal, Colchester).]

In the 1984 election, two additional seats were won by the NDP. Alexa retained her seat, and was joined by teacher John Holm for Sackville and legal aid lawyer Bob Levy, Jr. for Kings South. As a team, they were very effective, and the increase in seats began to lend credibility to the NDP having some momentum in Nova Scotia. But an incumbent government is not without the power to create temptations. When Jeremy Akerman and Paul MacEwan were elected in 1970, the overall picture was that

On the hustings, campaigning together with Alexa.

the Regan Liberals had ousted the Ike (George Isaac) Smith Tories, but with just 23 of the 46 Legislature seats. Regan proposed that MacEwan be Speaker, and suggested that Akerman join the Liberal Cabinet, which would have given the Liberals clearer control of the House. Both turned down the overtures. In 1988 though, Bob Levy accepted from John Buchanan an appointment as a family court judge shortly before the election, vacating the Kings South seat that then went Tory with Harry How. When Bob Levy was appointed to the bench just prior to the election, *Frank Magazine* ran a cover photo of John Holm embracing Alexa and added a thought-bubble saying, "I'll never Levy you, my love."[5]

In 1991, I volunteered on Robert Chisholm's campaign to win Halifax Atlantic. I took a couple of polls and canvassed them the traditional, pre-Internet and pre-email way: by knocking on every door, chatting with folks, and doing this three times. By the end of the canvassing I knew that he would get 42 per cent of the votes in those polls, and so it was, just as it was in the constituency overall. Robert had won a by-election in the old John Buchanan Tory stronghold. Surely this was a good sign for the party, at least in Metro.

When Robert resigned in November 1999, announcing his decision at a provincial council meeting in Dartmouth, very few people knew in advance. As Robert was speaking, press contact Ron Sherrard was going around the room to those MLAs present to tell them what was about to occur. This closeness with the information was, surprisingly to me, actually the basis for some criticism when caucus met together two days later. Some members took not having been informed in advance as a sign of lack of trust in their ability to maintain the information as confidential. John Holm took this view. Jerry Pye was more diplomatic, just saying that he had respected caucus confidentiality since 1998 and so felt worthy of being told; he also said he was disappointed Robert was stepping down. Darrell Dexter said he was also sorry not to have known since it takes weeks to catch up mentally. Robert made the lead point that he wanted to minimize the chance the story got out in a way he could not control. John Holm calmed down after the discussion, "the rant," he called it, and said he respected the decision, it was the right decision.

In fact Robert was not stepping down immediately. He stayed on as leader until the convention that was held the following July. There was discussion of whether he could do an effective job in the interim, but no one had concerns about that. Kevin Deveaux said we needed to know that Robert would still be engaged during the interim, and Robert assured us that his passion was still there for all the issues we would have to deal with. And indeed it was.

I was actually very sorry to lose Robert as leader. After the 1999 election, when there was discussion in caucus about what had occurred, the eleven of us who remained as MLAs had a very frank exchange. No one explicitly pushed for a resignation. It was clear that Robert wanted to stay on. I was among those who said the issue had to be looked at objectively and in terms of what was best for the party as a whole. The question, I suggested, was whether we could win the next election with Robert as leader, or whether the issue of his not having been forthright about his old drunk driving conviction had just caused an insurmountable problem with the public. I thought it had, which I regretted very much. Others thought it was entirely too difficult to predict the dynamics of the next election, which was three or four years in the future. Unlike what transpired with the leadership of Helen MacDonald later on, there was no active push; Robert was left to reflect.

As with all leaders, Robert had a distinct mix of characteristics. The topic he knew best was labour relations, reflecting his time working at CUPE (Canadian Union of Public Employees). This was highly useful, as the Hamm Tories unwisely picked fights with the province's paramedics and nurses, fights that were high profile and damaging for the Tories. Robert was much weaker in his grasp of the economy or of environmental matters. This was problematic because both of these were of great importance, and party

With Robert Chisholm in the 1999 election.

Robert Chisholm.

members and the public were looking for some inspiration on both. He was very good at listening to debate, and caucus was run on a reasonably open basis. In the Legislature and on other public occasions, his ability as a speaker improved markedly, to the point where he became very impressive: confident, articulate, and in command of his material.

During the time of his leadership the party evolved. Previously it had been a very small grouping with limited professional capacity. Under Robert, and with the financial resources that winning seats delivers, the caucus office became staffed with competent researchers, files were built up, polling was undertaken, outreach occurred. Talented people like Peggy Cameron, Floyd Kane, and Elizabeth Johnson came to join an office that for so long had just operated on a shoestring. Pamela Whelan had managed the office since Alexa had been leader, and always did it well. For a brief period, there were decent resources to allow support for the contingent of MLAs in the House and to develop policy plus get the message out around the province. All of this was trimmed very severely after the 1999 election when caucus size fell to eleven. But a start had been made.

Helen MacDonald was short-lived as leader, having been elected in a surprising convention in July 2000. She, Kevin Deveaux and Maureen MacDonald squared off after Robert Chisholm resigned [Dave Peters from the NSGEU (Nova Scotia Government and General Employees Union) and Hinrich Bitter-Suermann also ran, but were not serious contenders.]. I was a backer of Maureen's. In fact, along with a team of Paulette Sadoway from the CLC (Canadian Labour Congress), Leon Thomas, her constituency assistant, Cliff White, Marilyn Keddy, John St. Amand, Yvonne Atwell, Joan Gilroy, and Gilbert Daye, we managed her campaign, mostly out of my dining room. At the convention Maureen had to drop off the ballot when she polled third. In fact, there were not many votes separating the candidates (Kevin: 211; Helen: 207; Maureen: 177). But it was a big shock to Maureen's supporters that she was the one who had to drop out. There was a quick huddle, and Maureen decided to throw her support to Helen. The thinking was pretty straightforward. Kevin is someone we admired but he had run a bit of a pe-

Helen MacDonald

culiar campaign, with some policy positions we were not entirely comfortable with. But the key point was his relative age. The analysis was that neither he nor Helen was likely to be a success as leader (Helen had lost her seat in the previous election) and if so it would likely be easier to depose Helen than Kevin. Given his age, 33, he could be expected to be leader for a decade or more if chosen.

In fact, Helen became a liability almost immediately. For whatever reasons, the press decided that she was not an effective leader and treated her with little respect. For my own part, I met with her shortly after the convention and let her know my views. I told her that although I had not supported her candidacy, I was prepared to support her as leader and work with her, but that she had several things to do to establish herself as a credible leader with caucus: she had to overhaul the party office to make it effective as an organizing entity; she had to show grasp of progressive policy issues; and she had to win a seat. Unfortunately, she was not able to deliver on any of these points and ultimately there was a caucus revolt that led to her resignation.

Her most disastrous showing was in the Cape Breton North by-election in March 6, 2001. It was an unwise decision to run there (Fairview, which also had a vacancy due to the death of Eileen O'Connell from cancer the previous September, would have been a safe interim choice. But she was determined to try for a Cape Breton seat, although North was not where she had previously run and won.) Not only did Helen not win that election, she ran third. It was a grim contrast with the results the same night in the Halifax Fairview by-election where Graham Steele won handily, taking every poll. In the view of a majority of caucus members, Helen's days were numbered.

In the meantime, though, an interesting story had been unfolding. It had to do with prayer in the Legislature. One day in early February I received a phone call from Murray Brewster of Canadian Press. He asked if I was aware of a lawsuit in Ontario about prayer in their Legislature. I replied that I was not, but pointed out, as a lawyer, that the case probably would not succeed since the Supreme Court of Canada had ruled in a 1992 case that the *Charter of Rights* does not apply to matters that the Legislature itself regulates internally. Brewster then asked what I thought of the daily recital of the Lord's Prayer in our Legislature. I said that I thought it inappropriate since its daily use suggested state sanction for religious belief, and I favoured separation of "church and state." I was surprised a week later to see this interview appear as a front-page story in *The Chronicle Herald*: "Take prayer out of House – Epstein."[6]

The item provoked a huge amount of attention, from letters to the editor, to opinion columns, to phone calls and letters to my office and to the caucus office. Premier Hamm stated he favoured keeping the recital. Tory Deputy Speaker Brooke Taylor said the minority should respect the

Republished with permission from The Chronicle Herald.

Christian majority on this. All opinion columnists sided with me. However, my constituency assistant, Donna Parker, had to field some unpleasant phone calls. Some were plain disagreement: "Your comments don't reflect the opinion of your constituents," although I was reelected just a few months after that, and three more times thereafter. Some were more aggressive: "The only reason you object is because you are a Jew." This was accurate only in the sense that my upbringing sensitized me to these issues, not accurate in any way meaning hostility to anyone else's beliefs. Some were more problematic: "Five hang ups and two who blocked their number and refused to give their names. Both of these were offensive and insulting and don't deserve any attention." (Thank you, Donna, for dealing with all that.)

A small aside on anti-Semitism. I am the third Jewish member of the House of Assembly. The first was Martin Kaufman, a Liberal representing Cumberland County, a former mayor of Amherst, and MLA from 1945 to 1953. The second was Percy 'Pinky' Gaum, a Tory representing Cape Breton Nova from 1956-1970. My religion has never been a factor in elections. Nor does it seem to have been for Kaufman or Gaum. I sometimes have joked that I am the ideal candidate since I satisfy the views of those Catholics who would not vote for a Protestant and those Protestants who would not vote for a Catholic. But that is a joke. Religious background seems to have faded as a factor in Nova Scotia electoral politics. We are well past the point of an informal convention in which Protestant and Catholic mayors succeeded each other in Halifax, or in having separate schools. Although not quick to change, there is diversity in the Legislature. When David Rodenhiser interviewed me for his column on prayer, I said:

> I've been in politics for about six or seven years, and every year I receive probably one or two anti-Semitic letters or comments. I take note of them, but I don't worry about them. I think there's a very small – and I would emphasize really small – segment of the population that has those feelings.[7]

In the debate at the time, it sometime appeared as though my position was that of only one MLA. In fact, members of all parties regularly stayed

– and still do stay – outside the chamber while prayers are being recited. I estimate the number at about one-third.

The one comment regularly made that I did agree with was that too much time was being spent on this issue, and that the Legislature had more important things to be dealing with. This should not be taken as any backing off the core position I hold. And I certainly appreciate profoundly the support I did encounter. One comment came from a man later to be a colleague in the Legislature, Leonard Preyra, then teaching in the Department of Political Science of Saint Mary's University. He wrote:

> Offering minorities the option to exempt themselves from these religious exercises does not overcome the infringement (of rights) because it compels them to make a religious statement. [...] The recital of the Lord's Prayer ... blurs the boundary between church and state. If we accept the notion that an orthodox Christian group, acting in the name of the majority, can appropriate a legislative assembly and use it for religious purposes, there is very little in principle to prevent legislators from enacting faith based policies and programs.

These comments are especially pertinent as we look abroad and find

much to object to in lawmaking elsewhere in the world. In fact, I have often found it useful to test policies in that light: what would we think if we saw such a proposal coming forward in China or in Nigeria or in Myanmar? I have come to admire Leonard's work as an MLA. He is a careful thinker. It has also been fun to tell him that my real position was 'no Preyra in the Legislature.'

Though there was support, and extensively from individuals within the party, what was highly problematic was to find my party leadership not supporting me. A memo from

Leonard Preyra canvassing with MP Megan Leslie in the 2013 provincial election.

Dan O'Connor was quickly circulated after the first *Chronicle Herald* story to say that the response was to be: "Howard was expressing his personal opinion. It is not the NDP caucus opinion. If Helen is asked, she will say: She has no personal problem with the Lord's Prayer being said by MLAs who choose to attend. If MLAs want to make the prayer more inclusive, that should be considered." What was not on the table, apparently, was no prayer in the Legislature. Or support for a colleague. It got worse. Not long after this, caucus held an out of town meeting in Cape Breton, really as a way to allow us to show solidarity with Helen in her by-election contest, and use evenings to canvass on her behalf. Everyone, that is, except me. I was told that I was not to canvass because public opinion on the prayer issue would be stirred up. I could telephone but just refer to myself as "Howie" – no last name. Needless to say, I just went home. Some time later I learned that there were those in the party who were suggesting I had provoked the prayer story as a way to try to undermine Helen's chances in the by-election. This theory is, of course, complete nonsense. Helen managed to lose the by-election quite handily by herself, nothing to do with me.

Active journalist Parker Donham dug up the by-election story (not from me) and lambasted the NDP. He saw the "isolation" of me as, "convulsions of political cowardice," that were, "pandering to the lowest common denominator," and in line with the, "disastrous peekaboo campaign [Dan] O'Connor devised for former leader Robert Chisholm in 1999. Chisholm dressed respectably, said as little as possible, and tried to avoid frightening voters." Donham got it bang on. One of the dangers of Helen having acted this way was exactly that journalists would get on to the isolation story and publish it during her campaign, not after as happened. I wrote to Helen on March 8, 2001 about all of this (see: Appendix 2).

There was a meeting of the NDP provincial council a few weeks after the by-election loss. Helen made a speech in which she declared that she had no intention of resigning; there are always setbacks – you move on. Tommy Douglas, she said, had lost a couple of elections before becoming premier of Saskatchewan, and that was the model she was prepared to follow and we all should too. She said that the leadership race was over, but if there was anyone out there who thought they could do a better job as leader they should challenge her at the next party convention. It was a tough speech, well-delivered, but it convinced no one. At caucus Bill Estabrooks and Frank Corbett used to sit at the back of the room and when Helen came in they would sing-song chorus, "Good morning, Mrs. MacDonald," playing the bad boys to her school teacher style. They indulged in this male belligerence from day one. Which did nothing for her credibility around the caucus table (or anything much for the general tone of the place, come to that).

Helen's bold attempt to stay on when she had completely lost credibility prompted a formal move inside caucus. Six of us explicitly, and a couple of others who were reluctant to declare themselves openly, agreed that she had to resign. Three of the eleven MLAs did support Helen's staying on. Helen was sent the message of lack of caucus support via fellow Cape Bretoner Frank Corbett, and after some hesitation, did resign, with serious bitterness. She had lasted nine months.

This whole process raised the respective roles of the party and of caucus. Helen had certainly been elected as leader by the party, which is a source of legitimacy. But those closest to the political process, and who stood to lose their seats had arrived at a view that the party could not win the next election with Helen as leader. With no formal power to force out a leader, caucus nonetheless has the practical power to force the issue of leadership to be dealt with.

It is worthwhile looking at where all of this left the party. Helen had come to the leadership through deep roots in the party, and long-held friendships. She was always prepared to refer to her closeness to unions and the Cape Breton working class, but the themes of her time were of moderation and her closest friends inside the party were those who sought to bring it to power by trimming positions. She was bland on policy. Internally, she was not prepared to reorganize the party office or to develop constituency associations or to recruit good candidates. Helen never tackled any of this. Combined with her election loss and scornful treatment by the media, the result was predictable.

During the time Helen was leader she attended the Legislature by sitting in the library to be available to the press. In the chamber itself, John MacDonell was designated "leader in the House." When Helen resigned, John became a candidate to succeed her. But before that contest happened, there was another fascinating episode that did little to foster good collegial relations.

Caucus held a discussion about an interim leader. John Holm took the initiative by declaring that in his view there was only one member of caucus who could do that job, and that was Darrell. As we started to discuss this, Graham Steele intervened to point out that whoever was interim leader would have a big advantage in the convention to choose a permanent leader, and he suggested that no one should be interim leader if they intended to be a candidate for permanent leader. Everyone agreed to that. Everyone. Subsequently, of course, Darrell became a candidate for permanent leader while holding the position of interim leader. At no point did he resign as interim leader, or make a statement to caucus that he had changed his mind. He just did it. And during the leadership contest, the press learned of this arrangement made in caucus. (Not from me, I should add. I was put out by it but I took John MacDonell's direction that this was objectionable but not a matter for external talk. Nor do I know who the source of the press leak was.) What happened was that Bill Estabrooks, a Darrell supporter, flat out denied in the press that any such arrangement had ever been made. With the rest of us unwilling to discuss it publicly, this untruth became the public record.

Premier Darrell Dexter

Dexter was a well-qualified person to be Premier, although deeply flawed. He is a lawyer, he has served in the Navy, and he was a municipal councillor. His family is from rural Nova Scotia, but he also grew up in the city. His dad was a sheet-metal worker. He had lived for a while in a housing co-op, he plays basketball, he served on the board of a credit union, and also of the Dartmouth General Hospital, and was a part of the Downtown Dartmouth Business Association. And he loves politics. He especially likes talking, telling stories; he remembers everyone and their pertinent facts. Much of this is highly useful. In the end though, he would have been best placed as a cabinet minister and not as premier. He would have done a highly effective job if given direction. What he is missing is the essential vision for a transformative agenda. He is someone who is focused on crisis and administrative management and not so much on overall direction. He should have rowed rather than steered.

In seeking power Darrell sought out candidates who might well have run for any party. He was looking especially for candidates with established profile in their community. Often this meant people who had been elected to the school board or municipal council (e.g., Becky Kent and Sterling Belliveau). This is not a poor strategy at all. Though it did lead to some anomalies and problems. The anomaly was that although Darrell was very interested in recruiting politicians from the local level, he had no interest in helping Dippers get elected at the local level. That is, he wanted to stay away completely from promoting or supporting established NDP members who wanted to run municipally. The problem with this is that, in looking to recruit already elected people, he was competing with the other parties, and recruited people who could just as happily have joined any other party likely to help them build a career. This meant a growth in caucus members who were not established Dippers, or whose understanding of NDP thinking was limited at best. It is much better to seek to get already committed NDP members on to municipal councils or school boards.

As for internal discontent, this arose over the nominations for Cole Harbour–Eastern Passage after Kevin Deveaux resigned. Anne Marie Foote, a long time party member, assistant to Alexa and then to Megan Leslie, and a completely wonderful person, wanted to seek the nomination. As a courtesy she met with Darrell to tell him, and was astonished to be bluntly told he did not want her in his caucus. She was not mainstream enough. She had been too long associated with troublesome elements in the party. In the end, who he wanted was Becky Kent, who had already been elected to HRM Council, though not previously a New Democrat. This rejection of Anne Marie was widely resented within the party. A very similar situation occurred for the Chester–St. Margaret's nomination where long-time party member Jane Matheson was actively resisted for the nomination by Darrell, who favored Denise Peterson-Rafuse, not a person with roots in the party.

This was Darrell through and through. He is talented, but not in the way he thinks he is or wants to be. I once saw Darrell act impromptu the part of a dinosaur, a stegosaurus, the ones with big triangular armour in a line up their backs. It was at a fundraiser for Dartmouth's Eastern Front Theatre. Local celebrities were brought onstage and put through various acting experiences. Darrell as a dinosaur was terrific. He put his open hands up on his head and on his back and was instantly transformed. The audience was enraptured, and as the applause came, he called out, "You love me, you *really* love me!" Now this was certainly a Sally Field (perhaps also *The Mask*) reference, but there was something about the delivery that made it sound as though his soul was being exposed. Perhaps I read too much into it.

Darrell wants to be the smartest person in the room. He is given to trying to talk authoritatively about all points that come up. At caucus this was problematic because it stifled debate: better he should listen. He is also cynical about human nature. One of his favorite stories is the fable of the scorpion and the frog. He told it several times: There was a fire near a river. Various animals were trying to escape to the other side. Among them a frog and a scorpion. "Let me ride on your back," said the scorpion, "and we can escape together." "I would, said the frog, "but I am afraid you might sting me." "Why would I do that?" asked the scorpion. "If I did that we would both drown." So the frog lets the scorpion get on his back, and off he swims. Halfway across, the scorpion stings the frog. As they are drowning, the frog asks, "Why did you do that? We are going to die!" and the scorpion replies, "I know, but it is in my nature."

His cynicism and highhandedness resulted in a dysfunctional caucus. Instead of a productive gathering in which a range of opinion was welcomed, overall Darrell's approach was to inform caucus of what decisions had been made. Caucus was told, not asked. And Darrell's demand for loyalty meant he would snap at anyone resisting his views. For example, in one of the discussions about negative advertising aimed at Stephen McNeil, Darrell responded to objections from Gary Burrill by telling him that Darrell's long experience in elections made him a better judge of the effectiveness of negative advertising; then he went on to point out that Gary's son had resisted using party-generated literature in an election but had not shown any good results: a completely irrelevant point, with its message perhaps being that dissent and un-wisdom were in the Burrill genes. A terrible way to discuss things.

More often, Darrell would just not bring topics up. To my mind one of the most memorable occasions for this was the week in the summer of 2010 just after the Queen had been here for a visit. At the top of the caucus agenda is the "Leader's Report." Darrell thanked everyone for organizing Her Majesty's visit and making it a success. But just after the visit, two by-elections had been held in Glace Bay and Yarmouth. We were thumped in Yarmouth (6.5 per cent of the vote) and did not win in Glace Bay, even though we had been told we had a very good chance (the NDP received 42 per cent of the vote; the Liberals 54 per cent). Darrell did not mention the by-elections, just rambled on about the Queen. Gary Burrill had to ask him about them to elicit any comment.

If Darrell is in the mould of typical Nova Scotia premiers, it remains to be asked if he was an actual *NDP* premier. It is not obvious that he was. What seems clear is that Darrell, like his favoured candidates, could probably have run for any party. It seems accidental that he migrated to the NDP. Darrell, when resisting criticism over particular policies or – especially – over his choice of preferred candidates, has been fond of saying, "There is no DNA test for what is an NDPer." But in fact there are a lot of markers: Has the person been a member of the party? Does the person believe in progressive taxation, i.e., that the more you earn the more you should pay? Does the person believe in co-operative endeavors? Does the person have instincts to advance the interests of the marginalized in society? Do they value sustainability for our physical life support systems? Do they have a healthy skepticism about big business? Do they believe in public ownership of essential services? And do they have a history of standing up for these things, a history of accomplishments? On all of these Darrell and his closest team are weak at best.

Darrell's Chief of Staff was Dan O'Connor. In one of the later Sherlock Holmes stories, the great detective mentions his brother Mycroft. Dr. Watson, never having heard of the brother before, gets the impression he is "something in the government." "It would be more accurate," Holmes says, "to say that Mycroft *is* the government." This was Dan O'Connor. Nothing happened in the NDP – in or out of government – unless Dan O'Connor knew about it and had reviewed it. He is a very fast typist who maintains a prolific email correspon-

Dan O'Connor

dence. He is a classic micromanager. He is also profoundly cynical. He reminds me not only of Mycroft Holmes, but of that Renaissance bishop of whom it was said that he could never tell a lie, but he could not tell the truth either. You have to listen very carefully to what Dan says. He is highly skilled at what he does, including the attack: "If one would give me six lines written by the hand of the most honest man, I would find something in them to have him hanged." (Cardinal Richelieu, 1585–1642). This quotation is well worth remembering around Dan O'Connor. He often sits at the side of the room, working his phone's game function – he seems to be a big fan of solitaire. For the most part he walks to work. He looks like the Boston Irish writer George V. Higgins, bearded, slim but with a high waist, a happy imbiber of beer, a shambling walker given to ancient battered shoes.

Dan is a survivor. When Robert was about to finish his term as leader, he brought a motion to caucus to recognize some time Dan had spent away from Nova Scotia as part of uninterrupted service. This was a peculiar idea, and was presented nonetheless as a routine matter with no consequences. In fact, the consequence was that under Nova Scotia's employment laws, an employee with ten years of continuous service could not be dismissed even with notice, except for cause. Clearly this was an attempt to bind the hands of the next leader as to choice of chief of staff. It was an attempt to keep Dan in his position no matter what. The scenario Robert was anticipating was the possibility that Kevin Deveaux would become leader, and Kevin had identified Dan as a problem. This illustrates how closely tied Dan always became to every leader, as a support. Alexa relied on him, even with rough times. Robert did; Helen did; Darrell certainly did.

I first got to know Dan when he was on the Board of the Ecology Action Centre and I was the Centre's executive director, in 1990–94. This connection never really amounted to much. If Dan carries around core convictions that are oriented towards sustainability it has not been evident. Though it was an environmental issue over which Dan did once offer me an apology, a rare event in NDP politics – not apologies to me, but apologies of any sort. What happened was that during the 1998 election Robert was in Cape Breton, and met with the mineworkers union. The union was facing the prospect of closure of DEVCO (Cape Breton Development Corporation) supported coal mines, which had to do with the poor quality of the coal (high sulphur content, high ash content, i.e., dirt) and its high cost. After the meeting, Robert issued a statement about some steps that could be taken to deal with the coming changes in employment in coal mining jobs, and the high unemployment situation in Cape Breton generally. The last point on the list was a statement that if the Kyoto Protocol meant the loss of coal mining jobs in Cape Breton then Canada should not ratify it. When I read this I hit the roof. The environmental community was solidly behind Kyoto. And Kyoto had nothing to do with the coming closure of the Cape Breton coal mines – that was going to happen anyway. I registered my protest, and was so put out that I was considering resigning as an NDP candidate. Dan phoned me to talk it over. He urged taking the long view, that staying in to debate the issue would be more productive. He said the point was put forward at the urging of the union, and was not so much the product of party economic thinking. And then he said that although he was not authorized to say it, he wanted to apologize to me, this should not have happened. I don't think I ever heard anyone in the party leadership seriously apologize for anything, either internally or publicly, ever again. Energy politics, especially around coal, were to be an ongoing theme in the party.

Dan was later involved in a peculiar, murky, and embarrasing incident in May, 2010 in which he was accused by *The Chronicle Herald* of posting comments using the name 'O'Dempsey' and then of denying it. *The Chronicle Herald* had published a story about the $42 thousand cost of a public relations event and booklet boasting of the government's energy strategy for renewable electrical generation. Dan, using the 'O'Dempsey' name, then accused *The Chronicle Herald* of being like *Frank Magazine*.

The NDP held tenaciously to the position of opposition through four provincial elections: 1998, 1999, 2003, and 2006. The numbers went up and down. From 19 in the 1998 breakthrough, down to 11 in the 1999 election that brought John Hamm and the PCs from third to first place, up to 15 in 2003, and then to 20 in 2006. It was a long slog.

It took a long time for the NDP to advance as we did so markedly in 1998. In a minority situation, it is to be expected that another election will come within two years. The task of the party from March 1998 on was to get ready for the next election, to make the push to achieve government. That was explicit in internal thinking, and was the focus of all public political commentary: could the NDP win the next election? In any event, the Liberals lasted less than eighteen months. But the 1999 election did not produce the hoped-for gain of a government. The party campaigned well, but Nova Scotians were not quite ready. John Hamm's Tories adroitly moved from third to first place. They did so by offering a detailed plan, through the force of Dr. Hamm's personality, and through one significant gaffe of Robert Chisholm's, the statement about his old drunk-driving conviction.

The result was loss of some very good people from our caucus: Yvonne Atwell, Hinrich Bitter-Suermann, Don Chard, Peter Delefes, John Deveau, Rosemary Godin, Helen MacDonald, and Charlie Parker. Charlie later came back in 2003 and held onto his seat through two subsequent elections, and served as Speaker as well as Minister of Energy and Natural Resources. Helen succeeded Robert as leader in 2000 but failed to win the seat she tried for, Cape Breton North, and was later forced to resign. Rosemary Godin was publicly very upset with the party. She was unable to find work, including being passed over for a job at the caucus office, and spent some time on welfare. Godin pointed out something not well known, but a significant fact for those considering running for office: MLAs are not eligible for unemployment insurance. She was being dunned by the bank over her constituency association's loan, which she had co-signed as a guarantor, and so was stressed. She said she felt "thrown to the dogs." She also blamed her election loss in part on out-of-province staff who had been pushed on her by party organizers who did not know the local scene well enough.

But that 1999 election loss was in the future. In 1998 there were some immediate problems. Just after the election I heard through other lawyers that one member of our caucus was under formal investigation by the Barristers Society for improprieties with his trust funds (client monies held by a law firm temporarily). Reeves Matheson was elected MLA for Cape Breton East (Glace Bay). Ultimately he pled guilty and was sentenced to two years less one day of house arrest, and was required to reimburse the Barristers Society insurers some $117 thousand to compensate clients. At the first caucus meeting after the election I spoke privately with Robert Chisholm to warn him that trouble was probably about to come and become public over Matheson. He already knew. Matheson was suspended from caucus and never returned. This was a big embarrassment because there ought to have been a thorough screening process in place for candidates. In fact there was, but it did not work. Matheson was able to game the screening, and independent checking, if any took place did not turn up anything. Unfortunately this sort of misleading self-presentation occurs frequently, and not just in politics. It happens that searches of social media sites turn up highly problematic information about candidates or elected officials. They might have gone on record with objectionable opinions (racist, homophobic), views that are at variance with their party's policies, or shown themselves to be irresponsible in some way. All parties have suffered this. For the NDP, where a part of our public image has been to attempt to differentiate ourselves from the old line parties especially in terms of honesty and uprightness, these incidents are especially troubling. We had run into this previously a decade earlier in 1988 when the husband of one candidate admitted to growing marijuana.

At the very start of the 1998 term, how the minority dynamics would play out was completely unclear. But having achieved such a surge was enough to put us on the national stage. Former Saskatchewan NDP Premier, the late Allan Blakeney (with his origins as a Nova Scotian), came to speak with caucus about political maneuvering. He emphasized that there is a long list of political issues always before a party, and that it would be best to select just a few to make our signature pieces. A very good book about the NDP in government in Saskatchewan, *Dream No Little Dreams*,[8] documents how the events played out there. But that advice was focused on what to do should we become the government immediately. At the time, there was speculation that the NDP and the PCs might work out an agreement to oust the Liberals (both opposition parties had run on similar platforms) or that the next Liberal budget might be defeated and, instead of an immediate election the Lieutenant Governor might turn to the NDP to see if it could govern.

Things did not turn out that way. Instead, the Liberals held on for sixteen months, and then the 1999 election went to the Tories. I, though hardly alone in the party, was very disappointed. Somewhat intemperately I commented that John Hamm would have a tough time forming a good cabinet, and I called a lot of the new Tory MLAs, "no-name, know-nothing, nobodies." Oh, dear. It is never good to lose your temper. And personal remarks are beside the point. Sticking to the issues is what makes sense. I later apologized in the House to the new members. And I have tended to remember the lesson.

Why did we fail to win the 1999 election? The geographic results were clear: the Liberals were reduced to a base in Cape Breton; we maintained Metro; and the Hamm PCs took the rural and small town mainland. This was quite an accomplishment, to win a majority of seats with no real presence in Metro at all. It was done by taking virtually all of the non-Metro, non-Cape Breton seats – a sweep of the mainland. Expectations had been widespread that our party under Robert Chisholm would win the election. A lot of the press coverage was focused on him, in the adulatory style that goes to handsome political leaders. This drove Robert crazy. He is certainly a handsome man, but I am sure that it is not what it feels like to be him. He does not get up each morning and think how the world owes him glory because he is good looking. He is from a successful insurance family in the Annapolis Valley, but chose to work in the union movement, with CUPE. He and his wife Paula Simon have had a significant sorrow with the early death of their son. Robert threw himself into politics, and while he started out, even as leader, with an uneven speaking ability, he became very accomplished over his term. We lost the election through looking a bit overconfident, and in a moment of electoral wavering about whether to choose the NDP for the first time, and because of a misstatement about an old and irrelevant criminal conviction.

I tend not to give much weight to anti-union bias as a factor, though there certainly are some voters for whom the traditional ties of the NDP with labour are problematic. I do think that the memory of the Bob Rae years in Ontario was still fresh. The NDP took power in Ontario for the first time in 1990, just at the start of a serious recession, and had a terrible time struggling through it. They managed to alienate their own base, and faced an unrelentingly hostile press from the very beginning. The entire experience played into the hands of those who promulgate the opinion that the NDP has no expertise in managing an economy. I think this was a more potent factor here in 1999 than any anti-union issues. The 1999 campaign also marked, in visual terms, the start of the change in thinking inside the party leadership about centrism. Robert campaigned, in a hot summer election, in a suit and tie. The intended message was of business attire, and of business friendliness. Taking this sort of tack is advocated for as "immunization" i.e., protecting ourselves from a possible attack as being anti-business by showing that we are just as pro-business as the next party. In the party's formal post-election review, this approach was seen as flawed. Subsequently, leaders have chosen to ignore this party verdict.

One of the stars of John Hamm's team was Jane Purves. A true Halifax establishment person, Jane was managing editor of *The Chronicle Herald* newspaper but moved to electoral politics, taking the south end (Halifax Citadel) seat. She became Minister of Education. But just a couple of months later, she had to admit to a serious drug addiction during her teens and twenties. In a September 22, 1999 press release she said:

Earlier today ... I was asked about my past and, specifically, about past drug use. While I consider this matter to be private, given my current position of public trust, I felt an obligation to answer the questions honestly and to share this information with Nova Scotians. [...] I sought professional help and, with the support of my family and friends, was able to recover. I have been free of the addiction for more than 20 years. But there have been lasting consequences. I have a criminal record for possession of marijuana. I lost custody of my only child for a number of years. And, I learned that I had contracted Hepatitis C as a result of drug use. [...] Drug use could have ruined my life. It didn't.[9]

Jane Purves

What was most striking about all of this is the contrast with how Robert Chisholm was treated. Jane Purves drew sympathy. The prevailing attitude was that everyone goes through difficult periods in their lives; that the episodes were very much in the past and that although she could have been more forthright before the election the focus now should be on her performance in her portfolio. Robert had a conviction for impaired driving dating from when he was nineteen. And nothing since. No addiction. No intravenous drug use. No problem with his spouse over child custody. But he did fail to answer a question forthrightly. There were two errors. One was not to have put the facts on the public record years before. That would have been the easiest thing to do. No one would have cared one whit. The matter would have been a non-issue. The other error was to deny any criminal conviction. But the press he received was very bad, in stark contrast to how Jane Purves was treated just three months later.

Being Education Minister is a tough assignment. Nova Scotians value education highly, and any minister who shows wavering dedication to high quality is at risk. This happened to Purves in the following election. She was turfed following high profile strenuous fights over proposed school closures in her constituency. And while technically the responsibility for these decisions was in the hands of the School Board, a separately elected body, all school boards operate within a legal and financial framework set by the province, and so Purves as both the minister and the local MLA was constantly called to account. She herself was hugely frustrated since the Board was closing a French immersion school that was high quality, popular, and that she would probably have kept. Her constituency, Citadel, then elected a Liberal, becoming one of only two constituencies (the other being Preston) to have voted in representatives from all three parties in quick succession. Later she came back to the political process as John Hamm's chief of staff, after Jamie Baillie left to acquire business experience as a prelude to seeking his party leadership. When Jane died young (at age 63) in 2013, of cancer, many people noted that she had a wicked sense of humour, and was a person of integrity. All true. When she was caught up in the controversy over school closures, buttons appeared that said, "Calamity Jane." During an anti-government demo at Province House, she made sure to ask for one as a souvenir.

Years later, Lori Errington, who has had something of an inside look at the operations of our Legislature, having been an NDP caucus researcher, later working for the Lieutenant Governor before a stint as a civil servant, wrote her MA thesis entitled, "The experiences of female Members in the Legislative Assembly in Nova Scotia."[10] She conducted interviews with eight women MLAs from all three political parties. As she pointed out this represents 26 per cent of all the women ever elected in Nova Scotia. No one is identified by name: the subjects are referred to, for example, as "Woman # 4." Women are decidedly likely to state that they entered politics to effect change, to help others, and to be disappointed at the posturing that they find at every turn. Woman # 6 is quoted by Errington as saying:

It's odd because we were in these different political circles and we just fight so hard not (to) get along, it seems. It's just ... there's so much work to be done, and electioneering should be kept to elections. And in-between times, when we're put in the role of leaders of our communities, spokespeople, and we find ourselves, whether it's in government or opposition ... we really owe it to our constituents to really, to take off the political striped hat and really work together to get things done ... but we don't and that's the unfortunate part.[10]

To the extent any of the interviewed MLAs saw anything useful in the formal legislative process, it occasionally emerged in committee work. But overall, they felt intimidated and bullied, and part of a process where masculine values and style predominate. If in government, and in Cabinet, they were likely to be assigned the social portfolios: health, education, community services (exactly as Darrell Dexter later assigned his female Cabinet ministers before moving Maureen MacDonald to Finance after Graham Steele resigned).

I was not actually wrong about John Hamm's caucus and cabinet, as it happened. He had trouble with John Chataway (a minister for Housing and Municipal Affairs who got in trouble for owning rental properties with building code problems), with Bill Dooks (allegations of burying garbage and threats of prosecution under the *Environment Act*), with Mark Parent (for opening a committee meeting with a prayer that insulted the Irish – yes, this is true), with Rodney MacDonald (the classic helicopter ride), with Tim Olive (unpaid rent and business occupancy taxes), with David Hendsbee (offering to sell ad space to community groups on his MLA website) and with Ernie Page (leaving the scene of a car accident). It was not a joyous Tory time, except for the reporters. And for our party, which could just stand by and allow the new government to self-destruct.

And for those who wonder about that prayer of Mark Parent's:

> But if Ye have any favours to bestow or any good land to give away, give it to Thine own peculiar people, the Scots. Make them members of Parliament, rulers among Thy people, but as for the ungodly Irish, take them by the heels and shake them over the mouth of hell, but Lord don't let them fall in.

Let us, in all charity, assume that Mr. Parent, a Baptist minister, was only illustrating how partisanship can get out of hand.

Oh, and here are a couple more of the Tory messes that I am certain John Hamm hated sorting out. John Chataway was told by the Premier's Office the name of a journalist who made a *Freedom of Information Act* (FOI) inquiry about his department. The Minister approached the journalist and offered to be helpful. Friendly, but the province's Review Officer under the *Freedom of Information Act* had previously made clear that no one except the civil servant processing an FOI request should know the name of an applicant. The late Michael Baker as Minister of Justice refused to make good on an election promise made by the new Shelburne MLA Cecil O'Donnell to hold a public inquiry into events at the Shelburne School for Boys, opting instead for an informal review with a limited mandate. Jamie Muir as Minister of Health retracted a license from the Sisters of Charity to operate nursing home beds at the Mother Berchmans Centre located on the grounds of Mount Saint Vincent University, a license which had been promised by the former Liberal government and which the PCs had supported while in opposition. Bill Dooks (Eastern Shore) and Ron Chisholm (Guysborough) took a trip together to Ottawa at taxpayers' expense to lobby for improvements to Highway 107 but did not bother to arrange in advance to meet with Transport Minister David Collenette and so only got to meet with an aide.

So the promise of a reliable John Hamm led government on the comfortable model of the Robert Stanfield years did not really come to pass. There were problems from the start. But it was a majority government and so had a mandate for as long as the constitutionally permitted five years. The next election was called for the summer of 2003, at the four-year mark.

We went into the 2003 election tied with the Liberals in terms of seats held, both of us at eleven. We moved to 15 and the Tories were reduced to a minority with 25 seats. So it was something of a comeback, though not a win. It set the stage for a period of inter-party cooperation. At least to some extent. The parties cooperated because no one wanted another election immediately. The Tories picked us as their partner rather than the Liberals. The way this worked was a system of regular meetings between Dr. Hamm and Darrell, and Dan O'Connor and Dr. Hamm's chiefs of staff, Jamie Baillie and later Jane Purves. It was to be three years until the next reduction in PC seats, down to 23 in the 2006 election.

In 2003 one of the big election issues was auto insurance. In identifying this issue we were moved by forces that became part of how policy and electoral calculation interacted. For one thing, there was an actual problem of affordability. So it was a real pocketbook issue, and one that affected virtually everyone. For another, we could be seen to be taking the lead, showing ourselves as the party of ideas, a contrast with the others. There were also different models in place in other provinces, including publicly run schemes in British Columbia, Quebec, Saskatchewan, and Manitoba. So precedents for change existed. And in pushing for a public auto insurance system, we were showing faith in government-led initiatives. I quite liked this array, but was aware that a similar scheme had been abandoned by the NDP in Ontario, leading to a lot of internal party discontent.

What frightened the Ontario NDP about moving ahead with a publicly administered auto insurance system were demonstrations by the employees of insurance agencies and insurance firms. Ontario is home to significant numbers of insurance companies, and they convinced their employees that a public auto system would result in job losses. They turned out in great numbers. This was not the case here, although the insurance brokers were very opposed to the prospect of public auto. We had non-stop debates with the brokers. Later, after the scheme had been abandoned because the Hamm government adopted a regulatory system, and rates fell or stabilized, the insurance brokers made sure to hold regular annual dinners for MLAs to keep the dialogue going and to deliver their message that no wind-up of their business was necessary. Their 2003 debating foe, Graham Steele, became the usual friendly guest speaker at the dinners as Minister responsible for insurance.

The regulatory scheme adopted led to reduced rates, but also limited liability for insurance companies for minor injuries, a restriction later adjusted by us. A public auto insurance scheme was a minor part of the 2006 platform, but by 2009 public auto insurance was off the table.

Rodney MacDonald

My post-election comments for 2003 have already been cited. Basically, that election was built on the 1999 one as another attempt to position the party as centrist, as non-threatening, and as Tory-like. The 2006 election was much the same.

By then John Hamm had stepped aside and been replaced by Rodney MacDonald. The affable, handsome, fiddle-playing Cape Bretoner started out looking to be a good bet for the Tories as a new leader from a younger generation. He attracted adulatory national press coverage: "Music to the ears of Nova Scotia," wrote *The Globe and Mail*.[11] He turned out to be a liability. Just months after becoming Premier he called an election; the result being a loss of two more Tory seats, and a gain of five for the NDP.

Our theme for the 2006 election was, "A Better Deal – the plan you can count on." Many of the specifics that would later be implemented by us as government after 2009 were in the platform: taking the HST off of necessities, a tax credit for volunteer fire fighters, a restoration of the Arts Council, phasing out the large corporations' capital tax, and making Nova Scotia a leader in renewable energy. Overall, our aim was to make the ballot question a choice between a better NDP deal and Tory broken promises. The Liberals, under Francis MacKenzie, had a pretty solid platform but had not been out of office long enough to make a comeback. They drifted down to nine seats and MacKenzie resigned.

Platforms and slogans are an interesting aspect of politicking. Skeptics like British political journalist Jeremy Paxman see platforms as little more than a nuisance, "because they give a yardstick to judge performance"[12] while influencing few voters. This is not actually my view, though I join Paxman in amusement at the way slogans are shaped by advertising agencies and are recycled: "new", "hope", "tomorrow", "win", "action", "change", "together", "put XYZ first" are all examples.

The minority government years 2003–2009 gave the NDP the opportunity to influence the government, to good effect. In addition to pocketbook items like reductions in auto insurance rates, fairness issues such as seniors in nursing homes no longer being required to pay for their medical care, were agreed to by the government. The provincial portion of the HST came off of home heating bills. A 10 per cent surtax on those in the highest income bracket was adopted. The minimum wage increased. The NDP in the Opposition facing a minority Tory government, like the 1998–1999 period facing a Liberal minority, was the NDP at its best.

With Maude Barlow, National Chairperson of the Council of Canadians.

With Jack Layton.

4

That Was Then, This Is Now

While much was accomplished during our years in Opposition, some positions were staked-out that were not always followed through when we were in Government.

Labour

Traditionally it was said – and said accurately – that the Liberals were the party of big business, the Tories were the party of small business, and the NDP was the party of labour. This has evolved. In the time of Brian Mulroney the Tories became more the party of big business, and even with its later merger with the Reform Party, the Conservatives have never left that alignment. The Liberals have struggled for self-definition, federally and provincially, but have emerged somewhere in the mushy middle. And so too has the NDP. Without totally abandoning a traditional alliance with labour – in all its forms, organized and not, urban and not – the NDP has tried to broaden its appeal. However, ties to labour are still important, and do form a serious aspect of NDP politics. Before changes in the rules governing money contributions, unions were financially essential to the NDP. NDP members came to the party through their concern over labour issues, peace issues, gender issues, and environmental issues. But labour has long predominated. Indeed, until some changes in the party constitution, labour controlled votes at conventions because of assigned numbers of delegates. Although jibes are regularly offered to the NDP about its ties to labour, the party is not ashamed of them. But the actual delivery of support is a mixed story and this section should especially be read in association with the section on Health (below) to understand some of these major problems.

In Opposition, the party certainly took a significant role in the politics of labour relations, especially to defend labour from attacks from Liberal or Tory governments. Later, in government, the main issue became whether advances could be made on issues like labour legislation, minimum wages, and public sector bargaining. But during the Opposition years, the NDP was a reliable labour ally. We spoke for better minimum wage scales. We defended the right to organize and strike. We spoke up for better health and safety protection. We formally memorialized labour outrages such as the Westray mine explosion.

Because there were attempts to erode labour rights or to take a hard line in public sector negotiations, it was logical for the NDP to act as defenders of labour. Still, in looking back at Question Period sessions, it is striking that on occasion we were too preoccupied with labour matters. For example, on November 4, 1998 the first three questions put by the NDP to Premier Russell MacLellan had to do with negotiations over wage parity for continuing care workers. The questions asked by John Hamm were all focused on the economy: jobs associated with the Sable Offshore Energy Project (SOEP) and development of the Shearwater lands in Dartmouth.

There is a television ad made by unions in Australia, probably on the model of the Monty Python sketch of, "What did the Romans ever do for us?" It shows a group of businessmen sitting around a table, and they are dissing unions. Unions are useless, they say. They just take dues and do nothing for their members. It is only hard working business leaders who accomplish anything. Unions never accomplished anything. Nods all around. A pause. Then one fellow says, "Well, except the weekend." Oh, right, the others say, the weekend, that's not bad. "And the eight hour day," says another. Well, OK, the eight-hour day. "And ending child labour," points out another. "Workplace health and safety laws," mentions another. "Benefits like insurance," says another. And on it goes. But they don't really accomplish anything, they all agree. No. No. Nods all around.

Looking back I am happy to see that some of my own remarks are decidedly pro-labour. Our party's association with labour is something of which we should be proud. A part of my own experience has been as a labour lawyer acting for various unions. Others in our caucus have been union members or union staff. Labour issues come before the Legislature with regularity. Bargaining in the public sector, especially for health workers is a perennial topic. Framework legislation for union certification, the powers of the Labour Board, or the powers of arbitrators, have also appeared. Likewise for pension regulation and the minimum wage. So, too, have various aspects of health and safety legislation. All of these were important topics throughout our years in Opposition.

Dr. Hamm brought in legislation to amend the *Mineral Resources Act*, a bill with a variety of items, some emanating from the public inquiry following the explosion in the Westray Mine. Here are some of my comments:

> The Westray Mine was run by people who are no better than murderers and who ought to have been convicted in court for their actions. [...] This party should have taken the opportunity on this occasion, when dealing with amendments to mining legislation emanating from Westray, to act in the most scrupulous way possible and they have not done so. [...] In my opinion, and in the submission that was made by the Ecology Action Centre, no underground mine in Nova Scotia should be opened unless it has been subject to a Class II environmental assessment. A Class II environmental assessment is the highest level of scrutiny available under our *Environment Act*. [...] The only answer given by the minister the other day ... as to why he is hesitating to adopt this proposed change ... was that *The Environment Act* is due for review in 2000 and that is the time to deal with this. The time to deal with it is right now, when the very issue is in front of members of this House. [...] There is no necessity to wait. [...] There is a lesson ... Mr. Speaker, that if another underground mine goes forward and it has not been subject to a Class II environmental assessment and if something goes wrong in that mine and they fail

to act, having been specifically given the opportunity and the invitation today to act, it will be on the heads of the party led yet again by Pictou County Tories."[1]

My suggestions were not taken up. Legislation regarding bargaining by health care workers is dealt with in more detail in another section. Here let me just set out the major changes to labour legislation in the province over the last forty or so years, many instances, though not all, interfering with free collective bargaining:

1971
- Mediation to try to avoid strike/lockout introduced.
- Construction industry panel created.

1973
- Rules changed for certification of craft unions (first *Michelin Bill*).

1978
- Collective bargaining for government employees established.

1979
- *Michelin Bill* requiring multi-plant certification adopted.

1986
- Strikes in construction industry must be voted for by multiple unions.

1991
- Two-year contract freeze for government employees.

1993
- Five unpaid leave days for government employees mandated ("Savage Days").

1994
- Steen Bill allows unionized contractors to hire non-unionized subcontractors.
- Freeze on wages and other terms of employment for three years in the broad public sector implemented.

1997
- Highway workers included in collective bargaining.

1998
- Removing right to strike for police proposed but not adopted.

1999

• (Bill 9) Impending strike by paramedics banned, issues sent to binding arbitration.

2001

• Two-tier bargaining by teachers phased out.

• (Bill 68) Impending strike by nurses banned; issues sent to binding arbitration.

2004

• Police right to strike replaced by binding arbitration.

2005

• Expedited arbitrations added to *Trade Union Act.*

2006

• Firefighters right to strike replaced by binding arbitration.

2007

• Proposal to remove right to strike for health care workers; not adopted.

2008

• Arbitration for police widened in ambit.

2009

• Process of mediation/arbitration added.

2010

• New unified Labour Board established.

2011

• First Contract Arbitration (FCA) process established.

2013

• Impending strike by paramedics banned, issues sent to binding arbitration.

2014

• (Bill 37) All health care and Community Services workplaces to have essential services agreements.

• (Bill 1) Health bargaining units merged; arbitrator chooses union to represent workers.

It is clear that governments have not hesitated to freeze wages in times of financial constraint. In essence, such legislation is a cancellation of free bargaining process usually with the imposition of major terms and conditions of employment unilaterally. Such moves, with the major legislation having now come from all three parties, bring out the essentially political nature of labour relations. This is hardly new. The interactions between employers and employees, the struggles between classes, account for much of the story. Even seen only as a technical legal matter, the framework basic legislation, the *Trade Union Act*, is clearly designed to keep workers working. That is, the structure of the statute is to try to avoid work stoppages: thus all collective agreements must contain a provision for arbitration of grievances, and if they fail to, a model clause is deemed to be a part of the collective agreements. What this means is that in the case of a workplace dispute, the workers cannot "down tools" and walk off the job: disputes go the route of grievance/arbitration. The other main set of provisions designed to keep workers working is the structure for the bargaining process: thus the parties must bargain in good faith; the existing terms of employment are frozen while bargaining goes on; no strike or lockout is allowed until mediators become involved. Again, the object is to avoid work stoppages. Clearly all of this is designed to maintain economic production or protect the general public from even temporary loss of important services. This could be seen as something of a neutral stance on the part of the state, but probably tends to favor employers, which is no surprise. What has been the main feature of the special legislation that has altered, either permanently or for some set period the bargaining relations, is that it further favors employers.

Nothing illustrates this better than the 1979 *Michelin Bill*. As part of the arrangements for attracting investment to Nova Scotia by the French tire manufacturer Michelin, the government of the day (PC) agreed to change the law as it affects the establishment of a union and to do so focused particularly on Michelin. Starting in 1969 the company had established several plants in Nova Scotia, one in Bridgewater and one in Granton, near Pictou, and one in Waterville. Early on, the United Rubberworkers Union started to try and sign up members. (In later years the Canadian Auto Workers (CAW) would also try.) Up until the *Michelin Bill*, the law was clear that in any attempt to unionize, the target workplaces would almost always be taken to be one site, regardless of interactions be-

tween that one site and others owned and operated
by the same employer. This
had been established by
the Canada Labour Rela-
tions Board (CLRB) when
attempts were made to
unionize bank branches; the
banks took the position that
a union could not target just
one branch, they had to treat

The Michelin tire plant in Granton, NS.

a bank's full network of branches as one workplace and therefore sign up
a majority of all employees Canada-wide. The CLRB ruled that this made
no sense, and that precedent was widely taken as representing the state
of the law. What the *Michelin Bill* did was to alter that: where the location
sought to be unionized is part of an, "interdependent manufacturing location," the employer may claim that, "the unit appropriate for collective
bargaining is the unit consisting of all employees of the employer at all
such ... locations." This change in the law put a halt to the unionization
effort directed at Michelin here. Subsequent efforts, organized so as to
try to meet the requirements of the new law, have not been a success and
were abandoned.

This extraordinary alteration of the basic rules for establishing collective bargaining at a workplace was strongly opposed by all unionized
labour groups in the province. It was a major and bitter struggle of the
time. Obviously the bill favored only one company. It was a change in the
rules in the midst of the process. It went against the logic of what is a
natural unit appropriate for collective bargaining.

When the *Michelin Bill* went through the Legislature both the NDP
and the Liberals opposed it. Debate was heated. And it reflected the outrage in the labour community at large. Here is Paul MacEwan:

> Mr. Speaker, in Michelin we are not dealing with any run of the mill,
> private company. We are not dealing with a local family firm...We are
> dealing rather with a global giant which has risen to supremacy in
> the tire industry. [...] As has been demonstrated an essential element

of that strategy ... is the avoidance of any industrial areas having a history of ... trade unionism.[2]

Here is Jeremy Akerman:

The Minister of Labour ... went stumbling around this province muttering and mumbling about ... how horrible labour relations are ... and how something has got to be done. At the time when the statistics show that we had the best record in the country! Then ... after trying to cultivate public opinion to believe that the situation was bad ... we see the piece of legislation coming back into the House ... [then] the Minister of Development ... [announces] that Santa Claus will be visiting Nova Scotia this year in the form of Michelin Tire who are going to build a new plant and expand their existing operations. Now I ask you, Mr. Speaker, what person who has any experience of life at all ... can possibly doubt that all these events are very closely connected.[3]

NDP Policy resolutions condemned the Bill:

Resolved that this convention condemn the Buchanan Government for passing into law the so-called *Michelin Bill* thereby restricting the rights of Nova Scotians.[4]

Party resolutions included being scathing about government assistance to Michelin in 1997 when the MacLellan Liberals granted it some $27 million:

Resolved that a New Democratic Party government in Nova Scotia would work ... to curb the activities of corporate blackmailers like Michelin.

When Alexa was the new leader, she campaigned in the 1981 election promising to repeal the *Michelin Bill*. However, in 2009 we learned that Darrell had a different view of Michelin. "NDP wouldn't kill *Michelin Bill*," *The Chronicle Herald* told us:

"I have no interest in fighting battles that took place ... 30 years ago," the New Democrat leader said Monday during a campaign stop in

Halifax. "I think we've moved a long way and industrial relations have moved a long way since that time."[5]

Well, thank you for that Darrell. No point in holding to principle when there is an election in the offing. A decade earlier, during the 1999 election, our candidate in Lunenburg West, the Bridgewater area in which a Michelin plant is located, had said during a local debate that the NDP would not alter the *Michelin Bill* if it became government. But that was a local candidate, not the party leader, and did not reflect party policy.

And what did this get either Nova Scotia or the NDP? Was there ever any realistic chance Michelin would shut up its plants here and move? Highly unlikely. From the time the provincial government gave Michelin an $80 million low-interest loan plus a $7.6 million grant when the company first came to Nova Scotia, Michelin has enjoyed a cozy and profitable relationship with Nova Scotia governments of all three parties.

The 1992 text, *The Atlantic Provinces in Confederation,* says this in commenting on various attempts by the Nova Scotia government to attract business:

> Even more successful ventures raised difficult questions. In July 1969 the establishment of two tire-manufacturing plants in Nova Scotia by the Michelin company had been announced with great fanfare. In this case, there was no collapse. Michelin expeditiously built factories at Granton and Bridgewater, and in 1979 the company announced that a third would be added, at Waterville in Kings county. Large sums of public money were invested. Of the $150 million of projected investments in the original two plants it had been agreed that approximately two-thirds would come in one form or another from government sources. A price was also paid in the form of the power that the Michelin company would henceforth exercise over successive provincial governments. [...] This was reflected in the government's eagerness to act in the interests of Michelin's non-union policy.[6]

Our government played footsie with Michelin as much as anyone, promising money to help with an expansion of the Waterville plant. What it did get us was Dana LeBlanc, President of Michelin North America (Canada) Inc. (and every other false friend of the NDP government) coming to the Law Amendments Committee to condemn our Bill 102 on First Contract Arbitration (FCA). Perfectly happy to take public money over many years and perfectly happy to have had the *Trade Union Act* amended for its particular benefit, Michelin opposed changes to the *Trade Union Act* that it said amounted to, "a well-known union organizing tool to help organizers downplay or distort the reality of collective bargaining for employees."[7] In fact, what distorted reality was the 1979 *Michelin Bill*, a major alteration of the basic structure of labour law, unique in Canada. The NDP's FCA was a minor tweak, which reflected the prevailing approach in most other jurisdictions. In terms of sheer gall, LeBlanc's comments made his presentation a moment to remember.

Not only did the NDP fail to come to grips with the highly offensive *Michelin Bill* (although Darrell was at least frank in his position on that) it failed to come to grips with the very many weaknesses of the *Labour Standards Code,*[8] although quite a different indication was offered when we were in Opposition. (The *Labour Standards Code* sets minimum employment terms and conditions which apply regardless of whether a workplace is unionized. Thus, it governs most workplaces in the province.) At one time *The Chronicle-Herald* newspaper allowed the party leaders to write columns. Here is Darrell in 2001 on the *Labour Standards Code*:

> An increasing number of workers face unique challenges. There are part-time workers who receive few or no benefits. [...] It all means greater stress in the workplace and at home. That's why in the past year the NDP caucus introduced changes to the *Labour Standards Act* that would help attract and maintain a well-trained, highly skilled and productive workforce, changes to the *Occupational Health and Safety Act* aimed at making Nova Scotia workplaces safer. [...] Nova Scotia lags behind most other jurisdictions in all these areas.[9]

We still do. The term for this style of campaigning is "bait and switch." And as with virtually all aspects of public policy, good models do exist. In this case, the Nova Scotia branch of the Canadian Center for Policy Alternatives published a March, 2012 review, "Labour Standards Reform in Nova Scotia."[10] Not a peep out of our NDP Labour department.

Another of the dubious policies of our government regarding labour: one of the important aspects of getting Back To Balance was the proposal to reduce the size of the civil service by 10 per cent "through attrition." The loss of jobs mostly means a loss of services for the public, reduced opportunities for young people to start careers, and in any event was poor policy during the Great Recession.

Nor did job fatalities diminish during our term in office. The appalling long-term average in Nova Scotia is approximately 24 job-related deaths per year – both acute (traumatic injury) and chronic (industrial disease). During our term the number increased slightly to an average of 27 per year.[11] The NDP always participates in the Federation of Labour's Day of Mourning each April to remember those injured or killed on the job. Some useful pro-labour steps were taken when we were in government; these are described in more detail in chapter 14. But better we had done many more substantive things when we had the chance to in government.

Using Committees

Of the eleven years the NDP spent in Opposition after 1998, most of them were with minority governments. The first year and a half involved a Liberal minority, and then from 2003 on there were Tory minorities. Committees are especially useful for opposition parties during minorities. This is because membership on committees reflects seats held in the House, and so the government loses control of the committee agendas. Time and again we were able to use this venue to advantage.

Two examples are especially interesting. One was the investigation by the Public Accounts Committee of the involvement of the Liberal Premier and Minister of Finance in attempting to manage the contract for the new gambling casino. The other was the special (Select) Committee on Petroleum Pricing under the Tories. I had some involvement in both sets of hearings.

(i) Public Accounts Committee – Casino

The tradition for Public Accounts Committees (PAC) is that they are chaired by an Opposition member. This is true even in a majority government, where committees are controlled by the party in power. Being chair is not a powerful position, and is more symbolic than anything else because the agenda is the key question, and that will be set by vote if there is no agreement. In a minority situation, though, the PAC can become a powerful instrument for holding a government to account through public scrutiny (name/shame/blame). So it was in that first minority period of 1998-1999. As the opposition critic for Finance I became chair of the Public Accounts Committee. Fortune offered us an opportunity to poke around in the inner workings of the Liberal cabinet's business dealings. This involved an especially touchy subject, gambling.

There is no shortage of problematic gaming issues. Should it be allowed at all? What about Video Lottery Terminals (VLTs), which are notoriously addictive and attract the most vulnerable? Should there be casinos? What about relations with First Nations people? What about organized crime? How to deal with gambling addictions? Should these issues be left to local communities or should there be one province-wide policy? What about the Internet and online gambling? How should gambling be managed from a policy, administrative, and tax perspective? Can control technologies help reduce gambling addiction? All of this has been debated as strongly in Nova Scotia as elsewhere. In the end, though, gaming has proven irresistible, both for governments as a source of revenue and for many citizens as a diversion, and for an unfortunate group as an addiction.

The legal framework for gambling is not complicated. Gambling is a criminal offence unless it is organized and managed by government. This leaves room for the private sector, but only on contract to governments. The whole point is to limit the involvement of organized crime, as well as to control the profits, and, as with alcohol, to include programs for dealing with addictions. Since the 1970s Canada has had an Interprovincial Lottery Corporation to run games like Lotto 6/49 or Super 7. Nova Scotia's involvement is through Atlantic Lotto and our provincial agency is the Nova Scotia Gaming Corporation. The size of the enterprise is apparent through noting that by 1997 Nova Scotia was receiving some $120 million per year as its share just from the lotteries. By 2012–2013 net gaming revenue to the province was $312 million.[12]

Until the 1990s there were no gambling casinos in Nova Scotia. But during their term the Liberals under John Savage decided to allow them following a study conducted by the former warden of Halifax County, Lazlo Lichter. It then accepted bids from companies interested in their operation. Ultimately, a company called Metropolitan Entertainment Group (MEG), a partnership of the ITT Sheraton and the local company, Purdy's Wharf Development Ltd (the Lindsay family, at the time owners of the Purdy's Wharf office buildings) was chosen. The requirement was to build one casino in Sydney and another in Halifax. Both were opened in the summer of 1995. In Halifax, the casino was a temporary one located in the Sheraton hotel, with a permanent complex to be built by September 1999.

The Nova Scotia Gaming Corporation (NSGC) was chaired by Ralph Fiske, who was appointed in early 1995. The NSGC was to conduct and manage the gambling enterprise on behalf of the government, with direction allowable from the provincial Cabinet. All of this was set out in the framework legislation, the *Gaming Control Act*. Inherent in the legislation was some ambiguity as to the respective roles of the Cabinet and the NSGC. One of the thrusts of the legislation was that its management be arm's length from government. Another, though, was that there would be a link to government through the Minister of Finance, and Cabinet could put in place regulations. Also inherent in the whole situation was the potential for political trouble: in part because the government would always have to accept responsibility for anything that went wrong (an increase in addictions, a shortage of revenues); in part because complex business deals were involved; in part because there was always potential for political influence, meaning either companies influencing the government to their advantage, or governments interfering with the core business in some way.

Ralph Fiske was a businessman from Pictou County. He had been an MLA (Pictou Centre) and a cabinet minister under Premier Gerald Regan, resigning over ongoing government funding for the financially failing Sydney Steel mill. He was widely respected. It was something of a surprise, given that he had been the choice of a Liberal government to chair the NSGC, that he resigned in the fall of 1997. He offered some public statements about his resignation, but not in a great deal of detail. After the 1998 election that produced the Liberal minority, the two opposition parties were able to set the agenda of the Public Accounts Committee. How about we invite Mr. Fiske, we thought, and ask him to explain why he resigned from the NSGC? This turned out to be bombshell material.

Mr. Fiske read a statement on June 17, 1998 in an open public session of the PAC. In it, he detailed a troubled business relationship between the NSGC and MEG. There were disputes over how to account for HST/GST, and how to disentangle casino expenses from hotel expenses, disputes that ended up in commercial arbitrations. There was a dispute over MEG wanting to delay construction of the stand-alone casino, and an issue of whether just to leave the temporary hotel-based casino in place as the permanent arrangement. MEG at one point forbad its Nova Scotia staff from talking with the NSGC, something dubious under the *Gaming Control Act*. The political point, though, was that Mr. Fiske detailed interference by the Premier's Office in these interactions in a way to advantage MEG and disadvantage the public. They wanted one of the arbitrations to be terminated and independently negotiated a settlement that he estimated cost the taxpayers over $20 million. Mr. Fiske resigned, he said, because the inappropriate political interference had undermined the independence of the NSGC, especially his own authority. He took the view that his resignation was actually a dismissal, and he subsequently sued the province for wrongful dismissal. That case ultimately came to trial in 2000, resulting in a victory for Mr. Fiske. The province was ordered to pay him some $300 thousand in damages.

In a measured judgment, Justice David Gruchy found that the Premier's Office had undermined the proper authority of the NSGC in its business dealings with MEG, to the extent that Mr. Fiske had been constructively dismissed. He doubted the amount of money the province was out as a result of the interference was as high as Mr. Fiske had estimated. And on some points he thought Mr. Fiske's hurt feelings had colored his perception of events, but on every important item he preferred Mr. Fiske's evidence, which was confirmed by the documentation. One crucial point was why the Premier's Office became so deeply involved in the normal business dealings of the NSGC. The answer seemed to be that Premier Savage was leaving, and in the Liberal party leadership contest, in which Bernie Boudreau was one of the contenders, he was apparently favoured by Dr. Savage, and the casino was seen as something Boudreau had especially championed. The view, apparently, was that if a serious dispute between MEG and the NSGC over money became known publicly this would harm Boudreau's chances to win the leadership. And apart from that, the government had simply tied itself so closely to the financial success of the casino that it became vulnerable to the blandishments of MEG when MEG found itself called to account by the NSGC.

That was for the future, though. In the meantime, his testimony became the number one talk of the province. Some of those he mentioned asked to have the opportunity to rebut. The Committee found itself with an ongoing investigation on its hands. Mr. Fiske returned to the PAC on July 8, 1998 to elaborate his evidence. And on the whole show went. For months. It went on so long, that in Question Period in November, a testy Premier MacLellan responding to a question as to why there were no files on the casino in his office said: "Mr. Speaker, the committee has been meeting since the end of the Korean War. Surely they could take the initiative to ask Dr. Savage whatever they want to know."[13]

Dr. Savage testified. So too did his deputy, Bob MacKay, and lawyers John Merrick, Dara Gordon, Robbie MacKeigan, and Carl Holm. Premier Russell MacLellan and his Finance Minister, Don Downe, also came. The process of hearing witnesses took until November. The Liberal and Tory members of the committee early joined to resist an NDP proposal that the committee meet every second day for a couple of weeks so as to focus on the casino issues. The result was this drawn out process. In the end, this helped the NDP even though the 1999 election was to go to the Tories.

We submitted a seventy-page report on the evidence and issues as they emerged before the PAC in May 1999. The report was chiefly written by NDP researcher Richard Starr, with editing by Darrell Dexter and myself. The party was able to show itself as adroit at using a committee. It showed the Liberals in a very bad light. It showed the NDP as in charge, as tough minded, as competent, as having legal expertise, as being prepared to take on the establishment, as measured in tone, as looking out for the public good, and as able to handle complex material. The whole process had the effect of validating the voters' choice in the 1998 election to back the many NDP candidates that were elected.

Gaming, however, was not a focus of our government. The negative effects, especially on the most vulnerable, were well documented, but we brought in no changes in policy.

(ii) Petroleum Pricing

The cost of energy is not the only aspect of energy that is important, but it certainly does register with everyone. Price signals can definitely affect behaviour. If something is expensive people will try to find ways to use less of it. If it is cheap, not much thought is given to efficiency. For a long time, all forms of energy were cheap, but that changed abruptly in the early 1970s with the steep increase in oil prices. That first major shock prompted research into alternatives, increased efficiency measures, a search for alternative sources of supply, and no little prominence for environmental organizations, as well as a focus on the international politics of oil. This story had impact on all of the main uses of energy: for electricity generation, for building heating and cooling, and for transportation.

North American culture is easily seen as tightly tied to the automobile. The desire to travel, to feel liberated, is the core of advertising for cars. We have built our towns and cities around cars, to the extent that for every car there are four or five parking spaces, which amounts to a major commitment of land use. Beyond the personal use of cars, truck transportation for goods is also a major fact of our economic lives. No wonder that when the price of gasoline at the pumps rose to circa $1 per liter there was serious public concern. There was speculative talk of predatory pricing.

We should pause to note that actually the pump price of gasoline in 2004 was not exorbitant by most measures. On an international basis, Canada's domestic price was fairly cheap: throughout Europe, for example, the cost was double; in Japan it was almost double. But many of us look to the United States for many comparisons, and there the price to consumers was 15 per cent to 20 per cent less. And on a longitudinal basis, the price had been fairly steady, within a 70 to 90 cent range for about twenty-five years (2004 constant dollars). So it was probably the psychological impact of the approach to $1 dollar that was so attention-getting as the price went over 90 cents and stayed there.

The Hamm Tories tried to approach the dilemma softly. They introduced a bill to allow for advance notice to be given of impending fuel price increases. But this bill stalled in the legislative process. Basically, both opposition parties saw the public concern as a chance to square off against each other and against the government. The government bill was put on hold. Agreement to establish a Select Committee was forced.

The committee held public hearings throughout the province. The hearings were extensively covered in the press. Price at the pumps is made up of several components: crude oil cost, refining cost, federal and provincial taxes, and a marketing margin (the charges of the retailer). Many of these components seemed to shift over time. What was obvious was that nothing we could do in Nova Scotia was going to affect the price of crude oil, which is an internationally traded commodity. So unless the federal government was to revert to its earlier experiment of trying to control the domestic price of crude oil, this was beyond our reach. Likewise for refining. The costs of refining seemed to be high, since reports of profit margins for refineries showed it to be a robust business. But taking control of refining would mean thinking about nationalizing a refinery, which would be a significant undertaking. And for a small Atlantic Provinces market, it would be a risky undertaking. Reducing taxes was a possibility but was not seen as desirable. And the retailers were complaining that they could not make a living with small margins, especially at low-volume outlets. Closing more retail outlets (many had already closed over decades of consolidation with the takeover of independents by the oil companies) would have negative impacts on customers in smaller or remote communities, who would have to drive significant distances to access a gas station. What to do?

Faced with a complex international business, the committee actually took some bold steps in its recommendations. Regulation of price by the Utility and Review Board (UARB) was always in play as a possibility, and indeed such a system had previously existed in Nova Scotia. But instead of moving there immediately, the committee had a look at retail divorcement as a preferred approach. Retail divorcement describes separation of ownership between companies that produce oil or refine it and those that sell it to customers. The point about retail divorcement is that it tries to allow for some real competition in the only part of the marketplace that a province can control. The hope is that independent retailers could more effectively bargain with producers, i.e., the refiners. What the committee recommended was that retail divorcement, which was in place in some US states and parts of Australia and New Zealand, be tried, but that if the government were to be unwilling or if it proved unsuccessful, then the UARB be given authority to regulate the price. An Irving representative called the proposal "Stalinist."

What was interesting about the whole exercise was the extent of party agreement on retail divorcement. Everyone on the committee, except Danny Graham, signed the report. Retail divorcement would have been a significant government initiated change in the marketplace. It certainly would have affected the Irving interests, along with those of the international oil majors (Shell, Esso) that owned retail outlets. But the Tories signed the report, as did Liberals' Russell MacKinnon (Cape Breton West) and Gerald Sampson (Victoria-The Lakes). In the discussion sessions of the committee Danny Graham was vehemently opposed. But his inability to persuade his party colleagues probably reflected the tenuous hold he had on the leadership of his party. The fact that everyone else was prepared to contemplate, and advocate, a change in the oil marketplace that would have brought on a public fight with the Irvings was amazing. In the event, the retail divorcement proposal went nowhere with the Hamm government and gasoline regulation through the UARB became the accepted framework.

Rereading the August 31, 2004 Report of the Select Committee now, a decade later, it is striking how good it is. For example, in discussing the possibility of reducing the provincial portion of HST payable on gasoline, the committee resisted this idea, citing the proposal for allocation of some greater portion of the revenues to efficiency measures, as well as the likelihood that any reduction in tax would just create room for producers, wholesalers, and retailers to increase their charges with no resultant benefit to customers. What was mentioned was reducing the HST on home heating fuel, a proposal that later became central as a pocketbook policy that was so successful for the NDP. Indeed became one of our signature policies (combined with its removal from electricity). And on the environmental aspects of petroleum, a slew of recommendations came forward; such as the province leading by example with energy efficiency in its buildings and fleet; such as revisions to the provincial Energy Strategy to increase the emphasis on reduction in fossil fuel use; and such as more support for public transit. All of these became standards of public policy.

What the exercise did politically was to show the NDP as engaged and informed, and as leading on an important public issue. It was a step in familiarizing the public with the NDP. Frank Corbett, Charlie Parker, and I all had the chance to ask questions on behalf of the public, and to write a report that touched on a complex industry, one with pocketbook as well as environmental aspects.

Inevitable Struggles: Health

Polling always shows that, given an unstructured opportunity to identify their top political issue, the Canadian public names health care. There is both truth and potential for misunderstanding in this. Medicare is rightly seen by Canadians as a blessing, as a signal accomplishment of public life, as an expression of a caring community that fits a self-image, and as

associated with the NDP because of
the initial push for it under Tommy
Douglas when he was Premier of
Saskatchewan. Half of each provincial budget goes to the health care
system. The system is a major employer. It is sophisticated, and also
accessible. People know what they
want. They want the system to be
free. Where it is not free, as for pharmaceuticals, they want it to be inex-
pensive. They want a family physician. They want emergency services

Tommy Douglas

to be available. They want no undue delays in access to specialists. They
just want appropriate help when they need it.

All true. But is it as important a factor in elections as the preoccupation suggests? It has always been my view that health has huge potential to be a vote loser, but limited potential as a vote winner. Messing
up health issues may well lose a government voter support (and this is
always a risk for a government and not so much for an opposition). But
competent delivery of the services does not usually attract votes. Competent delivery is what voters expect as a given.

When in power, the NDP made the error of thinking that because it
was doing a creditable job in the health portfolio, that this would attract
votes. This was a weak theory. Certainly voters liked the improvements
that were promised at the end of the term (more dental care for children,
insulin pumps). But basic competence, and even incremental improvement, was expected. In opposition, however, health was front and centre
for the NDP as it attacked governments. As a negative for both the Tory
and Liberal governments, health was crucial.

The focus was on nursing positions and their collective bargaining;
it was on the costs of long-term care for seniors; and it was on charges
associated with long-term care. Each of these was worked endlessly and
adroitly by the NDP as issues. In the end, both the Liberals and the Tories
lost some public credibility because of mishandling of health issues.

For the Liberals, some major issues were grappled with in the 1990s. Restructuring the system to reduce the number of health boards, to move from only having boards at each hospital, to creating regional boards, was a contentious issue. So, too, was struggling with Federal government changes to the money transfers for health, in combination with rising health costs. Some hospitals were closed. Wages were rolled back by 3 per cent. Wait times for access to specialists first emerged as a problem. There was great turmoil, and extensive adverse public feeling.

In the Tory years, for some reason they lost sight of the lessons that should have been learned from watching the Liberals struggle with health issues. Famously, and rather controversially, Jane Purves campaigned in Halifax Citadel with a pamphlet showing the closure of the Sysco steel plant in Sydney (which the John Hamm government did do in 2001) as implying the opening of a hospital bed. Not that the point was not valid, but it overlooked that financial support for Sysco had been a Buchanan Tory pet project for a long time, not to mention the very poor optics of the pamphlet in Cape Breton. Still, fixing health care was one of the main points that Dr. Hamm, as the man with a plan, put forward in the summer of 1999. Just a few months later he ran up against the paramedics.

By the autumn of 1999 the province's paramedics had been without a collective agreement for some fifteen months. On any reasonable comparison, they were not well paid. Plus, shift assignments allowed for very long times on duty, sometimes to the point of exhaustion and thus a compromised standard of care. Negotiations were not going well. A strike was a real possibility. The government's response was Bill 9, which prohibited a strike, and required the terms of a collective agreement to be set by binding arbitration.

Some background might be useful. Health sector bargaining and collective agreement administration is a big business in Canada. Labour lawyers, unions, employer organizations, arbitrators, labour relations boards, and sometimes judges, all get involved. Particularly in large provinces such as British Columbia and Ontario, there exist sophisticated systems. Academic writing studying health sector bargaining abounds. One of the main issues is the use of binding arbitration. For functions such as police, fire, and health care, many governments take the view that these are essential services and thus should be dealt with outside the normal framework of collective bargaining in which disputes can lead to strikes or lockouts. At the same time, free collective bargaining is now seen as a *Charter* protected right, and impairment of that right has to be on reasonable grounds, and as minimal as possible. It is also desirable that if binding arbitration is to be substituted for the strike/lockout mechanism, that both employer and employees agree to this different framework. What this implies is that it is not desirable, politically or in terms of effective bargaining, for a government to step in during the bargaining process and legislatively change the framework rules; not unless the parties request it.

The problem of withdrawal of services by health system workers, or their lockout by employers, remains: that is, some level of service is necessary in order to avoid health emergencies. The usual way this is dealt with is for unions and management to agree on some level of service that would be left in place in case of a work stoppage. Confusingly, such arrangements are also referred to as essential service provisions.

As for binding arbitration imposed by legislation, this should not be confused with First Contract Arbitration (FCA). Our government has amended the *Trade Union Act* to provide for First Contract Arbitration. Applicable only where the parties are trying to negotiate their very first collective agreement, the legislation allows moving the process to binding arbitration, but only after extensive attempts at negotiation and with certain procedural safeguards to try to get the parties to negotiate their own agreement.

Although as a government we improved labour legislation through adoption of FCA, a serious piece of hypocrisy was made manifest when we were faced with exactly the same scenario that Dr. Hamm had to grapple with in October 1999, the prospect of a paramedics strike. After the Hamm government was elected in the summer of 1999, the Premier assured the population that all was well and suggested everyone just go back to their barbecues and enjoy the summer. It rapidly became clear that the new government was accident prone, and this extended to its aggressive stance with the paramedics in October. Bill 9 forbade strikes, imposed binding arbitration, set the term of the collective agreement as three years, and even circumscribed the award that would be possible by forbidding the arbitrator from awarding any retroactive pay earlier than October 1, a serious limitation given how long the paramedics had been with no contract. Even Peter O'Brien of the Canadian Federation of Independent Business, a reliable friend of the Tory government, publicly criticized this provision in the bill as going too far.

The paramedics came to Province House in force to testify about the nature of their jobs, the inadequacy of their pay, and other problems at work. In the end, there was a strike for 18 hours before the Hamm majority passed Bill 9, albeit withdrawing the "no retroactivity" clause. The main point, though, was that the public sympathy seemed to be with the paramedics even though Jamie Muir as Health Minister tried to appeal to the fears of the public by referring to, "the risk to public safety." "To sit idly by and do nothing would have been an abrogation of our duty to protect public safety and was unacceptable," he said. He appealed to seniors:

> A province-wide strike by paramedics, even for a short period of time, would pose an unacceptably high risk to public safety. This is especially true in rural Nova Scotia where many residents often live considerable distances from the nearest hospital emergency room. The percentage of seniors living in many parts of the rural Nova Scotia is very high and this is a group that relies on emergency personnel to get them to and from hospital. Yet another reason why we can't allow our emergency services to be interrupted.[14]

During all of this the NDP Opposition was firmly on the side of no legislation. Here is Darrell Dexter on October 26, 1999 in a sarcastic Notice of Motion:[15]

RESOLUTION NO. 301
MR. DARRELL DEXTER: Mr. Speaker, I hereby give notice that on a future day I shall move the adoption of the following resolution:
Whereas All Hallows Eve is but a few days off; and
Whereas traditionally the province's children will be going from door-to-door dressed as ghosts, goblins and such other worldly specters as costuming will provide for; and

Whereas children will undoubtedly ask the age old question Trick or Treat;

Therefore be it resolved that this House recognize that only treats will be available this year as all the tricks have been used by this government in their dealing with the province's paramedics.

MR. SPEAKER: The notice is tabled.

Here he is that same day asking a question:

MR. DARRELL DEXTER: Mr. Speaker, with respect to this contract negotiation, the buck stops with the Minister of Health. Last week the Minister of Health assured the House that he had a contingency plan so that Nova Scotia's ground ambulance services wouldn't be affected in the event of a strike by paramedics. My question to the minister is simple. Is this undemocratic, oppressive and Draconian legislation your contingency plan?

[...]

MR. DEXTER: Mr. Speaker, the EMC contract contains clauses to protect the fleet of ambulances and the employer, but it does little to protect the rights and welfare of workers. It really doesn't protect Nova Scotians either, and it does not require the government or the employer to have a contingency plan in the event of a legal strike by paramedics. My question for the Minister of Health is, why didn't the minister work with EMC to amend the contract and to develop a contingency plan, instead of taking away the paramedics' right to fair negotiations?

We opposed this interference in free collective bargaining as an Opposition, but in 2013 did exactly as the Tories did in 1999 concerning paramedics and their bargaining rights and with not even any public acknowledgement of our history, even though the 1999 events were often cited by Health Minister Dave A. Wilson as having brought him into politics, and several of us were present through the Bill 9 debate. It is little wonder that during our mandate long-term party supporters severely questioned the direction of the party. Issues like this one have nothing to do with claims of "incrementalism" and everything to do with playing to the supposed expectations of the general voter in an election year.

There was a strong NDP position in 1999 against legislation that was anti-strike. But in July 2013 the line from the party leadership was that this time the situation was different, that everything had been tried and that legislation was a last resort. The House was called back for a one-day session to adopt a bill. At an early morning caucus gathering immediately before the bill was introduced, we were told that the essential

difference between John Hamm's Bill 9 scenario and our Bill 86, was that the union membership was being unreasonable in the negotiations, and had also refused to put in place any arrangement for emergency services. (Later in the day during the testimony before the Law Amendments Committee both of these points were challenged by paramedics who came to testify.) I was amazed to hear the paramedics blamed, and told my colleagues I would not vote for the bill – I would not vote against it or speak against it, but I would not vote for it.

Indeed during the day's debate, the Liberals made very effective points against us. In their resolutions, they pointed out that one of our claims in pre-election literature was that we had handled all labour negotiation without having had to resort to back-to-work legislation, so we should amend this claim since it was no longer true. In their speeches, they pointed to all the parallels with the 1999 situation, concluding, in the words of Michel Samson (Richmond): "What has changed? The NDP has changed." Exactly correct.

The position of organized labour was also interesting. The major labour organizations came to the Law Amendments Committee and said they did not like legislation that interfered with bargaining, but in this case they were not about to strenuously oppose it. At caucus we had been told a stronger version of this, that labour outright supported the bill. We were also told that labour would oppose a bill that tried to deal with emergency services and, according to Maureen MacDonald, at this point we did not need a fight with labour. What this touched on was the imminence of an election. The fear the government had of finding itself in a health care crisis with the disturbance that would mean in provision of services, along with the possibility of a patient's death, meant it behaved exactly as John Hamm had. The "No Difference Party" indeed.

Things only worsened when the Tories tried to deal with collective agreements for nurses a year and a half after taking on the paramedics. There was no evidence they had learned anything from their experience. Taking on nurses is a fundamental political mistake. There are many nurses, located in all communities, and they are inherently popular because of the work they do. But the infamous Bill 68 was brought forward, and we as the Opposition were in for a long fight.

In June 2001 in a speech very similar to that he gave regarding the paramedics, Jamie Muir again invoked, "the health and safety of Nova Scotians," as the reason for legislation to remove bargaining rights from nurses. This was particularly unbelievable since, unlike the paramedics, a working arrangement was in place between the nurses and the District Health Authorities for the provision of essential services in the case of a strike or lockout. Nor had the nurses even taken a strike vote. Essentially the government was focused on two things: the monetary side of any possible contract, and restructuring health sector bargaining so as to eliminate the possibility of strike/lockout in the future. It was not forthright about this agenda. It is impossible to read the provision in the bill that gave Cabinet the power to set the terms and conditions of the contract, and for a period of three years, as anything but a complete disdain for the collective bargaining process.

As allies of the health care workers, and at the same time very aware of the need for patient services, we took on active opposition to the bill, and used every procedural maneuver we could to delay and focus public attention on the ineptitude of the government. One response was for the government to set the sitting hours of the House on a non-stop timetable.

We sat 24 hours a day. This meant using the allowed time of one-hour speeches at 1:00, 2:00, 3:00, 4:00, and 5:00 in the morning, napping on the sofa in the members' lounge. Difficult and irritating, but we did it.

By this time Darrell Dexter was interim leader of the NDP, with a leadership convention coming in July. He spoke well against Bill 68. It was, therefore, particularly disappointing to see Darrell as Premier bringing in legislation in the summer of 2013 to interfere with a planned job action by paramedics by sending the dispute to binding arbitration. An alternative might have been to delay any walkout until the parties negotiated emergency services provisions and to impose those if the parties could not agree. Instead he removed the right to strike, exactly the opposite of what was advocated for by the NDP in the Bill 68 debates in 2001.

Auto Insurance

The NDP's campaign for a publicly-owned automobile insurance scheme was an example of the search for a popular issue that could attract votes, more than advancing a principled position. Thus, it was pushed aggressively in one election, and then dropped when the Tories caved to the extent of bringing in some degree of regulation of rates charged. Victory was declared and the party moved on. All of this is very peculiar but all too typical of the new NDP under Darrell's leadership.

Focusing on a widespread pocketbook issue made sense. Most Nova Scotians own and drive cars. Rates had been increasing. Insurance is mandatory and thus not an optional purchase. There was potential for almost universal benefit in attempting to control rates, and also the electoral advantage of being seen to stand up for consumers.

The policy choice of a publicly owned insurance corporation had successful precedents elsewhere in Canada. British Columbia, Saskatchewan, Manitoba, and Quebec all have such corporations. The Saskatchewan system, Saskatchewan Government Insurance, dates back to 1945. The other three provinces created their publicly-owned systems in the

1970s. Overall, these systems tend to have lower rates, and offer consumers efficiency and convenience.

The issue also served to bring out a philosophical difference between the NDP and the governing Tories. The Tories were inclined to rely on the private sector as their first resort for anything that looked to have a commercial aspect. For the NDP, there was a willingness to adopt public ownership, the general tests being whether the service was essential and whether it could or should be offered on a monopoly basis. It is certainly a judgment call but it is hard to see in automobile insurance how the private sector advantage of competition adds anything to the product: the product is the same, and the residual issue is price; in those circumstances monopoly seems the best choice.

The cost of automobile insurance a decade ago was a real public concern. Consumers were faced with significant rate increases over a two to three year period starting in 2001 while they also saw the companies that provided the coverage show big profits. This raised questions. An editorial from June 2003, *The Globe and Mail* said:

> The need for reform is obvious. Car insurance premiums climbed an average of 50 percent nationally in 2002. [...] The largely government-run insurance programs appear to have had the most success in keeping premiums in check. [...] Government-run systems have the advantage of efficacy. There is no profit margin built into insurance premiums. There is only one insurer, so no time is spent fighting with another company over who will pay costs. And there are economics of scale in underwriting insurance for a broad spectrum of drivers.[16]

The editorial went on to suggest that reforming the flaws in the existing private systems would probably be the better approach because it would be "expensive and disruptive" to switch to a new system; "jobs would be lost, and provinces would have to spend hundreds of millions of dollars to set up new insurance bureaucracies."

The problem had become increasingly apparent and in February of 2002 the Legislature's Standing Committee on Economic Development called in the Insurance Bureau of Canada to explain. All parties expressed their concerns. Initial sparring took place. Industry pointed to rising claim costs, especially for bodily injuries and including pain and suffering; basically, industry was blaming tort lawyers and the courts. They did not blame the cost of repairing vehicles. They suggested profits had not been good. The MLAs did not agree, although one point that did validly emerge was the small size of the market in Atlantic Canada.

This suggested that there might be a place for a regional public insurance system, perhaps a national one. But that possibility has not emerged as yet for any active discussion. The problem remained a province-by-province one.

Once the issue had been identified, the NDP moved on it. Everyone knew that this had been a big and problematic issue for the one-term Bob Rae NDP government in Ontario in the 1990s. Because of this we moved cautiously, which at the same time gave the opportunity to build public support.

In the end there was no follow-through. But the approach to public automobile insurance was a model of how to achieve some significant transformation of public life. Where real issues exist, bringing the public along through education about the facts, plus offering genuine opportunities for public involvement, will produce results. There is a widespread appetite for serious public interaction with government. I saw this in my years as a municipal councillor. People were keen to have the facts set out and to hear possible solutions, while at the same time being listened to. I never attended a public meeting, either as a councillor or as an MLA, in which I did not learn something from the public. No level of government is ever exclusively an undertaking for the experts; as valuable as expertise is, governance is in its essence participatory.

In March 2003 the NDP established a "Task Force on Lower Auto Insurance Premiums." Darrell, Frank Corbett, Graham Steele, and I were on it. Previously, Graham had participated in the UARB hearings on rates, and was widely seen as having done a good job on behalf of consumers' interests. As part of our campaign we collected "horror stories" to harass the government: steep increases over short periods of time; apparently inconsistent or arbitrary policies regarding how rates are assessed; the impact on seniors and low-income customers; fights over claims; the problems truckers encountered. There was no shortage of them.

Opposition to change came from the Insurance Bureau of Canada representing the companies, and the Insurance Brokers Association representing the agencies and brokers around the province. The brokers basically worried about their jobs, although public schemes usually need agencies around the province. Some lawyers had their own concerns focused on the issue of no-fault: not all publicly-owned automobile insurance schemes included no-fault, and one province, Ontario, has no-fault even though there is no publicly owned system. The real issue for consumers was the cap on claims that usually goes along with no-fault.

Tactically, the issue was very effective. In the 2003 election, the John Hamm Tories lost their majority and our seats increased from eleven to fifteen. The government was forced to act, and changed the insurance laws.

The Tory changes, though they did have some impact on rates, did so by limiting payments to claimants for minor injuries. Essentially, a cap of $7,500 was established. Because this had the effect of limiting payments, rates moderated. (Though in the view of many analysts, the problem for the insurance companies that led to rate increases in the first place never really had anything to do with claims but was attributable to declines in the returns from investments made by the companies with their premium income. As market returns increased, the pressures on rates lessened.) Subsequently, the NDP government (Bill 52 of 2010[17]) amended the *Insurance Act* to reverse these changes, or at least moderate them: the Tory definition of "minor injury" was far too broad and we restricted it to sprains, strains, and whiplash, in addition to allowing the cap to rise with the Consumer Price Index.[18]

So in terms of some real benefits to consumers this has to count as a small success. But it was not a, "driver-owned, non-profit car insurance plan for Nova Scotia," which had been the recommendation and promise of the NDP in Opposition. The party's final report from our Task Force was a thorough exploration of the various issues. It was asserted that a public system would bring:

The lowest and fairest premiums for compulsory auto insurance. Relying on private insurers to provide the basic, compulsory coverage has not worked. Auto insurance premiums have skyrocketed by 65 per cent Private insurers want rates to go even higher, and they want to limit benefits. The choice over how to provide compulsory insurance has come down to a choice between what is best for the province's drivers and what is best for private insurers. The NDP is on the side of the drivers. That is why we recommend that Nova Scotia provide its basic, compulsory insurance through a driver-owned non-profit plan for all registered vehicles without delay.

My signature is on the report. It was a good report. But I guess that was then and this is now.

Environment

At one point, I was referred to by an opposing party MLA as, "MLA for the Ecology Action Centre," a remark apparently intended as a slight, but I took no offence at all. I was happy to have regularly raised environmental issues. They are overwhelmingly important. And the Ecology Action Centre (EAC) has been the province's main citizens' environmental organization for decades. Our province has other, quite significant environmental organizations, such as the Sackville Rivers Association, the Sierra Club, Clean Nova Scotia, and the Nova Scotia Nature Trust. For the most part, though, they are limited in their focus by topic or geography, or are smaller groups, or disband after a particular problem has been dealt with. The EAC has no limits on its range of topics, it tries to operate province-wide, and it has persisted for over forty years, always with a physical location, volunteers, and staff. Survival, while it is a factor in the EAC's prominence, is not the main point: the virtue of the EAC is that it is independent and has consistently displayed scientific integrity. It is independent in that the main source of its funding is memberships, fundraising and donations. Its scientific integrity comes from writing solid briefs:

others might take issue with the Centre's policy perspectives but no one has ever found its facts to be inaccurate or its research to be poor. This is a precious accomplishment that has resulted in credibility. The press will look to the Centre for reliable commentary, and under the NDP, the EAC actually had some influence.

For more than forty years I have had an association with the environmental movement in Nova Scotia, based at the Ecology Action Centre ("Action is our middle name," they say there now). The EAC was started in 1971 as a Dalhousie University-based project. It was mainly the idea of Brian Gifford who, along with a group of friends, wangled federal grants plus the pledge of some office space from the university, and just got going. David Reynolds, Don MacLennan, Cliff White, Kathleen Flanagan, Tim Sullivan, and Ginny Point were all among the initial workers. Professor Don Grady was a mentor to the group. Later, Susan Holtz and Susan Mayo and then Lois Corbett were central figures. The first focus was on local projects having to do with recycling of paper, but more extensive issues were on the agenda including energy and land-use planning.

It was the land-use planning aspect that led to my involvement. In 1973 I was just finishing at Dalhousie Law School, where I had taken

Susan Holtz and Susan Mayo at the Ecology Action Centre in 1977.

both the land-use planning and environmental law courses. The EAC became involved in a major challenge to a planning decision of Halifax City Council; its approval via a development agreement of a large project for fifteen acres of land on Quinpool Road that belonged to the Roman Catholic Episcopal Corporation (RCEC). This block housed a closed orphanage and a monastery, and was mostly open land. The RCEC entered into a conditional sales agreement with local developer Ralph Medjuck, whose company, Centennial Properties, was already active in land development. The proposal approved by Council was for four 25-storey apartment buildings to be located at the corners of the land, plus retail/commercial space fronting on Quinpool Road. This would have put enormous pressure on the adjacent low-rise residential neighbourhoods to the north and south, and although intensification of the residential presence on peninsular Halifax made sense, this proposal was too far out of proportion. The EAC organized opposition and a formal appeal to the province's review body, the Planning Appeal Board (a predecessor to the UARB). It sought some help from Stan Makuch, a planning law professor at the Law School, who insisted that the Centre also recruit some law students. And that is how I became involved, not only in land-use planning issues, but in the EAC and environmentalism generally, and with a group of people who have been lifelong good friends.

My core conviction is that adoption of serious steps towards sustainability is a vital necessity. What we are abusing when we abuse the environment is our life support systems. This is too important to take second place to anything.

Although this is easily said, as indeed it regularly is by far-seeing Canadians such as David Suzuki, Elizabeth May, or David Schindler, it has been a long slog to make sustainability a serious matter for public policy awareness and action. Here in Nova Scotia we have, as a movement, had some successes, but not enough given the seriousness of what is at stake. It is over forty years since the EAC coalesced the environmental movement in the province. We can take stock. There is no nuclear power plant in Nova Scotia, and indeed Nova Scotia Power is prohibited by law from owning or operating one. There was a moratorium, now a ban, on uranium mining. Oil and gas exploration on George's Bank is not allowed. There is a reasonably modern *Environment Act*. Twelve percent of the landmass has been put aside as protected in some form. There is a significant shift to renewables for generating electricity. No hazardous waste incinerator has been built. Programmes exist to help conserve energy through building insulation. The Sydney Tar Ponds, one of the most hazardous industrial waste sites in the country, has been stabilized and encapsulated, albeit this remains controversial as to its efficacy. There are regulations to limit pesticide use. Sustainability is taught in the schools and in post-secondary education programmes. In some disciplines, such as Land-use Planning, it is of the essence of what is taught. All of these are real advances.

At the same time, much remains outstanding. We still have polluting industries, often associated with environmental injustice, which is a tradition of placing problematic infrastructure in or near marginalized communities. In Nova Scotia that has meant Aboriginal and Black communities. The Northern Pulp plant and the problem of Boat Harbour is an example, as is the Guysborough County community of Lincolnville and its struggle with a leaky waste facility.[19]

As environment critic I organized a major round table discussion in December 2001 attended by some twenty of the province's leading environmentalists. The objective was to signal to that community the party's serious interest in their issues, plus to learn in more detail about their concerns. Being Opposition critic for a topic always implies taking active steps to learn about the subject and meeting with the major players; it means serious research, the assembly of a set of files, ongoing communication, and searching for those particular items that can usefully be advanced through party politics. An elected official speaking to some topic, especially if it is a technical one, has a limited but important function. Politicians are generally not engineers or physicians or research scientists; when their opinions are offered or sought on matters involving specialized knowledge, it is not for their technical expertise. A politician taking up a topic signals that the topic is important, or that if elected, financial resources would be allocated to it, or legislation or negotiations would be adopted or changed. This public policy context is important, and always needs to be based in knowledge.

The round table was a success. Participants raised a variety of issues: forestry, fisheries dragging on the ocean floor, oil and gas exploration and extraction, energy policy, community development, green businesses, land use planning, lack of enforcement of existing laws, and pesticides.

The meeting lasted a couple of hours. Darrell had to leave early. As he was exiting he explained that he had other obligations. Then he said, "This reminds me of a bumper sticker I once saw. It said: 'Earth First.' [pause] 'We'll mine the other planets later.'" There was a stunned silence. He left, and we carried on. The remark, however, was revealing. It was clearly meant to be amusing but it mostly served to remind everyone that environmentalism was a big gap in the party leader's background. I am a big fan of jokes, but in them there is often submerged aggression. There is a reason the end is called a "punch line." So Darrell's joke always seemed to me to suggest an underlying hostility.

Skepticism about how urgent sustainability is as a principle has been widespread. To return to Paul MacEwan, here is a column he wrote for the *New Waterford Press* in 2001, attacking me:[20]

> The NDP recently held a caucus at Ingonish, where they played musical chairs once again, dividing up the department's [sic] of government and giving everyone a new assignment. To show their devotion to "old-line" ways, former Leader Robert Chisholm was made "Special Advisor" to current Leader, Darrell Dexter. And amazingly, Howard Epstein was made the party's official voice on the environment.
>
> This shows where the NDP really stands. For years, in this column, I have given a running report on the anti-coal views of Mr. Epstein. He's the chap who, in articles and speeches, has called for the shutdown of all coal mines and thermal power plants, and the replacement of these by wind-mills.

And my response:

> To the editor:
> Paul MacEwan is at it again, trying in his hapless way to abuse the NDP in general and me in particular. Surely it is time to recognize

how seriously out of touch he and his party are.

Let's look at the facts:

Mr. MacEwan seems to think that the only environmental issue is coal. As an NDP MLA and formerly as Executive Director of the Ecology Action Centre, I have dealt with numerous environmental issues of concern to Cape Bretoners including human health and pollution, PCB incineration, garbage incineration, sewage systems, the fishery, environmental assessment law revisions, and also, of course, energy policy.

More than a decade ago I predicted the Cape Breton coal mines would be closed by the Federal Government. Anyone clearly assessing the situation would have concluded the same, and have said so. By pretending that coal in Cape Breton had a robust future, Mr. MacEwan and the Liberals diverted community energies away from planning for the future. They seem to prefer waiting for crisis rather than planning early enough for inevitable change. Shame on you, Mr. MacEwan.

Another one of his comments suggests that Halifax NDP MLAs have no sympathy with Cape Breton issues. I want Cape Bretoners to know, first that I am a labour lawyer who has represented unions for more than two decades; second, that my late mother Leah was from Glace Bay. I never for a minute forget the needs of Cape Bretoners, or the legitimate and generous protections that are needed for workers. Neither do my colleagues. How the Hamm Tories have treated displaced Sysco workers is a disgrace. How the Federal Liberals treated displaced Devco workers is equally so.

I suppose this is both of us showing our partisanship in clear terms. Still, I was happy to have the chance to set out my visions on coal mining. It is inherently an unsafe and unhealthy undertaking for miners. Our province's coal mining history is replete with disasters leading to loss of life (e.g., New Waterford 1917, 65 deaths; Springhill 1956 and 1958, 113 deaths; Westray 1992, 26 deaths). We should have been happy to see the coal mines close, and have moved on. Instead, some community leaders – including NDP Deputy Premier Frank Corbett, MLA for Cape Breton Centre – have been public advocates for the re-opening of the Donkin Mine. The inherent nastiness of this, the poor quality of the coal, the disinterest

of Nova Scotia Power in purchasing it, and the availability of better options make the enterprise unlikely. But our party keeps on thinking it is
good politics to pretend there might be a coal mining future in the old
industrial Cape Breton. The parallel with Robert Chisholm's 1998 position that if the Kyoto Protocol meant the loss of coal mining jobs in Cape
Breton, then the Protocol ought not to be ratified, is very clear. Fantasiz-
ing about coal mining jobs is easier than actually engaging in effective
community economic development, but it is dishonest and misleading.
Even if the Donkin mine were to reopen, coal mining is no blessing; not
for the miners, and not for the environment.[21]

Causes

One of the features of the NDP in opposition was its links to progressive
causes. As individuals many of us were or had been members of groups
like Oxfam, Amnesty International, the Sierra Club of Canada, the Canadian Centre for Policy Alternatives, and/or subscribed to magazines or
online magazines (zines) or blogs that had information that added to
what is available from more mainstream news and opinion sources such
as the *New Internationalist*, Jim Stanford's *Facts From the Fringe*, Janet
Eaton's hourly bulletins, *The Progressive Economics Forum*, the *CCPA Bul-
letin*, *The Dominion*, *rabble.ca*, *Al Jazeera* in English, *Truth-Out.org*. There
is no shortage of information. Politics is a knowledge-based profession,
though the problem is getting to be how not to spend absolutely all your
time online and in libraries learning things.

When labour groups or students came to Province House to demonstrate, we would be there with them. We would be in the crowd, or would
address them from the steps of the Legislature. These were our friends.
This is who we were.

Many of the information and news
sources are focused on international
and national issues. Once in a while,
though, these matters show up in our

province. So it was with the G7 finance ministers meeting in 2002.

Demonstrations are a common feature of democratic life. One was organized for this event. Just as in 2003 as war in Iraq seemed imminent, people in Halifax joined those around the world who marched against the coming war. Or when President George W. Bush visited Halifax in November 2004. Such events are common and free speech and the right of assembly are constitutionally protected rights. For the G7, a march to the Grand Parade area occurred on a Saturday. The police had announced in advance that they would respect the right of demonstration, but it was something of an intimidating scene with full riot-geared officers arrayed in the square. Ultimately, tear gas was used. I sent a letter of complaint to the RCMP Complaints Commission.

The letter includes an account of the events that I witnessed at the Grand Parade Square in Halifax on June 15, 2002. It was a largely peaceful public demonstration that culminated with the RCMP deploying (without warning) tear gas. I concluded my letter to the Commission for Public Complaints Against the RCMP by saying:

> As I see it, the Force has its option of two choices of explanation of its actions. One is incompetence and the other is that it acted deliberately. I do not believe the former to be the case. I believe that the tear gas was used as a deliberate strategy of interference with constitutionally protected rights of assembly, free speech and political expression.
>
> So far as I could see the members who were on the line were disciplined, dressed in full protective gear, were not intimidated or nervous, and were in no physical danger. To the extent that demonstrators took actions that were or might have been illegal, no steps were taken by normal police methods to interfere or effect arrests. In my view the minimal amount of force necessary is all that is ever appropriate for the police to use. The mood of the event was not dangerous.
>
> In light of the experience in Canada that led to the APEC Inquiry, I believe that the Force should be aware of the legitimate rights of the public to assemble, speak, and express political opinion. I am not suggesting that in anything I saw individual officers took individual rogue decisions. I do suggest that the response was directed by

senior officers as part of a deliberate attempt to stifle constitutional rights belonging to the public, immediately in Halifax and probably in the context of the forthcoming meeting in Kananaskis, i.e., to send a signal to those thinking of demonstrating there that they should expect to receive similar treatment. That is not acceptable.

I ask that the Commission investigate fully, including explore the extent to which the Force and or those elected officials responsible for its operations attempted to interfere with the rights referred to.

Should you wish additional information from me, just let me know. I look forward to hearing from you.

Howard Epstein, MLA, Halifax Chebucto

The process for any formal complaint such as mine is that the Commission first refers the matter to the RCMP for its own investigation. And, some two years later, the final reply from the RCMP's internal investigation rejected most of the points that I raised, except for the lack of warning before the use of tear gas:

It is clear that no warning was provided and this is contrary to policy found within the Tactical Operations Manual. I wish to advise you that operational guidance has been provided to the Tactical Troop Commander with respect to not providing an appropriate warning to the protestors prior to ordering the discharge of tear gas. Also, the Commander and his Troop leaders have been upgraded through training with respect to use of Force.[22]

The Commission declined to deal with the matter further.

Many others have found the police to be very heavy-handed with demonstrators,[23] and also found the formal avenues of redress not to be effective. As a footnote, I do not think anyone was ever convicted of criminal activity for the initial G7 demonstration. Some thirty-one people were arrested, mostly to do with activities later in the day, after the police used tear gas. Some shops on Spring Garden Road were damaged. Eight people were charged. One of the leaders of the demonstrations, Chris Arsenault, was charged with unlawful assembly, but acquitted when his case was heard in December 2003. One young man, Sandy Munro, age 20, pleaded guilty to breaching the peace; he threw rocks, sticks, and coffee at police officers after they used tear gas.

There was considerable coverage of the events, though it is far from clear to what effect. One of the letters I received was from someone describing herself as married to a Halifax police officer, but it was unsigned. She was very indignant about the fact that a complaint had been filed. She suggested that no police member or their families would vote NDP: "They know they can expect no support for the difficult job they do from people like you, who instead want to molly-coddle those criminal types who choose to break the law. Shame on you!" The letter mentioned, "professional agitators," who apparently, "came to our beautiful city to bring media attention to their cause. Once the ringleader with the bullhorn told the demonstrators to remove the barricades, it was 45 minutes before police took any action with the tear gas. The demonstrators up front were verbally warned many times to move back. You have got to be kidding about having a formal complaint or investigation lodged! It is my opinion the police did an exemplary job in keeping things from escalating to a higher degree of violence." It was a four-page letter and I have no real reason not to think it genuine.

But a word about anonymous letters or voice messages. Often there is little reason to pay attention to them. Clearly they represent something, but it is not clear what. Many of us are prepared to speak publicly and to defend our views, and to take the criticism that comes, and of

Police in the Grand Parade during the G7 protests in 2002.

course even to change our views if presented with convincing facts or arguments. This is not just a peculiarity, but is essential for our democracy. We do our best to make public life safe by speaking with our names attached. A society plagued by anonymous denunciations or anonymous gossip or anonymous allegations is a society that is crumbling. Her stated reasons for being anonymous are in these terms: "I will not sign this letter, although I'm sure you would like the chance to defend yourself. [...] It's not because I am afraid to sign, but I do not wish any further correspondence on this matter. My husband is very professional and would not approve of my responding to this incident or to your dumb remarks." I certainly do not claim to always be right. I do believe, though, that it is important to be engaged in the debate. Openly.

Several years later in 2011, when the Occupy movement camped out in the Grand Parade in front of City Hall, not many of us attended their sessions or reached out to them. I attended a few times. With Remembrance Day ceremonies about to be held, the Mayor asked Occupy to move to another location. They did so, but then Council promptly had the police evict the group from Victoria Park. I called the councillors, "a bunch of sneaks," a view that seemed to be widely held, judging by the overall reaction.

For the NDP caucus being "in the struggle" has often been a part of our lives. Backgrounds or jobs have often been associated with social justice. Sometimes this has meant being a part of a union, or working for one, or being a social worker, or a member of an environmental group, or a volunteer in shelters, or organizing anti-poverty advocacy. The list goes on. As elected representatives our role shifts somewhat. But not so much that we should ever forget what has motivated us to look to the political world as a means of finding change. It is easy to become cynical: "In which other job could you expect to be taken seriously on subjects about which you know nothing?" is a jibe made not so long ago about British MPs.[24] It is easy to become lost. Struggles are endless but they are what we are for.

Occupy protestors being evicted from Victoria Park.

5

Off to a Bad Start:
Three Conversations

H ere are three memorable scenarios. I offer them as individual, but vivid, examples that convey something of what the flavour of NDP government was like for a backbencher. Each moment had a statement that suggests much about where we went wrong.

I am nothing if not a conventional fellow and one convention is to start with a learned quotation. Why is this done? The main reason is to indicate something of the essential lesson of the essay that is about to follow. An alert reader can thus figure out all they need to know, without the trouble of actually reading the full essay, unless they like detail. (In that regard I highly recommend a small book by a French philosopher, Pierre Bayard, *How To Talk About Books You Haven't Read*.[1])

So, enough with the blather. Here is the quotation:

> *For all the rest,*
> *They'll take suggestion as a cat laps milk;*
> *They'll tell the clock to any business that*
> *We say befits the hour.*
> — William Shakespeare, The Tempest, Act II, Scene 1

The relevance of this passage is explained at the end of the chapter.

Margaret Thatcher in One Government Place

In July 2009, I met with Darrell in the Premier's Office at One Government Place. Seven backbenchers had been assigned to various departments as Ministerial Assistants to work on some aspect of the Minister's portfolios. My own assignment was to Denise Peterson-Rafuse in the Department of Community

Darrell Dexter in his office at One Government Place.

Services, with my stated responsibility being for housing generally and co-operative non-profit housing in particular. Darrell wanted to talk about the assignment.

The co-ops portion was really his focus. He reminisced about the early years of his marriage. He and Kelly had lived for a while in a housing co-op, he told me. Nova Scotia legislation regulated housing co-ops as part of all other co-ops. He wondered if separate legislation might make sense so as to recognize the differences between worker or consumer co-ops and housing co-ops. He asked me to consider that. Then he pointed out that in his experience, housing co-ops tended to suffer from an imbalance among those prepared to volunteer time and work to make them viable. Some members, he said, tended not to volunteer to be on committees or to do physical work. This was unfair, and he said that he felt that if co-ops could become private property, then the individuals would have a greater commitment to them.

Oh, oh.

At that point I found myself talking with Margaret Thatcher, the hard line Tory Prime Minister of the United Kingdom, and not Darrell Dexter the first NDP Premier of Nova Scotia. For this was exactly what Thatcher thought and said in the 1980s. Take "council housing" (the UK term for public housing) and privatize it. The virtue of property ownership, she said, was a good in and of itself, and would also be likely to turn residents into Tory voters, or at least have a good chance of this. She embarked upon a major sell-off of council housing. In the UK, the housing market was and remains very different than in Canada. Council housing had been a dominant form of housing (pre-Thatcher circa 33 per cent; after Thatcher, circa 19 per cent). Here public housing is generally no more than 10 per cent or so of the housing stock. And co-ops, which are not public housing, are no more than about 1 per cent of the housing stock.

We have a range of housing types. Private ownership is the main one. Some 67 per cent of Canadians own their homes. The rest do not. The rest are renters in some fashion or other. They could live in privately owned apartments, or in public housing, or in co-ops.

Why do co-ops exist for housing at all? In fact, Nova Scotia has a long history of interest and involvement in co-ops: producer co-ops (Farmers Dairy), consumer co-ops (the Co-op grocery stores, credit unions), and housing co-ops. The housing co-ops are a very small niche, but appeal to those who believe in a co-operative lifestyle or who generally cannot afford private ownership. For some people, like Darrell and Kelly, living in a co-op is a transition phase in life, something done temporarily, perhaps while being students; for others it can be a lifelong experience.

Early on Nova Scotia had some "builders' co-ops." These did contemplate a transition to private ownership. The co-op ownership arrangement was specifically to secure mutual combined support to borrow money and to build the housing units. It was contemplated, and specified, from the beginning that after all construction was complete there would be a dissolution of the co-op and a sale of the units to the individual families. Arnold Housing, Canada's first builders' co-op was in Nova Scotia, in Reserve Mines in the period of 1936-38. This was a provincial response to the Great Depression, a programme that continued until about 1970. Some 5,500 housing units were built in Nova Scotia that allowed for transition to private ownership.

Most housing co-ops are not of that sort, however. Transition to private ownership was never a part of the basis on which modern, federally sponsored co-ops were created. Quite the opposite.

Although housing co-ops are few in number (1 per cent) there are some 250,000 persons living in co-ops in Canada. And there is a national organization that supports housing co-ops, the Co-operative Housing Federation of Canada (CHFC). The CHFC offers support to individual co-ops through education. Additionally, it tries to interest the Federal Government in putting in place new programmes to develop the sector, and generally advocates for affordable housing. The federal government financed housing co-ops through making long-term mortgage financing available. Unfortunately, it has stopped its support programmes and is letting the existing mortgages run out. There have been no new housing co-ops developed since 1993.

One of the positions of the CHFC is that there should be no diminution of the number of housing co-op units. Darrell's proposal would have run completely contrary to that. It was predictable that any such initiative would simply buy us political trouble.

Furthermore, the CHFC, of course, recognizes that not all members of co-ops pull their weight. This happens. The CHFC, which has a Nova Scotia office, offers education in ways to promote member involvement and participation. Thus, Darrell's proposal was an extreme measure to deal with a very small problem, one that was already being addressed.

Beyond that, how would the fairness aspect of privatization be dealt with? There would be past members of housing co-ops who had contributed to paying down the mortgage or doing repairs and maintenance. Would they be eligible for some share of any profits that flowed from sales, or would profits just go to those who were members at the time of sale (a sort of lottery)? Or would funds go to the public purse? Imagine a ten-unit co-op with its mortgage paid off. A sale might perhaps generate $2 million. Who would get those funds? If you were a founding member of the co-op and had lived there for ten years but then moved out and a year or two later the government authorizes a sell-off, would you not feel you were owed something? (Or even a priority opportunity to purchase?) The equities involved in all this are too problematic to make a sell-off practical.

At the Department of Community Services I wrote various memos outlining the issues, including the possibility of separate legislation for housing co-ops. It turns out that the legislation had been amended in 2001 and 2008 to address the specific differences between housing co-ops and other co-ops. It would have been possible to separate those provisions and package them as a "Housing Co-op" bill, but

Darrell Dexter and Denise Peterson-Rafuse

to little point really; the existing law is pretty comprehensive.

In the memos I pointed out all the problems with Darrell's suggestion about sell-off. This resulted in a meeting with Denise Peterson-Rafuse in which she scolded me, "Whose side are you on, Howard?" Say what? It was clear that she did not mean, was I on the side of the Liberals or the Tories? Or, was I on the side of co-ops instead of being supportive of private ownership? What she meant was, was I on Darrell's side or not? If the Premier wanted something, that was good enough. Party principles (i.e., a 1979 policy, "This convention reaffirms its belief in Co-op Housing....") and the facts should not get in the way.

Affordable housing as part of a poverty-reduction strategy should have been a high priority for an NDP government. It was not. For the first two years of the government's term, there was a preoccupation with accessing cost-shared dollars for housing upgrades, the so-called "shovel-ready" projects that the federal government put in place to get the country through the Great Recession of 2007–2008. That money was spent on public housing. Fair enough. But policy work should have been going on to articulate a serious housing policy. It was not. Late in the term a document was published on housing policy that was a disgrace. The 2013 Housing Strategy was trivial and came too late. It did contain some comments on co-ops including the statement that the province will be, "considering equity or builder's co-operatives," apparently as part of a, "new housing co-ops," scheme, although how this would occur or whether any money was to be on the table was left unsaid.

The poor are always with us. But are we with the poor?

What was to become the driving force of our term in government was balancing the budget. Nova Scotians will recall that Darrell promised in the 2009 election to balance the budget within one year, and to do so without raising taxes or cutting services. What an abomination of a thing to say.

First, it was simply unnecessary: the NDP was highly likely to win the 2009 election in any event. Furthermore, it was obvious from long familiarity with Nova Scotia budgets that we, as a province, were in big trouble: no budget balance was in the offing. Basically this was because the PCs had built into general revenues the offshore royalties to the tune of some $450 million, a sum that was about to plummet because the Sable Offshore Energy Project (SOEP) natural gas extraction was about to start winding down. Consequently, a major drop in royalties was about to take place. Third, with the Great Recession upon us there would likely be decreases in other government revenues (income tax, sales tax, corporate tax). Plus, in time of serious recession, government spending to stimulate the economy, even to the point of deficit spending, makes sense. Finally, it is pretty hard to take seriously a candidate for Premier who says such things as they are so obviously out of touch with the realities of basic economics. Amazingly, the first time former Premier's Office staffers spoke publicly about their experiences, in a May 2014 panel discussion of "communications," they repeated the claim that they had no idea of the true state of the Province's books until briefed by the Department of Finance after the 2009 election. Phooey.

So, the first order of business for the new government became how to get out of this promise of Darrell's. The first step was to commission a study of just how bad the deficit position was: the Deloitte study said that unless something was done, the annual deficit would reach $1.3 billion within four years. Then a group of economists were asked for suggestions.[2] The result was a push to raise the provincial portion of the sales tax, hence the HST would increase from 13 per cent to 15 per cent, as well as to reduce government expenditures. Graham Steele, as Finance Minister, went around the province to 'consult' about (read, 'sell') the necessity of this. "Back To Balance" became the theme of the government.

In caucus, there were serious concerns. The predominant one was that if the sales tax were to be increased, this would have a disproportionately negative effect on lower income families. Sales tax was seen to be a regressive tax, i.e., one that was harder for poor people to absorb than the middle class or the wealthy. No one objected to raising taxes. This was seen as necessary. There were those who tended to favour raising other taxes, but the concern over sales tax focused on the impact on the poor.

Ultimately, Graham Steele came to us and said that according to the calculations of the Department of Finance staff, with the HST increase of 2 per cent, there would be a cumulative cost to the lowest income quartile of families of about $50 million. What he proposed were various tax measures aimed at those families that would offset that negative impact. There would be an Affordable Living Tax Credit and a Poverty Reduction Tax Credit.

Illustration from NDP election platform documents.

In fact, he said, the credits would be worth about $70 million. Thus, the credits would more than offset the cost of the increase in sales tax for those families. They would be better-off to the tune of some $20 million.

But, he said, "We are not going to publicize that. Doing things for the poor does not go down well with the middle class."

Well, Jesus wept.

The middle class resents the poor, and does not want things done for them? First, of course, this is just wrong in the sense of inaccurate. Who does Graham think makes donations to the United Way, to charities that offer shelter housing, to church programmes that offer meals, to Feed Nova Scotia, and to furniture banks? It is the middle class, which in fact values building community through mutual aid. According to Statistics Canada, 22 per cent of Nova Scotian tax filers donate to charity, 42 per cent of those to "social services" charities.[3] This does not lead the country but is a solid, respectable number.

Second, redistribution of resources is a core NDP value. Using the mechanism of government to help in doing that is something we have always stood for. Redistribution means offering services where they are needed, and options for progressive taxation.

Third, let us try to put Graham's views in a favourable light. How about: "What you say is much less important than what you do." Thus, it doesn't matter that the NDP does not say it is helping the poor, just that it gets the job done. The benefit is what counts.

Well, no.

Government programmes are not private charity. For private charity we may as individuals follow the Biblical advice (*Matthew*, 6:2) to offer alms anonymously. In politics it is different. In politics it matters what you say, every bit as much as what you do. Politics is partly about influencing the climate of opinion. It is about debate. It is about challenging others. It is about setting out your principles, not about hiding them.

In caucus, Graham's statement became a central example often discussed among backbenchers of just how misdirected our government was. What is going on that we have ventured this far astray? Anti-poverty measures became the focus of a lot of caucus discussion held away from the leadership. The predominant view was not that doing a small bit for the poor was good enough, but that much more needed to be done, and that in not pursuing that agenda we were failing.

But our leaders thought that they understood electoral dynamics. Do not look too much like traditional NDPers; be moderate; look like the other parties; be "conservative progressives;" don't allow other parties to accuse you of using government to help those who are your friends.

And how did that work out for us?

Real people

One of the most disappointing features of the Dexter government was the extent to which Maureen MacDonald bought into his agenda.

Make no mistake. Maureen is someone I admire. She has a long history of doing good work. She and I worked closely together over the years. Her constituency adjoined mine. We were elected for the first time together in 1998. In 2003 we even ran a joint campaign, using one shared office. She is well known as the one who prompted Tory Minister of Community Services Edmund Morris to exclaim that Dalhousie Legal Aid – where she used to work – is just a training ground for the NDP. As a community worker, and later as a professor at Dalhousie University's School of Social Work, she has an admirable record. And as Minister of Health she did an excellent job.

But she was also an unrelenting supporter of the main points in Darrell's agenda, from "Back to Balance" to large scale grants to industry. Somewhere along the line she stopped being a critical presence and decided that loyalty to the leader and the inner circle was more important than what actually got accomplished. I am at a loss to explain it.

I do know what was said by the inner circle. A party cannot accomplish anything unless it is in power. That means being elected, and then getting reelected. To do that, go slow. Scorn was heaped upon those who would "rather be right than be elected."

At its core I think this shows a misunderstanding of why the NDP was elected in 2009 in the first place. The party inner circle explained the 2009 electoral victory by referring to two factors. First, voters were ready to toss the Tories out after their ten years in power; the NDP had been the Opposition for a long time and were best positioned to become the replacement government. Second, voters saw the new NDP under Darrell Dexter as moderate and therefore not threatening – as a safe alternative. While I agree on the first point, the second one is profoundly mistaken. I believe Nova Scotia voters were looking to the NDP not to be like the other two parties, but to be dramatically different. It was because we failed in that, that we were so decisively turfed in 2013. After all, if all the parties are more or less the same, there is no rationale for the NDP to exist at all: when voters are ready to switch governments all that is really needed is one alternative not two or more.

Maureen became a dedicated Darrell supporter, which meant a unity of voice, and a dedication to appeasing industry on virtually all occasions. Several times, Maureen would declare, in rejecting dissenting voices in

Maureen MacDonald and Darrell Dexter.

caucus, "suck it up, buttercup." This is not much of an analytical point. It relies on name-calling, and makes the underlying implied point that wiser heads have already made a choice, and that everyone should just follow suit.

One debate, which continued over several caucus meetings in May and June of 2012, had to do with the policy on forestry clear-cutting. The government had promised significant changes. Policy studies such as our own Natural Resources Strategy, had pointed to the need for major alteration in how forestry was conducted. The main point was to be a significant move away from clear-cutting. The particular point that came up for discussion was exactly how to define clear-cutting.

The Department of Natural Resources had a specific proposal (ultimately adopted) that was fairly extensively criticized at caucus, and had been seriously and publicly criticized by the province's main citizens' environmental organization, the Ecology Action Centre (EAC). The debate went back and forth. Maureen's contribution was to say that the Department's proposal should be adopted because to impose stricter standards would negatively impact 'real people with real jobs' that is, forestry workers. Apparently environmentalists and those in the public at large concerned with forestry policy are not real people, nor do they have real jobs.

Maureen's constituency, Halifax Needham, which is the north end of peninsular Halifax, is a fascinating place. In it, she often notes, both ships and beer are made. True. The Oland plant and the Irving shipyard are both there. But so too are a huge range of educators, small businesses, government employees, health workers, professionals, and community organizations and their leaders. Dalhousie Legal Aid, the Mi'kmaw Friendship Centre, Stepping Stone, Adsum House, the North End Community Health Centre, and the Affordable Housing Association are all in Needham. I have always thought that their employees are real people with real jobs. The EAC is in Needham. It is probably the leading non-governmental organization in Needham. I have always thought that its employees are real people with real jobs.

One of the features of our one-term government was a reluctant engagement with environmental sustainability. Measures were taken, but they were not a priority, nor were they central to the government's agenda. Jobs were the priority. But as we say in the environmental movement, there are no jobs on a dead planet.

And now back to that *Tempest* quotation:

> *For all the rest, they'll take suggestion as a cat laps milk.*

The folk who took suggestion so willingly were not just the cabinet ministers who were happy to embrace the Dexter agenda. I think a lot of the blame goes to all of us in the full caucus – indeed in the entire Party – who were too passive when it was clear that the way, the path, was just plain wrong.

Darrell lost his seat, as well as the government. A clutch of cabinet ministers were defeated. Graham Steele and Marilyn More bowed out of politics. Maureen came very close to losing her seat. There were lots of reasons behind this, but drifting out of touch with the traditional NDP agenda, and thus failing to deliver any significant change, explains most of it. A wasted opportunity. Our deluded years.

Walking the picket line with Mareen MacDonald in 2005 in support of locked-out CBC workers. CBC TV producer, David Pate, is on the left.

6

Whack-a-Mole

It began to be clear a full eighteen months before the 2009 election that the Tories were declining in popularity and the NDP was rising. Very good poll numbers for us came out in January 2008. At caucus, Bill Estabrooks enthused that, "Darrell Dexter walks on water," to which John MacDonell replied, "Well, it is January – come on." But now with the possibility of forming government becoming a tantalizing reality, what we were going to do became a major preoccupation for the party membership. By the May 2009 Provincial Council meeting there was some concern over the adequacy of the platform. Taking the pragmatic line, Dan O'Connor said, "There's not much point in having details about what we would do as government if we don't win government. So helping us win government is job one for the platform."

The internal rhetoric about what the new Nova Scotia NDP government would be had, in essence, two components. The first was to exhibit fiscal soundness through achieving a balanced budget. The second was to move towards progressive NDP ideals of social change, but to do so step by step. The plan was to imitate the NDP governments of Manitoba and Saskatchewan. Tommy Douglas, we were told, did not bring in Medicare until the province's books were balanced – fiscal discipline first. In both provinces successive governments had been elected. The plan for Nova Scotia was for three terms in a row. In fact, it is not so obvious that this second branch of what was said, was actually the plan. Looking objectively, the preoccupations were a balanced budget and job creation.

Ontario Premier Dalton McGuinty, Nova Scotia Premier Darrell Dexter, and Québec Premier Jean Charest at the Council of the Federation meeting in Halifax in 2012.

The actual story was of course entirely different. The attempt to show that a NDP Government could be fiscally disciplined was hopelessly compromised by the promise to balance the books in the first year of government, and to do so without raising taxes or cutting services. This was such a profoundly ridiculous, unachievable objective that it should never have been made in the first place. Trying to live up to the promise even in its modified form (back to balance in four years with a temporary increase in the HST) was also unachievable and had the unfortunate consequence of driving the rest of the policy agenda. It drove policy by requiring cuts to be made to the cost of services. This became, more than the broken promise, part of what offended voters.

Unfortunately, the Dexter government did not seriously lead public opinion into adopting a vision of where the NDP would go. In their 1999 winning election, the Hamm PCs talked about a 'plan' for Nova Scotia. Their plan was pretty thin, and focused mostly on managerial objectives. A plan, however, is not a vision. Visions are transformative. Visions invite hope. Visions invoke the future. Visions promise that we can all do better. Our government was not visionary. To the extent that ministers came up with policy documents, for the most part they were modest (immigration), late (housing; aquaculture; "Kids and Learning First"), or misconceived (jobsHere). What did characterize our time in government was being reactive to events as they happened to occur, rather than setting our own course.

The two policy documents that had actual substance, "Better Care Sooner"[1] and the Natural Resources Strategy[2] suffered different fates. The health policy, mostly about the delivery of emergency services outside of HRM's main hospital complex, and built on the basis of the Ross Report,[3] was implemented, though not without some difficulties. However, Collaborative Emergency Centres were not what many communities expected from the NDP after its time in Opposition and election talk of "keeping ERs open." As for the natural resources policy, hardly any of it was implemented. The section dealing with forestry was made completely subordinate to the desperate search for jobs.

Our four years in office were a lurch from one crisis to the next. The Province's books are found to be a mess? Panic. All hands on deck to get "Back To Balance." The Auditor General finds serious problems with the MLA expense system? Panic. All hands on deck to show that we can be as petty as anyone about spending by elected officials. Two pulp and paper mills are about to close? Panic. Never heard of this before, but all hands on deck to show that we can shovel out the cash with the best of them.

Inevitable Struggles: Rural Jobs

At a June 19, 2013 event held at the Dartmouth campus of the Nova Scotia Community College (NSCC), the fourth anniversary of the swearing in of the first NDP Cabinet, Darrell spoke of his dedication to, "relentless incrementalism," a recognition that not everything can be accomplished at once and that things take time, but the essential point is to be going in the right direction, and to be planning for the future. He specifically mentioned the coming demographic change, which would mean that by 2025 the percentage of the population over age 65 would have increased from 13 per cent to 25 per cent. We must plan for that, he said, "not wait for it to happen and let it overwhelm us." A perfectly good point. Too bad it did not characterize planning for other eventualities. Forestry, for example.

Earlier in the speech he had mentioned that the same day in the summer of 2011 when Jack Layton died, he was also informed of the closure of NewPage and the likely closure of Bowater. Part of his implication was that the mill closures were something of a surprise. Not so.

In 1991, the environmental community of the province, the Nova Scotia Environmental Network, issued a document called "Building a Green Nova Scotia". It was a submission to the Round Table on Environment and Economy that had been established by the government, and which had been holding some public sessions. One section of this document, which was written largely by a team consisting of Ishbel Butler, Lois Corbett, Jim Purdy, Charlie Restino, and myself, addressed forestry. Here is what it said:

The Forestry: an Alternative

Most of the use now of the harvest from the forest of the province – on the order of 80 per cent – is for pulp and therefore for paper products, chiefly newsprint. This is a sunset industry for several reasons. First, recycling is already making significant reductions in the call for newsprint. Eleven de-inking plants are planned for construction in Canada soon. Second, there is a very realistic possibility that fast-growing trees from warm climates will soon be a major source of raw materials for pulp. Third, the market for newsprint is a limited market, and, worldwide, newspapers are losing out to their news competitors, radio and television. Fourth, with the ending of the Cold War, there is a real possibility that the USSR will emerge as a major world supplier of newsprint. If there is no planning now for diversification, what will happen to the many people who now rely on forestry? They will have to move, and we will have clear-cut our population along with our forests, a double waste. Unless urgent steps are taken, in twenty years the forest industry in Nova Scotia will be unable to support people in anything remotely approaching the same manner as now.

A central point here is that the analysis of the need for profound change in forestry policy is based purely on hard economic facts, and is not reliant at all on an opposition to practices such as clearcutting. And in the end, the pulp and paper plants that did close or were reduce in size did so because of the external economics. Nonetheless, abuse of the resource

A clearcut in Nova Scotia.

has been a fact of life in forestry, and if the economics had continued to support pulp and paper for a bit longer, the problems with industrial forestry would have led soon to the same result.

The Environmental Network's submission has turned out to be remarkably prescient. But it was hardly an outlier view. The main history of forestry in our province, published a few years prior in 1986, written by forester Ralph S. Johnson, and issued by the province through the Department of Lands and Forests, said this: "Forests have often been harvested without regard to the future due to ignorance, poor logging techniques, and a demand for low-cost forest products. Today we are paying for the mistakes of past generations. Our children will pay more dearly than we for these past errors and for our current errors in managing natural resources."[4] In other words, what we have encouraged are fibre farms, not forests.

Another important book on forestry policy is *Trouble in the Woods: Forest Policy and Social Conflict in Nova Scotia and New Brunswick.*[5] The focus of its analysis was the conflict between small harvesters and the big pulp and paper mills, set in a context of a lengthy, aggressive overexploitation of forest resource by international companies abetted by successive governments. Amongst the things it highlights are:

In the 1920s, the most attractive and accessible forest lands in Nova Scotia were acquired by local pulpwood exporters, small ground wood pulp mills operating on a cut and run basis, and absentee pulp and paper companies holding land on a speculative basis as pulp-wood reserves. [...] The development of the pulp and paper industry in Nova Scotia was slow because of the scarcity of Crown lands. [...] By 1954 ... the pulp and paper segment first rose to industrial hegemony in the Nova Scotia forest economy. By 1965 pulpwood had become more important than saw log production. [...] The three major pulp and paper companies held Crown leases on most provincial forestlands, which amounted to 21 per cent of the total forest. [...] Small wood lot owners were the subject of repeated exploitation by the pulp and paper industry and the client states. [...] The government paid little heed to the aspirations of the wood lot owners. [...] As in the past, the favoured position of the pulp and paper industry prevailed, based on the arguments that the industry provided jobs and revenue. [...] The labour militancy (real and potential) and labour shortages of the 1950s prompted ... the development and adoption of mechanized pulpwood-logging methods. [...] Contemporary sources make it clear that small wood lot owners in the Maritimes practiced sustained yield forestry in the period up to 1930. [...] It was only with the introduction of the pulp and paper industry that small wood lot owners began to 'mismanage' their wood lots. But this 'mismanagement' was prompted by economic necessity. [...] Corporations now dominate the forest.

GPI Atlantic studied the province's forestry sector in 2001, producing a two-volume report that essentially confirmed the absence of sustainability in the traditional practices.[6] It showed a forest that is in dire shape. It later issued a 2008 update[7] noting that all the major indicators continue to, "demonstrate clearly that ... Nova Scotia's forests have been severely degraded over time." (pp. 43) Its conclusion was that, "A shift from clearcutting to selection harvesting, and from over-reliance on pulp and paper production to greater value-added production can increase jobs and value per unit of biomass harvested." (pp. 44)

When we were still the Opposition in 2007 our caucus held a meeting in Bridgewater, inviting local community leaders to talk with us about their issues. One that was identified was a concern that the Bowater plant might close. By the time the NDP came to power in 2009, no one should have had any reason to expect anything except crisis in the forestry.

Thus, there was no shortage of evidence about the perilous state of our pulp and paper forestry. As Hegel has pointed out, one of the main lessons of history is that no one learns the lessons of history. This is pretty clear with regard to forestry policy in our province. As with so many areas of public policy, especially those that have an environmental dimension, the barriers to change are generally not that we do not know a better way of going about our lives – information about better ways usually abounds. The barriers are usually adherence to the *status quo* because it is easier, and because profits are already being made. The human evolutionary advantage is supposed to be that we have creative brains, the virtue of which is the potential to imagine the future and anticipate consequences and options for change. When it comes to preserving our life support systems, there is not nearly enough evidence of use of this evolutionary advantage.

When we came to power in 2009, planning should have begun immediately for some transformation of those many communities that depend on this form of forestry. There should have been public statements warning people. And there should have been public economic development sessions to develop plans. To suggest that in the late summer of 2011 that a plant closure was surprising is simply not correct. Everyone who wanted to know, knew. Anything else was willful blindness. And was of no service to the people affected.

Bowater and NewPage

Our government went all-out to try to save the pulp and paper plants.

The attempts to assist Bowater were, in fact, fairly extensive. There was a package of measures totaling $50 million offered in the fall of 2011. Twenty-five million was to be a forgivable loan, $1.5 million for worker training, and $24 million for the purchase of land. In addition, there were to be breaks on power rates and property taxes. In the end this was not sufficient to keep Resolute Forest Products in business. The mill closed, with the province taking over its assets and liabilities in December 2012. In a stark contrast with the position of workers at NewPage, where pension values were reduced some 30 per cent, the liabilities the government assumed at Resolute included pension plan obligations of some $120 million. Even before the closure, while the first bailout package was before the Legislature, the Canadian Federation of Independent Business, the voice of small business, critiqued the move.[8]

The purchase of land, although perhaps legitimately criticized as too expensive per acre, was a good thing. It was in line with the policy of acquiring land for public ownership, in part because not a lot of the province's land mass is Crown owned (circa 23 per cent), and in part because it has been a formal target since the 2007 *Environmental Goals and Sustainable Prosperity Act* (EGSPA) was adopted to set aside 12 per cent of the overall land mass as protected. This is difficult to do with so little of the land publicly owned. In comparison, the British Columbia provincial government owns some 90 per cent of its land. There is a wide variance in Canadian provinces, but taking land into public ownership in Nova Scotia makes sense. In fact, moving significantly towards the 12 per cent target has been one of the best things our government has done in terms of the environment.

The pulp and paper plants in Nova Scotia are all different. Bowater was older, and had its own energy generation component, plus something of a dedicated market in that it was partially owned by a US publishing company, so its newsprint was directed there. The small Jodrey plant, CKF, in Hantsport, is oriented towards recycling cardboard and other post-consumer papers into boxboard. Even it has had to downsize. Northern Pulp's Abercrombie plant outside Pictou is not a modern plant, and is adjacent to a sizeable pollution problem, Boat Harbour. Its emissions-control system is not functioning properly. Recently it became public knowledge that the NDP government agreed to pay for half the cost of replacing it, something not previously known. It also became public that we had allocated 125,000 tonnes of fibre to the mill, to be taken from Crown land, primarily in the western part of the province. This was revealed by the Liberals; it had not been announced by the NDP. And NewPage in Port Hawkesbury is a very modern mill specializing in coated paper used for colour supplements and magazines, called supercalendrated paper, although it also produces newsprint.

The Premier's Office went into overdrive to save that plant. It paid for keeping it from deteriorating; it sought a buyer; it negotiated the sale.

The amount of money allocated to NewPage by our government ended up being $156 million. Here is how it was spent:

- $12.3 m for ongoing 'hot idle' plant maintenance pending sale.
- $24 m for a forgivable loan for plant improvements.
- $1.5 m for a forgivable loan for worker training.
- $40 m as a repayable loan.
- $19.1 m for forestry improvements on Crown land.
- $1 m as a forgivable loan for a marketing plan.
- $ 38 m to support sustainable harvesting and land management.
- $ 20 m to purchase 20,000 hectares of forested land.

Stern (Pacific West Commercial Corporation) purchased the plant for $33 million. But the province loaned the company $40 million. Even if the $40 million is allocated to plant improvements, Stern has too little skin in the game. It would not be surprising to see the plant closed and sold off within a decade. In a retrospective on the NDP performance posted in 2013 called, "Six things the NDP did wrong," journalist Parker Donham cited this deal as an example of how we were, "maladroit on big negotiations."[9]

In October 2012, Barrie McKenna, columnist for the Report on Business section of *The Globe and Mail*, wrote a critique of this specific bailout to illustrate just how questionable an undertaking such ventures are for governments.

Hewers of wood, drawers of water and givers of handouts. It's the sad, but all too common, story of single-industry towns in Canada. Thanks to the largesse of the Nova Scotia government, an oft-bailed out paper mill in Port Hawkesbury is back in business this week, cranking out rolls of glossy magazine paper for the first time in more than a year.

But the rescue doesn't come cheap. Nova Scotia is contributing incentives worth as much as $156-million, including the cash it has already spent maintaining equipment since the Cape Breton mill went bankrupt in 2011. That's the equivalent of $470,000 for each of the 330 jobs saved. If those workers earn an average of $45,000 a year, Nova Scotia will essentially underwrite the mill's entire payroll for more than a decade. Nova Scotia Power is also chipping in with discounted power rates, presumably paid for by other rate payers in the province.

Various companies have been making paper at the Port Hawkesbury site, dating back to the 1960s – Canadian, American and Finnish owners. And all of them have repeatedly gone to the government trough when the mill was unprofitable, threatening closure if the money wasn't forthcoming.

There are records of subsidies going to the mill, dating back to the 1970s. [...] The Canadian corporate landscape is littered with these pay-us-or-we'll-walk sagas. And they rarely work for long. Plants close, owners fail, workers and pensioners lose.

These kinds of bailouts raise a troubling question about the limits of ... regional development policies. What price is too high to save a job? [...] Bailouts don't occur in a vacuum. More money for troubled businesses inevitably means less money for something else.

When plants close, policy makers don't seem to make the obvious calculation. What's a better use of taxpayers' money – saving jobs that will likely vanish when the subsidies run out, or making investments that will pay dividends for decades, such as research-and-development or higher education? It's a choice between real work and artificial work. [10]

Is there another way to deal with these pressures? It is obvious that governments cannot invest in this way for all businesses. Are you opening a restaurant? A barbershop? An optician's? Offering yoga classes? Selling furniture? Motorcycles? Offering carpentry, electrical, or plumbing services? Creating a dozen or more jobs by doing that? Should the government calculate what amount of taxes these jobs will generate over the next ten years, and grant you an amount equal to that? Or maybe as a forgivable loan if the jobs are created and maintained? Or perhaps not the full amount, but a rebate of "payroll taxes?" In principle it could be a government function to do all this, but it involves government embarking into the banking business. If government is to do this – if, in the terms set out on the Nova Scotia Business Inc. (NSBI) website, your company, "finds it challenging to satisfy your financing needs through other lending agencies" – what criteria should determine eligibility? The prospects for success of the business? The economic fragility of the specific community where it is to be located? Whether the jobs are in sectors the government wishes to see advanced? How big the business is through spinoff benefits? All of these?

In any given year recently, Nova Scotia businesses created 4,860 new jobs. This is a fifteen year average, covering the period of 1997 to 2012. In recent years it would be quite optimistic to achieve these figures. In that period the workforce increased from 323.6 thousand to 396.6 thousand, i.e., by some 73 thousand jobs. But the bulk of them were created in 1998-2001, 2003, 2004, and 2006 – some 65.7 thousand of them. In the last six years, the average increase has been about 1,700 jobs per year. Being optimistic and using the fifteen year average jobs number. if the province were to rebate the amount usual for job creation deals approved by NSBI (circa ten per cent of gross payroll). the annual cost to the government would be $20 million in contemporary dollars and using average wages. Such an investment is not realistic under any conceivable scenario, partly because of the expense and partly because of the administrative complexity involved.

And in any event, the NewPage/Stern jobs were not new jobs, they were jobs "maintained." It is a term that appears often in NSBI statements of, "jobs created or maintained." Maintained means not lost. In plain terms, the government has given in to political blackmail.

Should NewPage have simply been allowed to close? That was certainly an option, and if the government were going to get involved it could have spent public money otherwise. It could have gone to support the pensions of retired workers who found themselves facing reductions of some 30 per cent. It could have invested in retraining for workers losing their jobs. It could have invested in community economic development to try to change the base of the area economy. There are strong arguments against some of this, especially the bailout of a private pension plan where the employer and employees negotiated the contribution levels that led, at least partially, to the underfunding. But overall, these sort of investments are probably a better approach than the one chosen, which bets heavily on the ongoing success of an industry that has shown itself completely incapable of surviving without public monies.

The parallel has to be with Sydney Steel. Nova Scotia governments subsidized that industry well past the point at which there was any realistic prospect of independent success. They ignored the marketplace realities for the steel business. And while it is certainly true that communities need to have an effective partnership with government, it should be based on clear appreciation of the overall economic facts. If the choice made is to offer public support to some business that cannot be successful on its own, in general that might better be allocated when the business is an emerging one rather than one that is on its way out. Change is a fundamental fact in the structure of the economy. Helping transitions makes more sense than trying to pretend that no transition is occurring.

On top of the economic naïveté there seemed to be a hope that the public subsidies for NewPage/Stern would result in electoral success for the party in the newly restructured constituency of Richmond because, we were told, the government's decisions were hugely popular in Port Hawkesbury and the surrounding area. Port Hawkesbury had previously been a part of the Inverness constituency, but with the redrawing of electoral boundaries, it had been shifted to Richmond. Why this change in boundaries would be expected to make any difference was not completely clear. Inverness was Tory held and Richmond was Liberal held.

Both would be hard for us to win no matter what. And although the decision to subsidize the mill was greeted with relief and praise from local municipal officials, and the union, there were still discontents: the loss of half the jobs, the hardball by Stern over municipal taxes and prices paid to wood suppliers, and the reductions in pensions for retired workers.

In the end, the problem is one that is an enduring part of the structure of the Canadian economy: being so dependent on natural resources, especially unprocessed or only slightly processed ones. Michael Porter at the Harvard Business School has focused in some special studies on the competitiveness of the Canadian economy.[11] His prescription – that skills upgrading and productivity growth, more research and development, more education generally, high regulatory standards, and conservation and renewal of natural resources – bear economic fruit, all make sense for governments to promote. There are also other important features of the Canadian economy, features that are as true in Nova Scotia as throughout Canada: a small domestic market, a high degree of foreign ownership, a high degree of corporate concentration, and a high degree of reliance on one main trading partner. I tend to see these as problems; others do not. But they are fundamental features of our economic life. And the first item on the list, natural resource dependence, is highly problematic in the forestry sector. I predict that Stern will be gone in a decade. If we have indeed bought ourselves those years, we should use them to prepare.

The Convention Centre

Despite all of the ink dedicated to it, I wonder if the issues around the Convention Centre remain fixed in the public mind. As I write, there is an enormous hole in the ground, two storeys deep, for two full blocks in the centre of the Halifax downtown on the slope leading up to Citadel Hill. Cranes are in place for the towers being constructed. And as the months go by towards the target completion date of late 2016 or early 2017, residents and visitors will be regularly reminded of what some of the contentious issues were: height, mass, disproportion to surroundings, distraction from and blockage of the view. But internally for the party, and to some extent with the public, the whole convention centre episode has represented the quintessence of the problem with this NDP government: not different from other political parties, a limited ability or willingness to think creatively, a serious fear of being seen as anti-business, and the willingness to offend its base.

For upwards of forty years, Halifax has controlled development in its downtown by setting a restrictive height limit – 40 feet generally, and 25 feet adjacent to the harbour – and then leaving it to developers who propose something larger to apply for a Development Agreement (DA). There were other controls as well, including policies about compatibility with nearby existing buildings, and both specific and more generally worded protections for the views along the streets to the Harbour and from Citadel Hill. This system worked well for a long time, but became subject to criticism from the development community, which wanted to avoid long public debates about new proposals, wanted greater as-of-right height limits, and did not want appeals to the provincial oversight body, the Utility and Review Board (UARB).

This resulted in Tory legislation to change the overall legal structure for land use planning in the Halifax downtown. This was to implement HRM By Design, a series of policies developed by the Halifax Regional Municipality (HRM) to set out objectives for the downtown, and it was adopted in the context of a desire to use a new planning method. The new method would give greater as-of-right height, though building design would be subject to review by an appointed committee. Because the system relied on as-of-right heights and review was by a committee there would be no formal public hearings and no appeal to the UARB. Essentially, the public opportunities for serious participation in the decision were to be removed.

I did not support the bill, and voted against it, although the rest of our caucus in Opposition led by Darrell supported it. Darrell did not have planning policy reasons for supporting the bill; it was clear that he was responding to pressure from the development community, which had mounted a very loud campaign to complain about development in the

downtown being held up by the existing legal process. This was not in fact the case. Development in the Halifax downtown was stalled for economic reasons, not the planning framework. Essentially, developers and city hall planners found public involvement to be inconvenient. Darrell was trying to show the party as being business friendly and this was simply a good opportunity to do so. It avoided the possibility of an allegation of being anti-development. So the question that came forward around the caucus table was not whether this was good or bad for Nova Scotians, but whether it was good or bad for the electoral prospects of the NDP.

Most of the specifics as to height set out in the HRM By Design by-laws had been debated publicly and consultation sessions had been held. There were flaws in that process, but it had occurred. It is important to remember that the process did include policies for what is called the "upper central downtown" i.e., the area that includes the two blocks bounded by Argyle, Prince, Market, and Sackville streets. The height limit was 72 feet, or six or seven storeys, with the possibility of a bonus of an extra two storeys if some public benefit were included. That was it. Also, buildings had to be stepped back at four storeys above the street line so as to allow for light to reach the street, and to minimize adverse wind effects. When the by-laws came to HRM Council a change was proposed: on those particular blocks, the bylaw was to say, if a publicly funded convention centre were built as part of a development, then the allowable height could almost double and go up to fourteen storeys on one block and eighteen storeys on the other.

Why did this proposal come forward? It implies private discussions, and the specifics have never become publicly known. This proposal, discussed *in camera* by HRM Council, came from the Rodney MacDonald PC government in 2009, just before the provincial election. But the change was adopted, flying in the face of the results of the only formal public involvement allowable by the HRM By Design rules.

With these new rules in place the three levels of government then started to consider the extent of their financial commitment to a new convention centre. By this time the NDP had formed government, so at the provincial level it was our party that had to grapple with this topic. What the NDP government decided was crucial. The municipality on its own would not finance the project, and the Federal Government tends to assign capital project dollars according to priorities set by the province. The Convention Centre became a major public issue, with nonstop coverage in all news media, for a very long time. In favour of public support for a convention centre were the following points:

- Halifax needed a new convention centre to attract larger events;
- Convention centres are publicly supported elsewhere;
- The downtown needs the stimulus of a new anchor building;
- The benefits would roll out across the province as tourists were attracted to the convention facility and then stayed on.

Against the proposal:

- We already have various event locations;
- The evidence is against such a facility attracting much new business;
- The amount involved is too great;
- In any case, this is not the best location;
- The public will not own the centre; it is another P-3 (public-private partnership) scam;

• Public funding will trigger a right to build towers on top, to a height not appropriate.

Many of these points were focused on the Convention Centre component, but doubts were also raised about the complex as a whole. It promised to add significant office space to the downtown, but the overall vacancy rate in offices in the central business district was, and remains, high. And if there was future demand for office space it could be met through much lower buildings, more compatible with the traditional character of Halifax.

The political problem for the government was that many core party supporters were opposed to a public subsidy for a convention centre, for many of the reasons listed above. People resigned from the party in droves when provincial government funding was finally announced, and they became particularly embittered.

In the middle of all the debate on the merits of public subsidy, whether a new facility was needed at all, and whether the projections of future business were reliable, there was a diversion over my own role. For a long time, the amount of money being sought from the various levels of government was not publicly disclosed. In September 2010 caucus was told that the amount was $156 million, to be shared by the three levels, federal, provincial, and municipal. It happened that Tim Bousquet, a reporter for *The Coast*, the free weekly newspaper that had an intense focus on Halifax politics, called me to talk about the Convention Centre. Because I had been on the record for years on land use development matters, and because I had publicly criticized HRM By Design, including voting against legislation to facilitate it, and because I had also been on record as opposed to the Convention Centre, I talked with him. In the middle of that conversation I let slip the amount of public money involved.[12] This was a new piece of information and could be expected to be reported. This was on a Friday. Because *The Coast* was published every Thursday, I thought I had a few days to figure out what to do.

It turns out that there is an online version, something I had not known, and Monday morning my phone began to ring. Big news. Big kerfuffle. Including at caucus, where there was resentment that I had revealed information given to us in confidence. While the press milled about outside, caucus met on Wednesday to discuss all of this. I explained to my colleagues what had happened and that the leak was inadvertent not deliberate; that I recognized that the information about cost was for the Minister to state and not for individual caucus members to reveal. I went on to say that because I was so opposed to the Convention Centre, caucus might not think my account credible. I invited them to consider several points: that I did not know Tim Bousquet, and if I had wanted to leak information I would have gone to reporters I had worked with for years and knew I could trust; that he had called me (not the other way around); that if I were going to leak, I could have leaked anonymously; that when Bousquet phoned me he already had some details of the previous week's caucus briefing, and that there was already a leak that was not from me: all of this was consistent with the information having slipped out during an interview rather than being deliberately revealed. I answered some questions and then waited in my office while my colleagues discussed the matter. (While I was waiting, I went out the rear door to use the washroom, only to find myself in the midst of a media scrum. I explained that I had spoken to my colleagues and was just waiting to hear from them, then excused myself. CBC reporter Paul Withers quipped "Speaking of leaks...." Two points for Paul.)

In the end, caucus accepted what I had to say, and we moved on. But Convention Centre issues were to remain present in one form or another throughout our term. When the provincial government did announce its commitment of money, I published an opinion piece in *The Chronicle Herald* (at their request) outlining the case against the Centre. Not long after that, caucus was presented with a set of policies on caucus solidarity, which was adopted, over objections from several of us. It essentially said that all MLAs should support government positions, and if they object they should raise the matter with the leader and if accommodation cannot be found, to resign to sit independently. What this did was to make the traditional rule of Cabinet solidarity in which a Minister must support a Cabinet decision or resign, into a caucus rule. No such rule applies in either the UK or the USA Congress, where caucus members frequently go on the record as dissenting from their party on various matters. No one there sees this as an occasion for panic. For whatever reason, the touchiness around range of opinion in caucuses seems to be common in Canada. I see this as political immaturity. It also ignores the principle that collective responsibility should have a corresponding amount of collective decision-making.

There was also an ongoing focus on the reliability of the business projections done by Trade Centre's staff.[13] The Auditor General later examined them, and concluded that further and independent reviews should be done. They were not. Experts in the convention business spoke about the highly competitive environment in North America for the convention business, and the significant problems many cities that had built or subsidized new centres encountered. The design of the Convention Centre component of the whole project, now called the Nova Centre, was widely criticized, because so much of it was underground. It was redesigned. Polls showed people completely divided even after years of debate and a non-stop selling job by the business community. A *Chronicle Herald* editorial from July 2012 said: "Whether a new convention centre is a good deal has been hotly debated for a long time. [...] But it's a done deal now. [...] Ready or not, Halifax is getting a new publicly financed $164 million convention centre embedded in a privately financed massive development downtown. Doubts about the suitability, desirability and viability of the $500 million Nova Centre will now be resolved not in the public square, but in the real world."[14]

But in that real world, Rank Inc., the developer, has not been able to announce one tenant, except for the government's tenancy of the Convention Centre component, for the 14-storey financial office tower (later two towers); the other component is to be an 18-storey hotel. Why not? If there is a solid business case for the Nova Centre, where are the tenants? On another political aspect of the project, so concerned was our government about negative reaction that it sent out a team from the department of Economic and Rural Development and Tourism (ERDT) to sell the Convention Centre to the rural parts of the province over the summer of 2012, as an opportunity for tourism operators and small businesses beyond HRM to benefit.

The Nova Centre under construction.

Since the 2013 election, some details of the redesign of the Convention Centre have become public. It turns out that between moving the underground components above ground, and rearranging the location of the towers on the site, the Convention Centre no longer meets the Request for Proposals (RFP) criteria for size of the facility. The ballroom of the existing Convention Centre is 20,000 square feet, the RFP calls for 35,000, and the revised plans are for 30,000. The exhibition hall of the existing Convention Centre is 40,000 square feet, the RFP calls for 52,000, and the latest plans are for 25,000. Given that the original rationale for a new Convention Centre was the need for a larger space so as to be able to attract larger events, these numbers are stunning. The failure to meet the requirements of the RFP offers the government an off-ramp, but there is little indication that it will be taken.

One result of the whole debate was some inspired journalism. Tim Bousquet wrote well and regularly in *The Coast* about the cozy relationship between the local business elite and government. The *Chronicle Herald* columns were generally full of uncritical boosterism (by writers such as Roger Taylor and Marilla Stevenson) but it did publish one fine piece by local University of King's College academic and Cape Breton native Laura Penny. She contrasted government support for the Centre with its lack of support for the universities, a much better investment:

"When the NDP were elected, I was glad. I hoped for the same thing I ask my students for: 'Please, guys, make new mistakes.' But the NDP's endorsement of the Convention Centre proposal is an all-too-familiar mistake. Nova Scotians have already seen the Very Special Episode where we buy the Big New Thing that saves the Economy. Repeatedly. I'm not against development. I'm against politics-as-usual passing for development. The idea that one big capital project will save us is old. [...] We need to work on our R&D skills, not our 'coffee or tea?' skills. But this will never happen. Our ostensible leaders, in business and politics, do not see our universities and community colleges as assets we should develop. They're just big tax sucks that need to be cut. [...] We can live off tips from people who come from places that still have industries. [...] And if factors such as fuel prices, or a strong Canadian dollar, adversely affect tourism, I guess we can sell plush lobsters and souvenir sou'westers to each other."[15]

At the moment there is a lawsuit with respect to the Nova Centre, brought by the Thiel group of companies focusing on a decision of our government to try to enable a fast-tracking of the project. The Thiels are rival developers of downtown land. Their point is interesting. They are questioning an order of the Minister of Municipal Affairs to, "exempt the development of the Nova Centre ... from complying with the requirements," of existing HRM by-laws that would otherwise apply. The Nova Centre is missing revised design drawings, an encroachment license, and street closure authorization, which means it could not have obtained building or other needed permits.[16] It is far from clear that the sections of the *HRM Charter*, which the Minister relied on to issue his orders, can actually apply. The initial court decision has been to uphold the legality of the Minister's order, but the Thiel company is appealing.[17] They object to the implication that the Minister can sidestep all usual orderly development processes at will.

Yarmouth Ferry

If you are looking for a wonderful read, the late Alistair MacLeod is probably our province's finest writer. I am especially fond of his 1976 short story about a group of Cape Breton mineworkers who do jobs abroad but summer at home every year. It is called, "The Closing Down of Summer." It includes this passage about tourism in the province:

> This is a record year for tourists in Nova Scotia, we are constantly being told. More motorists have crossed the border at Amherst than ever before. More cars have landed at the ferry docks in Yarmouth. Motels and campsites have been filled to capacity. The highways are heavy with touring buses and camping trailers and cars with the inevitable lobster traps fastened to their roofs. Tourism is booming as never before.

That was an exceptionally good year. Still, the value of tourism has grown to be worth almost $2 billion, a very significant portion of a GDP that is about $40 billion in total. The Southwest Nova region, with not a lot of other economic activity, is very sensitive to fluctuations in tourism.

One of the early decisions that was indicative of inexperience, haste, misplaced priorities, and stubbornness, was the decision to pull fund-

The "CAT" while it was still running between Maine and Yarmouth.

ing for the CAT, the ferry travelling between Yarmouth and the United States. The opposition never ceased referring to this, and so the odds of the NDP re-winning the Yarmouth seat, which we held briefly in 1998-1999, anytime in the forseeable future are now astronomically small. Southwest Nova is lost territory for the NDP. In retrospect, the problem is clear: pulling financial support with no alternative in place was rightly seen as a harmful economic move. Tourism was especially impacted. It was widely agreed that the particular ship working the route was not the right vessel. It had no capacity to transport commercial vehicles. And overall visitors from the USA via the ferry had declined from 40,000 in 2006 to 23,000 in 2009. And the federal government was not participating in the costs. And the government subsidy was expensive. Yet our government was seen as high-handed, not consultative, and acting recklessly of consequences.

Just before the 2013 election, Shelburne MLA and Fisheries Minister, Sterling Belliveau, said, "If I could hit the reset button, this is the one issue I would do again, " obviously meaning he would do it differently.

What led to the decision? It is not completely clear. To the extent a caucus member can judge, it was a move prompted purely by the first months' panic over the province's finances and the need to cut spending. It appears to have just been one of those items that happened to come forward early for review. But we went full steam ahead, reckless of the shallows. One aspect of the decision, which may have misled many in caucus, was the implication of a clear message to businesses that came to government seeking financial support for an enterprise that was in trouble: the new NDP government would not be an easy mark. As it turned out, any of us who thought that were seriously in error.

Many of the broad and also specific economic decisions of the government were made by Cabinet and did not involve advance consultation with caucus. With respect to the CAT, though, caucus was consulted, and though the course of action came with a recommendation to end the funding, it was open to all of us to think more creatively, and we did not. This has to be identified as one of the characteristics of the operation of caucus: for the most part we tended to go along with suggestions made to us. We failed to be critical, to raise serious alternatives, or to bring what is actually quite a good array of personal history and expertise to the table. It is not clear why. But that was largely the way it was. There are exceptions in the group. Gary Burrill and Jim Morton especially, though with distinctive styles, could often be relied upon to raise serious and important questions. On some topics, for example education, or forestry, or road paving, or cultural matters, other individuals did speak up. But it was not encouraged. Caucus was not structured as a place for informed debate so much as a place for a cursory review, a place where people were told what had been decided and were given the lines to recite back home. It was not a healthy dynamic.

Aquaculture

The sad story of our approach to fin-fish aquaculture is another illustration of much of what went wrong with our government. The basic approach was wrong; it was to encourage this industry, through approvals, talk, and money. What was missing was any policy analysis except that directed towards creating jobs. It was crisis management again. Ultimately, the government claimed to be committed to world-class standards for the industry, but this came very late in the process, and there was little in it to convince anyone that the commitment was sincere. A better approach would have been to announce from day one that we were committed to world-class standards, and to hold off on further development until those standards were in place.

In some parts of the province fin-fish aquaculture was not controversial. In Digby and in parts of Shelburne there seemed to be general support. But along the Eastern Shore and in Queens County it was otherwise. The industry had cultivated MLAs as actively as it cultivated mussels. Every year there was a reception for MLAs in the lobby of Province House with farmed local fish and seafood on offer, plus of course alcohol. The events were very popular.

The controversial activity, of course, is fin-fish aquaculture, not that for mussels. At one point, the NDP caucus held a retreat in Shelburne, and some opponents of an aquaculture proposal near Port Mouton turned out to demonstrate. All of the small crowd were elderly and peaceful and were traditional NDP supporters. Disgracefully, Darrell walked through them without stopping to talk, surrounded by tall staffers. As if there were any threat. Police were also in attendence.

Alexandra Morton, a British Columbia-based investigator who has become a foremost authority of salmon aquaculture there, was invited to speak at Dalhousie for the Ransom Myers Memorial lecture in October 2012. I also had the opportunity to meet with her directly. The late Ransom Myers was an ocean ecologist with a worldwide reputation. The science done at Dalhousie about ocean sustainability is of major importance. We are blessed in Nova Scotia to have scientists such as Myers, and now others like Boris Worm, who introduced Morton. She explained that she had become involved in examining the British Columbia aquaculture industry when it came to the remote coastal community where she lives. On the regulatory front, she found split jurisdiction between the federal and provincial governments with some resultant confusion. Additionally problematic was the low level of community involvement in decisions around whether aquaculture should be allowed, and if allowed, with what conditions and subject to what public release of information.

As to the science, she pointed to a variety of concerns: the presence and spread of pathogens, treatment with pesticides, the presence of sea lice, interbreeding and competition with wild salmon stocks (it is mostly salmon that is farmed in Canada), the general absence of baseline data about locations where pens are placed, problems for breeding of other species if their spawning beds are polluted by feces. Often the installations are nuisances in their communities and constitute

The late and greatly acclaimed Ransom Myers (RAM), a leading marine biologist and formerly a professor at Dalhousie.

an interference to fishing and swimming, or by waste being discharged into the water. It is possible to have fish farming, she said, if there are baseline studies, if there are good rules that are properly enforced, if the pens have closed-containment, and if not they are placed so there is no competition with wild stocks, especially away from migration routes. She thought aquaponics works better for trout, sea bass, and halibut.

Everything Morton had to say about aquaculture in British Columbia applies here in Nova Scotia.[18] One of our main east coast researchers on aquaculture is New Brunswick's Inka Milewski, who has also looked at some sites here in Nova Scotia. Her research confirms the existence of problems. But our government was an uncritical booster of the industry. There was also a structural problem in that the department responsible for promotion of fisheries was under the direction of the same minister responsible for advocating for the environment. Sterling Belliveau was minister for both and he was adamant that the industry is beneficial.

Scandalously, in 2012 we even gave Cooke Aquaculture some $25 million to expand its operations in Nova Scotia. By that time, the public noise about aquaculture, and New Brunswick-based Cooke in particular, had become very loud. Silver Donald Cameron made a film about aquaculture, *Salmon Wars*.[19] It featured Darrell Dexter making a pre-election speech to residents in Port Mouton that sounds a lot like a promise not to allow more fish farms. The film prompted nasty comments from Darrell about Silver Don at caucus. When the money for Cooke was announced, Raymond Plourde of the EAC called it "obscene."[20] The money was for expansion of facilities in Shelburne, Digby, and Truro. There was a $16 million loan, a $4 million forgivable loan, and a $9 million grant. "They should be paying us millions for the privilege of polluting our coastal waters," Plourde added.

The controversy about Cooke was fueled in part by Environment Canada charging Cooke's subsidiary, Kelly Cove Salmon, with causing a lobster kill by releasing a pesticide into waters off Grand Manan and Deer Islands in New Brunswick. The charges were laid in 2011, and in 2013 Kelly Cove Salmon entered a guilty plea and was fined $500,000. Aware of its controversial status, the industry ran a billboard campaign to promote its image. "Farms don't stop at the land," was its slogan.

In the meantime, matters in British Columbia had led to the appointment of a commissioner to report on the decline of sockeye salmon in the Fraser River. British Columbia Supreme Court Justice Bruce Cohen reported in November 2012 after three years of work. He identified no single smoking gun, but did point to a variety of stressors including climate change, infectious diseases, contaminants, industrial activity, wastewater, and aquaculture.[21] He was particularly alarmed about aquaculture in the Discovery Islands and said installations there might have to be closed.

In the midst of these debates, Rick Williams, the Deputy Minister of Policy, went to Scotland and Norway to investigate their approach to aquaculture. And then a report was commissioned from two Dalhousie Law professors, Meinhard Doelle and Bill Lahey. The only thing wrong with this is that it came so far into our term, and after we had already established a public position of boosterism of the industry. Basic to Nova Scotia's *Environment Act*, and stemming from international norms, is the idea of the precautionary principle. Not only have we tended to ignore that, we should have been committing the province to the highest standards. The Doelle-Lahey Panel seems likely to promote that. Its interim draft report[22] cites "state-of-the-art" standards for sustainable development, environmental protection, and social well-being including economic opportunity. The draft makes clear that aquaculture is, "not appropriate for all coastal waters" (pp. vi), that, "a fundamental overhaul of the regulation of aquaculture is called for" (pp. v), and that there are places where it is suitable and compatible with other uses.

Journalist Silver Donald Cameron speaks with Conservative party leader, Jamie Baillie, at a salmon aquaulture protest at Province House in 2012.

A rally in the Grand Parade in Halifax protesting the government's aquaculture policy.

7

Expenses Scandal

I f anything illustrates just how much no one person or body has control of the public policy agenda, the Auditor General's report on MLA expenses certainly does.

No one was looking to deal with expenses as a main priority. But this became a long running story after the Auditor General reported in January 2010 on abuses of the expenses system that supports MLAs in running their constituency offices. The ultimate result, played out over the next three years, was criminal charges against four MLAs, all convicted. The immediate impact was an enormous public preoccupation with the issue, and the occasion for blanket criticism of all elected officials. The underlying belief of critics seemed to be that dishonesty prevailed, that this was no surprise since all political parties were culpable, and that everyone was just in it for the money. For the NDP, the impact was highly problematic, since it fostered a belief that all parties are indeed the same.

In its antecedents the system of payment for expenses had been an occasion for Graham Steele to establish some unpopularity with his colleagues. He had gone on record in 2005 via an opinion piece in *The Chronicle Herald* specifying the flaws in the existing system, and plumping for an end to global payments (such as for postage and use of a vehicle) and a switch to a pure reimbursement system based on receipts. It is certainly a defensible view, but he published it without consultation, and the tone was unfortunate. The proposal was also somewhat problematic, since it would require (and now does require, under the new rules) record keeping for each business-related car trip. This certainly is common in many workplaces, but in this instance it does ignore the widely accepted fact that the annual global payment for vehicle use and postage has been a way to offset salaries that are seen to be somewhat low by most MLAs – too low on a national comparative basis, and too low to attract a good range of candidates.[1]

Compensation is a topic related to expenses. Some MLAs have denied that the drift upward of amounts for expenses was a way to increase compensation that was below what it ought to be. But that is exactly what it was, as Graham Steele also frankly acknowledged in his book.[2]

Expenses are for the running of the MLA offices: staff, rent, phone, equipment, postage, travel, and related items; plus, for out-of-town members, accommodation expenses. There is certainly room for serious transparency and accountability; indeed these arrangements contribute to the overall democratic vibrancy of the enterprise. At the same time, the system needs to be effective in allowing MLAs to do their job. Likewise the financial side of the job needs to be such that it will allow a representative range of the population to contemplate serving as an MLA. Inappropriately low compensation would limit service to either those in the most comfortable of circumstances or those in the worst of circumstances for whom the pay would be an improvement on their circumstances. Surely that is not desirable. Some sort of arm's length arrangement makes sense for setting compensation of elected officials. And indeed such a system has long been in place, though ignored by premiers when they want to make a political point, or pander to columnists who have stirred up public opinion. Thus, a series of written reports on MLA compensation by Graham Walker in 2000, Arthur Donahoe in 2003, and a group consisting of Barbara McDougall, Gordon Gillis, and George MacLellan in 2006 were all ignored, although the legislative framework required their implementation.

At the same time, a focus on the expenses of elected officials was not unexpected. Scandals had occurred in Newfoundland and in the UK the previous year. Additionally, expenses were something that had frequently been tinkered with. The Auditor General's investigation of MLA expenses was known to be in the works. Matt Hebb warned caucus to think about their use of the expenses allowance. "Who bought something really dumb?" he asked in July 2009.

Having been swept up in the mess myself, I can say it was not much fun. (Anyone wanting to get the flavour of the general press hysteria should have a look at *Frank Magazine* for March 2, 2010.) The Auditor General noted that I spent some of my office allowance on books, which he termed as, "out of the ordinary" – which basically meant I was the only MLA buying books. (Not only that, I read them.) The report was clear that this was not fraud or outside of the rules, just that it was unique, and apparently not contemplated. He made no request that the amount involved ($2,500 or so over three years) be repaid.

It has always been clear that allowable expenses include television, cable connection, radio, Internet, newspaper and magazine subscriptions. The obvious reason for this is to allow the MLA to learn things that are useful to them to do the job. A book is just a better form of information, but columnists did not see it that way, and I took a lot of ribbing. It is still my view that being an effective MLA requires serious attempts at self-education, and that books are an integral part of that.

As a footnote on the topic of books, my colleague Leonard Preyra cleared out his caucus office when he was appointed to Cabinet. As a longtime political science professor at SMU, he has a large collection of interesting texts. He put several boxes of these books in the caucus office, free for the taking. I helped myself to some, but the remainder stayed there month after month, untouched. So it goes.

More problematic were items that seemed to be unusually expensive or were outright fraudulent, either in that they had no relation to the running of a constituency office (Richard Hurlburt's generator) or were claims for items not paid (H. Dave Wilson's overtime pay to staff or Trevor Zinck's charity donations and office rent which were claimed for but not paid to the named recipient). Darrell Dexter was caught up in the criticism for having purchased an expensive camera; John MacDonell for expensive office furniture. And, unaccountably, Charlie Parker for a replica of the ship Hector, central to the Scottish history in Pictou County, to adorn his office. None of these items were actually forbidden, but the public pressure pushed these MLAs to offer to repay the amounts.

Much later on, a small joke went the rounds in the Legislature:

Q. A car goes by with Richard Hurlburt, H. Dave Wilson,
and Russell MacKinnon all in it. Who is driving?
A. The Police.

This was a lot funnier on our side of the chamber before we had to add Trevor Zinck, then an NDP MLA, to the passenger list.

How the Auditor General's report was dealt with was the occasion for an early example of erosion of the caucus's faith in its leadership. Their reaction was entirely driven by attempts to mirror the opinions of the newspaper columnists. Craven is the only word for how the leadership behaved. Thus, with the publicity in full swing, at the Legislature's Internal Economy Board, the Liberals' Manning MacDonald came in with some proposals for new rules, one of which would limit advertising expenses to ten percent of the monthly claimed expense. There is no real accountability rationale for such a rule; clearly it was an attempt to hit at Members such as Bill Estabrooks who ran a very economical office and so had a lot of scope for purchasing advertising. Instead of turning the proposal down or delaying it until it could be discussed in full caucus (especially desirable since it affected everyone) the members of the Board just agreed with the proposals so as to look to be doing something. There was quick cancellation of the annual cheque for "travel and postage."

The whole scandal – and it was a true scandal in that there were illegal acts – brought to the fore the voices of those who think that elected officials deserve no pay or benefits, or nothing more than symbolic remuneration. That the salary is too much; that there should be no pensions, or very restricted conditions; that scrutiny of constituency office expenses should be approached on the assumption that the system is likely being abused.

In the midst of the general hysteria, there were some reasoned comments. Retired professor of public administration, Paul Pross, wrote, "They don't deserve the abuse being heaped on them." The common spending on cameras, he noted, has to do with the fact that, "This is an electronic age and photographs are an important part of making the work of the MLA visible to voters."[3] Parker Donham wrote, "The public nurses an attitude of begrudgery toward politicians, and the media fans these embers at every opportunity. This is not our most attractive quality, and it makes it almost impossible for MLAs – who by definition must set their own salaries – to pay themselves appropriately for the work they do."[4]

In response to the Auditor General's report, the government brought in (as its first order of business in the Spring 2010 session) a bill to establish a Management Commission for internal financial oversight at Province House, replacing the Internal Economy Board. It was to meet in public, and adopted a set of regulations governing MLA expenses that included extensive changes. An update by the Auditor General reported two years later that no irregularities had been found under the new rules.

But the cravenness that attached to the Expenses Scandal has also characterized the overall matter of compensation. Rightly, MLAs tried in 1992 to remove themselves as much as possible from the process of setting their own remuneration. The system adopted was to appoint an independent commissioner to report, with a legislated undertaking to adopt the recommendations, no matter what they were, whether good or bad for MLAs. The moment, though, that a report suggested a significant raise, the publicity started and John Hamm as premier caved in to it. The recommendation from former Speaker Arthur Donahoe to tie MLA salary to that of MPs was rejected, and a freeze was adopted. So, too, did Premier Dexter simply cancel the mandated annual review and freeze salaries for two years, partly as symbolic during the recession, and partly because of widespread criticism due to the Expenses Scandal. This did not go down well in caucus, where the impact of the freeze plus cancellation of the global postal and travel amount was generally a 15 to 20 per cent cut in income, much less for cabinet members, however.

The expenses story went on for the full four years of our government. Trevor Zinck did not come to trial until June of 2013, with sentencing in August of that year. Like H. Dave Wilson he was given prison time. And Darrell Dexter again responded to the fulminations of columnists and brought in special legislation to strip Zinck of his pension, something not done with respect to the other three MLAs convicted. It was an unprincipled moment. I and some others in the caucus absented ourselves from the vote. The problem with it was that it was after the fact (terms of employment should be known by candidates in advance of an election, and if they are to be changed, the changes should take effect after the next election); that it treated one MLA differently than three others in exactly the same circumstances; and that it had no regard for what a pension is, namely deferred wages and a means of late-life support for all members of a family, not simply one person. At caucus, Darrell said of this legislation, "This is repugnant to me in ways I choose to ignore," a profoundly revealing remark. But the instinct to just play to the lowest common denominator of public opinion prevailed. It was during the time of the Senate expenses scandal and of the Charbonneau Commission inquiry into municipal corruption in Montreal, and the antics of Toronto Mayor, Rob Ford. The political class was certainly not showing itself at its best all across the country. Nonetheless, a line was crossed here.

Trevor Zinck was undoubtedly responsible for his own undoing. His circumstances seem complex. As events unfolded, it became apparent just how little we knew about our colleagues. Was Trevor an addicted gambler? Was he just incompetent? Was he going through some personal crisis, the nature of which remained unknown? We learned that he had borrowed $5,000 from one another MLA and the amount remained owing. He was offered the help of caucus staff in organizing his office expenses but avoided cooperating. It was a sobering and sombre experience. We deal with each other every day, yet much remains hidden.

In terms of the government's popularity, the Expenses Scandal, combined with the reversal of the promise to balance the budget in year one without raising taxes, seems to have been the point at which profound skepticism set in. For Darrell personally, this first year undermined his credibility with the public. For dedicated NDP supporters, it was the lack of wisdom of the anti-deficit and tax policies, later combined with the clear alignment towards big businesses that formed the basis for their alienation, not so much the Expenses Scandal.

Former MLA, Trevor Zinck.

8

Ships Sink Here

T om Traves, who was President of Dalhousie University for eighteen years starting in 1995, wrote an interesting PhD thesis, which later became a book, *The State and Enterprise.*[1]

> The idea that the Canadian economy developed under the protective wing of the state is now a familiar notion. Tiny markets, heavy overhead costs, persistent foreign competition, and the external control of necessary development capital and technological innovations impelled the state to sponsor measures to expand the reach of Canadian enterprise. (p. 3)

We should pause to note that hardly anything has changed since then. The overall picture of the Canadian economy remains the same. As Dr. Traves says, in 1979 this was already well recognized.

> What this led to was "a variant of state capitalism. [...] In this case, state capitalism does not refer to public ownership of the means of production. Rather, the term is used more loosely to describe the enormously expanded role of the state in capitalist societies. This phenomenon is often referred to by various terms such as ... pentagon capitalism." (pp. 155–156)

The standard approach to economic development in our nation has been for the state to assist the private sector as much as possible. There are serious problems with this. For one, it puts governments into an entirely too cozy relationship with just one sector of society. This can mean that health and safety or environmental concerns (the duties of the state as regulator) can become subordinate to the drive for supporting industry. Think of Westray. Think of Boat Harbour. For another, it tends to leave the state out of public ownership, even where that might be appropriate, for example in delivering necessities that are what economists call natural monopolies, activities where competition, the stated strength of capitalism, is not really relevant. Think of Nova Scotia Power. For another, it blurs the different interests of different classes. Workers might want jobs, but our lives are not defined by our usefulness to employers as units of labour.

In fact, the cozy relationship has had a distinct downside, namely the emergence of something of an indolent entrepreneurial class. The plain-talking former NDP Premier of British Columbia, Dave Barrett made a trenchant point back in 1975: "When you give money to people you call it welfare. When you give money to business you call it grants. Well, I'm changing that. From now on, when we give money to people it'll be grants, and when we give money to business, that's welfare." Good to remember. It also focuses us on whether and how public monies ought to go to business at all. Amazingly, it is sometimes still said by Dippers that we need an economic policy, that somehow we are lacking in this respect. It just ain't so.

The NDP in Nova Scotia has a set of economic policies, most well thought out and characteristic of our priorities. They could certainly do with some refinement, but our analysis and approaches are practical and mature. Where they could do with some modernization has to do with the interaction with environmental sustainability policies, with exactly how welfare to business should be structured (taking equity, tax credits, payroll rebates, etc.), the appropriate measures of wellbeing (Genuine Progress Index vs Gross Domestic Product), and how public ownership is best used. But the essential points in our policies – that along with some central planning there is a strong role for community economic development, local decision-making, and ownership – make sense.

The problem has been that the press has promoted a view of the NDP that implies we are not good on the economy, and some Dippers have internalized this – they have come to believe it. This allows for drift into imitation of the other parties.

Ships Start Here

"Big bucks for big business" became one of the bases for Liberal and Tory attacks on the government, and was a point on which the general public felt quite skeptical. It certainly made many Dippers uncomfortable. Financial subsidies for an Irving company were a prime example.

The federal government awarded the main part of its $25 billion shipbuilding contract to the Irving's Halifax Shipyards in October 2011. Six months later, in March 2012, the province announced its financial contribution to the project. The deal was for $304 million. It was structured as a forgivable loan of $260 million and a repayable loan of $44 million for human resources and technologies. In the immortal words of *Frank Magazine*: "Forgivable, meaning, you know, it's on us."[2] In the CBC news report about the deal it said: "Jim Irving, CEO of Irving Shipbuilding Inc. made no apology for accepting taxpayers' money. [...] Irving said his company needed provincial support to be the winning bidder for the shipbuilding contract. [...] Premier Darrell Dexter told reporters he doesn't think he'll have a hard time convincing taxpayers of the investment's worth. 'It is about the fact that we will move from having the slowest growing economy in the country to having one of the fastest growing economies...' said Dexter."[3] Dream on.

The issues are complex. It can be said that public money directed to such projects supports jobs rather than the company. It can be said that

the economic spinoff and even the tax flow to government, offsets the investment. It can be said that under the terms of the federal government's call for proposals from shipyards, support from the local provincial government was a requirement. It can be said that part of the investment was in training through the community colleges. It can be said that the investment would bring returns over a long period. And, of course, the govern-

ment said all of this regularly. And yet, something grated with the people.

The other side of the case also has its complexities. Three hundred million is an awful lot of money to put into one project. The Irving group of companies is hugely wealthy, and does not need a public subsidy. In fact, why are we in the business of financing businesses anyway; is that not for the banks? Anyway, most of the dollar value of the federal contract will go toward the design and electronics and that is not what we will be doing here. We will be assembling the ships, the physical side more than developing knowledge-based skills and businesses. And these are vessels for a defense strategy based on war; the federal programme may not fit our best long-range national coastal needs.

Of these, the general suspicion of big bucks for big business was the most potent. The Ships Start Here[4] project was seen in the same light as the failed bailout of Bowater, the money put into the Stern paper mill, the shares taken in Daewoo, benefits offered to Michelin, to CKF (Canadian Keyes Fibre). All were big businesses, and although it is clear that they have brought jobs to Nova Scotia (employers require employees) the mutual benefits were not enough to persuade the public. And some of the money ($620,000) went on an advertising campaign regarding which the responsible federal minister, Peter MacKay, told us: "Any lobbying, advertising, arm-twisting, and tub-thumping was just like pouring that money into Halifax Harbour. It made no impact on the decision."[5]

That the Nova Scotia public collectively did not like these subsidies shows tremendous independence of thinking, because all of the so-called "leadership" of the province endorsed them. The government praised itself. Jim Irving praised the government. The Chamber of Commerce spoke in favour. The shipyard union certainly supported it. *The Chronicle Herald* newspaper thought it was the right thing to do. Every publication showed photo after photo of cheering government and business leaders, throwing up their arms with big smiles as the federal government announcement was made. But in homes across the province, George and Martha were saying to each other, "WTF? The Irvings get $300 million?" And Darrell and his inner circle did not understand this. They did not get it, to the extent that as the 2013 election approached they made certain to hold a celebration of the winning of the contract, which just drove home to voters a very concrete example of what they did not like. Even post-election, Darrell in his interview in the *Globe and Mail* expressed shock at how the voters failed to understand.[6]

One of the most fascinating revelations in Graham Steele's book[7] is that the nature of the provincial government's support to the shipyard was not fully worked out until a year after the federal government had awarded Irving the contract. What this implies is that the Department of National Defence (DND) "National Shipbuilding Procurement Strategy"[8] of 2010 did not require this large measure of financial support. (This is the name for the programme under which Irving was awarded the contract to build combat vessels, "Arctic/Offshore Patrol Ships" and "Canadian Surface Combatants.") The federal government did not demand such a large investment. It was negotiated by the Irvings with our government. And was still being refined as we left office. Certainly the federal government required some provincial government support. But it could have been courses through community college system, plus some limited financial involvement. Why such a large amount? A discussion of this issue never came to caucus, except as an announcement. Perhaps someday we will hear more of the details. Regardless, it did not go down well with the public. And rightly so.

Policy and Priorities

One of the peculiarities of the Dexter government was the narrowness of the expertise it was willing to draw upon. The Premier's inner circle had some talented people, but the party at large includes some spectacularly able and experienced individuals. To a large extent, they were not consulted. I do not say never, but it was so limited as to be virtually *pro forma*. I have in mind people like Richard Starr, the author of a biography of former New Brunswick Premier Richard Hatfield, a book on energy issues in Nova Scotia (*Power Failure?*), and now one on Canada's experience with the federal/provincial equalization system (*Equal As Citizens*). Or Pamela Harrison, provincial coordinator of the Transition House Association. Or Wayne MacKay (Dalhousie Law professor, former head of the Nova Scotia Human Rights Commission, former President of Mount Allison University) who was commissioned to deal with cyberbullying. Or Ray Larkin, the province's leading labour lawyer, former president of the Barristers' Society, gold medalist at law school, and a brilliant legal and political mind. Or Michael Bradfield and Lars Osberg, both former chairs of the Economics Department at Dalhousie. Or Sue Wolstenholme, expert on early childhood education. Or Brian Gifford, founder of the Ecology Action Centre and later an expert on affordable housing. Indeed, the NDP has many very able people who accurately felt that their views and potential contributions had inexplicably been marginalized. Who we got instead was Rick Williams.

Many in the progressive wing of the party were encouraged when Darrell Dexter appointed Rick Williams to be deputy minister in charge of policy. Rick had been a faculty member in the School of Social Work at Dalhousie, but left to work as a consultant to unions, particularly those in the fishery, for municipalities, and for economic development organizations. He was seen as both scholarly and practical. Rick had been an associate editor and regular columnist with *New Maritimes*, a very progressive magazine that flourished between 1982 and 1996. Rick, Gary Burrill, a United Church minister newly elected for us in 2009 as MLA for the Musquodoboit Valley, Gary's brother Roger Burrill, Scott Milsom, Erroll Sharpe, and Valerie Mansour published a high quality magazine for some fifteen years. Rick was good friends

Rick Williams

with Ray Larkin, and altogether tightly connected to the left wing of the party. There were reasons to be optimistic about Rick's appointment. During the 1990s he had written coumns in *New Maritimes* that focused on many progressive ideas. Here are some comments about cooperatives that Rick made after a 1993 trip to Nicaragua to learn about its lobster fishery:

> It has never before been quite so clear to me that cooperatives are the only real way to confront underdevelopment at the local level. Communities need to have the collective means to socialize wealth and direct its use towards economic diversification and the development of social infrastructure. Without this control and this ability to discipline the use of wealth ... places ... have little ability to survive the ups and downs of commodity markets controlled by the imperial centre.[9]

Nova Scotia's economic development strategy under the NDP has not really emphasized cooperatives; they are mentioned but have been given no more support than under Tory and Liberal governments. Here is Rick on the Free Trade Agreement and how to approach NAFTA:

> Official unemployment rates have never gone below 10 per cent and averaged 12.1 per cent over the 1982–91 period. [...] Nova Scotians' personal per capita income as a percentage of the Canadian average reached a peak of 83.6 in 1986 but has fallen to 82.3. Similarly, average weekly wages fell from 92.4 to 89.6 per cent of Canadian levels over the same period. [...] These figures speak of the failure on the national level to solve the problem of regional disparity. [...] Our federal and provincial governments seem less and less willing or able to assist in the industrial restructuring and worker adjustment needed to cope with a more competitive environment.[10]

Our NDP government did very little to help workers adjust to a new economy. Instead, the approach has been, as with Resolute and NewPage, to try to prop up sunset pulp and paper, a failing strategy.

Here is Rick writing about the Department of Community Services:

> The social services systems in Nova Scotia and New Brunswick are unfair and inadequate. Hostility to the client is a feature of both.

Any way you look at it, the solution to the poverty problem in an advanced technology society with high structural unemployment is a guaranteed adequate annual income (GAAI). By this I mean an income which is automatically delivered to people, whether employed or not, who fall below a certain threshold and which fully provides for their food, shelter, clothing and personal development needs.

Such a system would replace all existing income support programmed from disability allowance to old age security to social assistance. [...] It is obvious that the Maritime Provinces could not afford such a system, and we cannot force the federal government to set one up. We could, however, go a long ways towards laying the groundwork.[11]

Nevertheless, not a single word came from this government about a Guaranteed Adequate Annual Income (GAAI). In no campaign did the party run on this. And in government, the idea sank without a trace.

Here is Rick on planning the economy:

When Canadian politics does shift back to demanding a constructive and positive role for government in the economy, as it must, nobody will want to go back to a highly centralized, super-bureaucratic planning system. People are clearly interested in smaller-scale approaches, which will offer more control to workers and consumers of services.

The challenge will be to find more democratic, popular and accessible methods of planning to translate these goals and desires into practical economic activities. It will still be government's job to build and manage an economy which will do for society what it wants done, but no longer will the state make these decisions on peoples' behalf without their full involvement, and their full comprehension of what is going on.[12]

Again, serious local community decision-making was completely absent during the tenure of the NDP government.

Despite the optimism of many party members about the appointment of Rick Williams, it did not turn out as we had hoped. For the most part, his team seemed to have had little influence in the government.

Universities

In one key topic, Rick Williams was especially off base. This was on post-secondary education. I met with Rick soon after he was appointed. In that August 2009 conversation, Rick brought up the university system, suggesting that it needed a good look, to increase efficiencies. I tried to head this off. I had spent seven years working for the organizations representing university faculty associations, both here and in Ontario. My time included close involvement with the Royal Commission on Post-secondary Education[13] chaired by Rod McLennan in Nova Scotia, and a similar commission chaired by Edmund Bovey in Ontario,[14] both focused on the university systems. I knew the university systems, their issues, their weaknesses and their strengths, and had long ago concluded that any aggressive government intervention would be ineffective and was probably misplaced.

What I said to Rick was that as a new government with a majority mandate, we had a lot of dark and dusty corners that needed sweeping but that the universities should be a long way down the list; that the system was robust and already had achieved important efficiencies (an integrated library system, common purchasing, agreements to use common panels for graduate students, and coordination of programmes to be funded on a Maritimes basis through the Maritime Provinces Higher Education Commission) and that if there was anything particular the government wanted to suggest, that it should say so and leave it to the universities to accomplish since they were generally responsive. I should have saved my breath. Rick was determined to achieve some restructuring of the system, and the Cabinet had already identified the universities as an expenditure envelope to be reduced.

This initiative manifested itself in a commissioned study by economist Tim O'Neill.[15] O'Neill had taught in Nova Scotia at Saint Mary's University (SMU), and moved on to become a vice president at the Bank of Montreal (BMO). Thus, although he'd had some background in the university system, like Rod McLennan before him or Edmund Bovey in Ontario, he was brought from the business world to scrutinize the university system.

Before going into more detail, a few comments on university politics in Nova Scotia are in order. First, the system is a wonderful boon to the province: education is a core Nova Scotia value, and the economic benefits of having a large and diverse system are enormous, ranging from the spending of students to the attraction of federal research grants, to the potential for commercialization of research, to the inherent value of having an educated citizenry. And yet governments regularly think that they need to do something about the universities. This comes up for a variety of reasons.

First, any government that is in a period of expenditure restraint will look at every area of expense and try to reduce it. But also, the transfers of federal monies intended to support undertakings such as universities are tied to provincial population and not to numbers of students; thus, Nova Scotia receives less money in transfers than it thinks it should, because the university capacity is larger than the provincial population generates, meaning a lot of students come from out of province but are not taken into account in the federal funding formula. Third, governments are focused on developing the economy, and see post-secondary education (universities and the community colleges) as sources of labour and of research that can be commercialized. And while the employment market is extraordinarily difficult to predict, i.e., it requires looking forward for the career of individuals and generations of students, governments are often tempted to try to adjust student enrollments in subjects, especially if they are going to be the employer or if demographic trends appear clear. Thus, for nurses and other health professions, and for teachers, governments have been especially prepared to make changes.

In Nova Scotia the government closed the Atlantic Institute of Education (AIE) in 1980, with one week's notice. The AIE was a very tiny institute offering graduate degrees in education, something the government saw as simply an expense since holding an advanced degree moved a teacher up the collective-agreement pay scale while bringing relatively little to the classroom. Another reason for government interest in the universities is the chance to make public hay about sabbaticals and tenure. Typically this is a preoccupation of anyone without deep exposure to universities. Governments with little representation from the Halifax

Regional Municipality (HRM) or from towns with universities are more likely to attempt to stir this up.

Which raises the geographic dimension. Universities are located in Sydney, Antigonish, Wolfville, Pointe-de-l'Église, Truro, and HRM. No one is going to suggest anything drastic for any of the universities outside of HRM; this would strike too much at what in smaller places is rightly seen as a mainstay of the local economy. The focus therefore tends to be on HRM. The three NDP MLAs from the Halifax Peninsula have one clear thing in common: we all are tied to the universities. Maureen taught at Dalhousie's School of Social Work, Leonard in the Political Science Department at Saint Mary's University, and I have taught at the Dalhousie Law School as an adjunct professor for many years. Leonard and Maureen are tenured. This common background is not an accident. Knowledge work is a big part of what goes on in HRM. This means the universities, the federal and provincial civil services, the Navy, the financial institutions, the business world, the entire health care system, and the professions. Admiration of education accomplishments is a core value in HRM, and indeed throughout Nova Scotia. And post-secondary education and all the other knowledge-based enterprises are big employers. A government forgets this in HRM at its peril, as the 2013 election made completely clear.

O'Neill reported in September 2010, just as the existing three-year framework for university-government joint planning, the memorandum of understanding (MOU), was coming up for renegotiation. The MOUs traditionally cover global funding levels and tuition. They are also an opportunity for government to advance any other policies. O'Neill wrote, "a core objective for future collaboration between the government and the universities should be to manage growing financial pressures and looming system over-capacity in the face of anticipated enrolment declines."

Associated with this, according to O'Neill, would be restructuring the system. This meant a focus on the Halifax institutions, although Acadia University was probably the institution with the most pressing financial problems, and St Francis Xavier University was also carrying significant debt due to an aggressive building programme. While formally putting aside the creation of a, "university of Halifax ... at least over the next five years," (p. 4) something close was mooted in that O'Neill advocated exploring the potential for merger or significant affiliation of Mount St. Vincent University (MSVU) with Dalhousie University or Saint Mary's University (SMU), as well as integrating the Nova Scotia Agricultural College (NSAC) with Dalhousie (which has been done), and to explore both merger and internal restructuring for the Nova Scotia College of Art and Design University (NSCAD). He also proposed more university administrative integration, though one longstanding real concern – students being able to take courses at a variety of institutions for credit – was glossed over and was treated as a minor aspect of administrative efficiency (pp. 118–119). Basically, the O'Neill Report formed the government's university policies for the next several years, stirring up trouble.

As I note elsewhere, a provincial government has limited control over the major factors in our economy. Banking and interest rates are under federal control. Our main trading partner, the USA, has its own dynamic and changes there, which affect our trade and tourism, are well beyond our local control. And on it goes. What we do have control over is quality of life and education. These are factors that can make a difference in economic activity, and in how attractive a place Nova Scotia is to live and do business in.

Education is itself a good business to be in. In Nova Scotia it is especially advantageous because we bring in a higher proportion of our postsecondary students from elsewhere than is typical of other provinces. Students bring tuition dollars, rent money, and their day-to-day spending. Faculty attract federal dollars from the national granting agencies. If students stay after graduation, we have added to the population, particularly to the educated population. We should have been celebrating universities as one of our major assets. Instead, we took the view that they are just another cost, to be trimmed and prodded.

The provincial government certainly has a legitimate role in keeping an eye on universities. A lot of public money does support them, even if the percentage has diminished over the last few decades, with a consequent increased reliance on tuition and private donations. One aspect of this oversight should have been limiting the growth in numbers of administrators, and some extraordinarily generous remuneration for presidents and other senior administrators.[16] Universities are established by statute, and typically the government gets to appoint members to their Boards of Governors (though, for no clear reason, this is not the case for King's and Saint Francis Xavier). It should be the role of these appointees to let the government know of problems, but that does not seem to have occurred. In the last few years, King's, Acadia, and St Francis Xavier have all had financial difficulties; for the most part these have not become public knowledge, and in some instances the situations seem not to have come to government attention either. For NSCAD it was different. Its experience has been very public.

For a variety of reasons I have had close ties to the NSCAD community. In the past, I was director of the provincial organization representing all faculty associations in the province and thus knew NSCAD faculty who were active in their union. At one point I sat on an arbitration panel that set remuneration for a group of NSCAD instructors. I have family ties to NSCAD faculty. Thus I have been well positioned to know details of the stresses at our art college.

Throughout my government's pressuring of NSCAD I objected. I have always been puzzled by the initiative. It fits the approach to the universities the O'Neill report set the direction for, but was profoundly mistaken. Other university faculty took note. They saw the push on NSCAD as a message to the university system as a whole, or at least in Halifax. The message was that the institutions are vulnerable to serious government direction, with no clear limits. NSCAD has been an amazingly successful institution. But it got into financial trouble through building a new campus on land rented from the Halifax Port Authority, next door to Pier 21 and the new Halifax Seaport Farmers Market. The required

The gateway into the Nova Scotia College of Art and Design University.

funding for this development was only partially in place, and the loan debt was expensive to service, especially for a small institution that saw itself as underfunded. The underfunding came from the province's funding allocation formula, which assigned relative weightings to different programmes; NSCAD saw itself as too lightly weighted given the need for space and energy use required to teach the arts and crafts. It also had the misfortune to be housed in its main buildings on valuable real estate in the downtown core, designated heritage buildings that could lend themselves to development when the local builders were ready.

It is the case that NSCAD has had serious administrative problems. A succession of presidents were unable to set it on an even keel. Paul Greenhalgh, who had charmed his Board of Governors into the port lands site expansion, was the one most often blamed. When at one point, while we were still in Opposition in 2004, I spoke in the Legislature's Public Accounts Committee to criticize money management at NSCAD[16], there was an editorial in *The Chronicle Herald* snapping at me.[17] In the end though, the hard fact is that the stage was being set for a serious financial squeeze. At least *The Chronicle Herald* spoke from a positive attitude towards NSCAD, and saw its value to our cultural enterprises. Unfortunately, as with the Yarmouth ferry, our government was shortsighted. It wanted to save money. It wanted to "rationalize" space use. Quality was not relevant to the calculus. What a mistake. *"Art hath an enemy called Ignorance,"* wrote Ben Johnson in 1598, and it is still true today.

The push for NSCAD to eliminate its deficit has resulted in serious erosion of the quality of the institution's offerings. Art and design are a strength in our province, but were little appreciated inside our government. The final reports about NSCAD supported its continued independence, but the years it took to arrive at that conclusion did damage. Now King's is in financial difficulty, partly from enrolment drop but also through mal-administration. Already, David Wheeler, the president of Cape Breton University, has brought up the possibility of a University of Halifax again. King's and NSCAD are both tiny, specialized places that need nurturing. There is nothing wrong with a frank public discussion about our university system, but it should start from an attitude of respect not negative criticism.

Economic Development

For obvious reasons, economic development is always a major preoccupation for any provincial government. No approach to economic development should be considered in isolation from tax policy, desired government programmes, and debt. All of these are interconnected. And in my view they are generally not understood correctly since they are usually discussed apart from environmental sustainability. No conventional economic activity takes place apart from our fundamental reliance on the natural world.

Economic development is something provincial governments can influence mostly indirectly. The main economic tools of a government are in the hands of the federal government in Canada. Banking, and thus the interest rates and money supply, are federally regulated. This controls or strongly influences credit, and thus investment and spending. International trade as manifested by treaties such as North American Free Trade Agreement (NAFTA) is also a federal matter, setting rules for foreign ownership, foreign investment, tariffs, protected economic sectors. Major transport infrastructure such as pipelines, railroads, airlines, and the St. Lawrence Seaway are also federally controlled. As are all aspects of telecommunications. There are more examples, but this illustrates the nature of the problem for provincial governments, which would like to be able to claim credit for their economic development expertise, but in reality are quite limited in their powers. To that should be added the basic nature of modern economies: they are often global. An example with special significance for Nova Scotia is newsprint, but this is equally true for fish, tires, agricultural products, building materials, metals, and even energy.

What, then, can a provincial government do? Perhaps start with an analysis of our circumstances. The Canadian economy and hence Nova Scotia's is characterized by several main facts: it is resource-based; we have a smallish domestic market, i.e., not a huge population; we have one main trading partner; there is a high degree of corporate concentration; there is a high degree of foreign ownership. People differ on whether they think these factors are problems, opportunities, advantages, or just facts. But in any event they are generally accepted as some of the most pertinent descriptors.

In this context, provincial governments have some residual powers to exercise. For one, they can lead by example or through public education efforts. The most important steps are to respect and rebuild as necessary the robustness of the natural world, and to invest in education. These are the most important contributions provincial governments can make to economic security. An educated populace is best able to thrive in a modern and quickly evolving economy. Families in Nova Scotia have long recognized this, and respect for education is a core value here. Indeed, according to a recent poll, 60 per cent of Nova Scotians would pay more tax in order to make post-secondary education more affordable.[18] So daycare, a good school system, community colleges, and universities should always be a priority for a provincial government. Next is planning, especially with public involvement. This means community economic development exercises carried out on a regular basis, not just in response to the latest crisis. As an adjunct to planning, the gathering and publication of data is always a solid government function. So, too, would be support for and encouragement of co-operatives, both producer co-ops and customer/consumer co-ops. Co-ops have a long history in Nova Scotia but have never really flourished as they should. Although the province has a Cooperative Council, the main emphasis of the Department of Economic Development has long been on grants, loans, and equity investment, primarily in larger corporations – often ones lured from elsewhere – rather than on co-ops.

What was our actual approach? Not much different from our predecessors. Successive governments have issued economic development plans. Preoccupation with "jobs and the economy" has always been a theme of government. Starting with the Stanfield government that relied for leadership on a new entity it created in 1958, Industrial Estates Ltd. (IEL), we can see a combination of approaches: an articulated plan, reliance to some extent on a quasi-independent body directed by leaders from the business community, plus some residual discretion for Cabinet. Industrial Estates Ltd. had mixed success, with major criticism focused around Clairtone Sound (a stereo and TV manufacturer), and a Deuterium of Canada heavy water plant meant to supply nuclear power plants. Both proved to be expensive failures. Other businesses lasted for a while but later folded, for example Cosmos Imperial Mills in Yarmouth, the hardboard plant on the south shore. We were drawn into ownership of the steel plant in Sydney when Hawker-Siddeley announced a pending closure in 1967. Two major pulp and paper mills started: Stora (Nova Scotia Pulp Company) in 1958 at Port Hawkesbury, and Scott in 1963–1964 at Abercrombie, just across the harbor from Pictou. Michelin has been the standout survivor, now employing some 3,500 people at its three plants. Ultimately IEL morphed into Nova Scotia Business Inc. (NSBI), which just like its predecessors, is directed by a board made up of some of the province's principal business people. Its board is now more broadly based yet it remains, as its website says, "Nova Scotia's private sector-led business development agency." The Liberals have supplemented NSBI with "Invest Nova Scotia," another private sector led entity with funds to invest, and chaired by Tom Traves.

Going into the 2013 election, some commentators said that the policy differences between parties were minimal, hence there would be something of a focus on the personality of the leaders, including personal abilities, e.g., the NDP on Stephen McNeil: "we don't know much about him," and, "too risky." On economic development, there really have been minimal differences. Why? Traditionally, the NDP has advocated policies that would have moved in a different direction: public ownership; tight environment regulation; worker health and safety; co-ops; community economic development; local benefits; fair taxation; investing in infrastructure, especially housing, water and sewer. All of these were regularly a part of NDP rhetoric, yet the party has also long been attacked as lacking credibility on jobs and the economy. Disastrously, many NDP insiders have internalized this point; they have either come to believe it or have come to act as if they believe it. The major electoral campaign in which the NDP failed to move on a serious and overwhelming economic issue was the 1988 federal election that was largely about the Brian Mulroney-proposed Free Trade Agreement with the USA. The NDP had criticized the deal in Parliament but chose not to campaign on it, focusing instead on health care, while the Liberals under John Turner stirred the country and united the anti-free-trade agreement vote. In Nova Scotia, the NDP under Darrell Dexter chose to present itself as being very much like the Liberals and Tories on jobs and the economy, and in office have behaved pretty much as the other parties would have.

One of the main features of the NDP time in office was its willingness to take an active role in economic development matters. In this it is not really out of line with tradition in Nova Scotia, or indeed with the general approach of most provincial and federal governments, even when they have official stances that might suggest otherwise. Conservative governments, for example, often speak of the value of free enterprise and open competition. They do not mean it. All governments are prepared to take some steps to try to protect indigenous wealth and the means of wealth creation. The real focus is on specifics: whether particular sectors of the economy are favoured, whether there is public ownership of some enterprises, how foreign ownership is treated, the approach to corporate concentration, how public spending is allocated, whether there is reliance on deficits when overall circumstances reduce revenues, how the tax system is structured. Abstract views are generally not a good guide to these points.

By the Dexter government's taking an active role in the economy, I have in mind the willingness to accumulate debt to invest in infrastructure, to do so especially during years of economic turmoil, to step in to try to support industries like pulp and paper in areas of the province where the plants and associated functions are major employers, to associating itself with major undertakings such as the Irving Shipyards' "Ships Start Here" bid for federal work, or the Emera Muskrat Falls/Maritime Link proposal. For the most part all of these choices have been politically disastrous for us. In terms of economic stimulus, the results have been mixed, which has been the story with all Nova Scotia governments.

For the most part, the Stanfield IEL model has prevailed. This has meant "hunting the elephant," the tag term for attracting capital investment from elsewhere, preferably large companies: Blackberry, IBM, and Daewoo are examples from our time in office. The Liberals and Tories have had some highly problematic adventures in economic development.

The Liberals brought us P-3 (Public-Private Partnership) schools and a toll highway. The Tories, while setting out some quite sensible ideas under John Hamm (for example, minimizing equity positions in companies and emphasizing payroll rebates tied to job creation; and trying to bring high-speed internet to the whole province), still ended up relying extensively on the instrument of call centers. Call centers were scattered around the province, but have clearly demonstrated the weakness of this approach. The companies come here, primarily in response to the inducements of government subsidies; for the most part they rented premises rather than purchased; the enterprise is inherently mobile; and they often left when the subsidies ended. For the most part, call centers were never anything more than stopgaps for communities in trouble, but the government failed to acknowledge that, or to use the stopgap time to develop and adopt effective plans for the next stage of a community's life.

Attracting investment from elsewhere can be a useful element in an overall economic strategy. But it cannot be central. Nova Scotia has a generally balanced economy: we have fishing, agriculture, some mining, some energy, forestry, some manufacturing, tourism, educational institutions, and government presence including the Navy. No one sector dominates, so we are not vulnerable to downturns in any particular sector. We have a small population, split about 50:50 between the main urban area, HRM, and the rest of the province, which is primarily rural and small towns. There is a decent level of education. Transportation infrastructure is present. If we took better care of it, our environment would be excellent, though as it is we are still in good shape. And it is beautiful. Living here is a complete treat. But it has been a century since there were protected freight rates; the opening of the St. Lawrence Seaway had a negative impact, and overall – though in company with all of Atlantic Canada – our standard of living (if measured by incomes) is lower than the rest of Canada. Additionally, our population size is stagnant and ageing.

Infrastructure investment can be a good step. Our choices were not necessarily the best. To a large extent, capital grants were made to businesses. But land was purchased, and roads were repaired, and public housing was renovated. Yet we put money into the dredging of Sydney Harbour to little apparent point. Our contribution was $15.2 million, 40 per cent of the $38 million cost; the federal government paid 50 per cent. There was certainly a local call for this, the ostensible idea being an improvement to the potential of Sydney as a port would allow it to better compete for business. Politically, the motivation was more about elections. The Harper government hoped to elect Cecil Clarke as an MP, and the NDP hoped to keep its two seats in the area and possibly to increase them. The economic potential was dubious. Freight transportation for imports or exports through Sydney depends largely on a rail connection, and that had been and continues to be precarious. Also, there is only so much port traffic likely to come through Nova Scotia and Halifax already has well-developed port facilities. Furthermore, other proposals such as Melford were in the works. What the Sydney port does handle is coal – an import. A dredged harbour may assist in that traffic, although only by allowing larger vessels to use it. The dredged material has been used to create more land, touted as a potential site for a container terminal.

Under Percy Paris, the Department of Rural and Economic Development and Tourism produced a plan, "jobsHere" in November of 2010.[19] In terms of its politics, the purpose of the plan was to draw attention to the cumulative failures of the Tory and Liberal predecessor governments: "Nova Scotia is at a crossroads – we can cling to vestiges of the past and take the future as it comes, or we can look to the future and shape our destiny with a forward strategy. If things stay the same the results will be the same. That could mean twenty more years of slow or no growth, mounting debt, and in some parts of the province, steady decline," it de-

jobsHere

the plan to grow our economy

clared. The twenty years of poor growth was referred to regularly by the Premier in the Legislature.

The *jobsHere* plan set out three overall themes: skills development, innovation, and the ability to compete globally. As a plan it was somewhat sketchy at best. Where it was specific, its proposals were undercut by the actual decisions of the government. The main way in which this contradiction appeared was in how the government approached the universities, especially NSCAD. The education and skills section ignored the universities. The industrial section referred to the universities as a source of Research and Development (R&D) and of commercialization of their research. This is a legitimate but extremely limited view of the university role, and it is inherently problematic to look to the universities to be a source of saleable research if the institutions themselves are put in a position of struggle, which has been the case. It is a very narrow and mistaken view of university level research to think that governments can target money at projects that can quickly be commercialized. A much more *laissez faire* approach works better. And while there are certainly university departments or faculties in which a significant part of the research work is directed towards wrestling with immediate real world problems – medicine, agriculture, and engineering – there could be no advances in these endeavors either without the benefit of other, general, so-called pure research. It is clear that the NDP government was keen only on commercializeable research and did not have much respect for the rest of the university enterprise.

Along with misunderstanding the universities, the other main problem with *jobsHere* was its failure to understand some of the basics of competitiveness. An expert on this is Professor Michael Porter of the Harvard Business School, author of *The Competitive Advantage of Nations*.[20] Following Porter's major study, the Business Council on National Issues, the entity representing the political interests of Canadian big business, along with the federal government's Ministry of Industry, Science, and Technology and International Trade, under Michael Wilson, retained Porter to investigate Canadian competitiveness. The result was a small paper, *Canada at the crossroads: The reality of a new competitive environment.*[21] In polite language, Porter identifies the main problem: not labour skills, or the basics of education, but management and cronyism. In the section entitled, "The Comfortable Insularity of the Old Order," Porter writes:

> The preceding section presents a picture of an economic system that had served Canada well in many respects, but leaves the economy ill-equipped for the future. This old economic order was an internally consistent system in which the determinants were mutually consistent and reinforcing. This makes change exceedingly difficult.
>
> Canada's abundant natural resources have been the bedrock of the economy. In many cases, these resources allowed Canadian firms to be profitable by exporting relatively unprocessed commodities rather than through upgrading. Strategies based on basic natural advantages often limited the demand for advanced technology. This in turn constrained investment in R&D and demand for highly skilled employees, which was reflected in enrolment patterns in universities and in the nature of educational programs. The virtual absence of leading edge related and supporting industries inhibited another possible source of technology.
>
> These tendencies spilled over into other sectors of the economy where Canada did not have such advantages. Many firms, insulated from external and internal rivalry, were content to exploit the profitable home market. The rate of innovation was slow. What emerged was a tendency to administer existing wealth rather than to invest vigorously to create new wealth.

The other important point to emerge in the Porter's study is the importance of serious imposition of high standards of safety, protection of the environment, and of probity.

I conclude from this overview of our involvement in economic development, not that the NDP as a whole is not capable of solid, productive measures, but that this particular government did not start from a position of any useful understanding of what needed to be done, or if it did then it lost sight of it very rapidly. In a time of serious economic crisis there was nothing wrong with increasing tax revenues, capital spending, and running deficits. Even serious right-wing economic writers like Richard Posner have endorsed that, however much they would normally advocate for free enterprise and low taxation.[22] But Darrell was trying to balance the budget, and saw the increase in HST as just an embarrassment he wanted to be rid of. These were exactly the wrong policy choices at the wrong time.

None of this should be interpreted as favoring an ongoing unbalanced budget. There is an upper limit on how much debt a small jurisdiction such as Nova Scotia can carry. We have been paying about ten per cent of our expenditures to service the debt. Obviously this is money that is not going to support programmes. But the percentage is half of what it was a decade ago. Balancing our budget is generally desirable, but the issue is when and how. Keynesian economics suggests the way to get through recessionary times is for a government to run deficits and/or spend on capital projects. The hysteria shown by the Auditor General about debt in 2012 was uncalled for.[23]

What have been the results of our efforts? When we took office, the unemployment rate in the province overall was 9.2 per cent; 45.5 thousand people were looking for work. (The Canadian rate of unemployment was 8.7 per cent.) When we left office, the rate here was 9.1 per cent; 45.3 thousand people were looking for work. (The Canadian rate of unemployment was 7 per cent.) When we took office there were 371.4 thousand people working full-time, and 79.6 thousand working part-time. When we left office the number was 361.6 thousand working full-time and 91.2 thousand working part-time.[24]

These numbers tell a stark tale. The Canadian employment situation has improved, but ours in Nova Scotia has not. Discouragingly, there has been a loss of almost ten thousand full-time jobs and an increase of almost twelve thousand part-time jobs. The situation is not any better with other traditional measures such as average wages, household incomes, purchasing power, and poverty levels. Small wonder that when voters asked themselves in 2013 whether they were better off than they had been in 2009, the answer was no.

9

Carbon, Climate Change,
Nova Scotia Power

There is no shortage of energy related issues in Nova Scotia: the offshore and its oil and gas reserves (and royalties); electricity for costs, supply, reliability of the system, and pollution; coal, with its long history; tidal power's potential; whether to go nuclear; fracking; whether to introduce a carbon tax. All of these are related to the pressing issue of climate change and have been tied up in politics. But none more so than the offshore, and electricity – although fracking has rapidly become a major focus of current debate. On all of these our government had a dubious record.

The main focus was on electricity, even though the three main forms of energy use (transportation, buildings, and electricity) emit roughly the same amounts of greenhouse gases. To some extent there are policy reasons for that. In terms of transportation, it is certainly true that vehicle efficiency is generally beyond the reasonable jurisdiction of the province to lead the way. EGSPA, as originally adopted under the Tories, promised moving to California-style vehicle efficiency standards, but this was probably unrealistic for a small jurisdiction, and was altered somewhat by our revisions to the *Act*. What we could have done was to lead the way in promoting public transit, and not to pander to excessive reliance on private vehicles. This would have meant talking about vehicle efficiency and alternatives in a concerted way, as well as modifying the amount of money put into road paving. None of this really occurred. Instead Bill Estabrooks as Minister of Transportation declared in the Legislature,

"Pave, baby, pave." And the money put into public transit remained miniscule. As for buildings, this had been shuffled off to Efficiency Nova Scotia where it took a secondary place on the public agenda. Efficiency Nova Scotia had been doing a good job, but needed a higher profile. This government did not really offer that. Home energy assessments, rebates on some energy efficiency purchases and construction work, low interest loans – all of these are available to assist homeowners but could and should have been spoken of more often by ministers.

Bill Estabrooks

The Offshore

Ten years too early and a billion dollars short. That should have been the headline for the end of the Sable Offshore Energy Project (SOEP) in 2013. SOEP is Nova Scotia's first serious hydrocarbon extraction project. Sable was heavily promoted by the Liberals of the 1990s as a revenue generator for the province. Eleanor Norrie, as Minister of Natural Resources, forecast $2.7 billion in royalties over the expected life of the project, from 1999 through 2025.

The project is ending early because the first projection as to the amount of gas that was economically recoverable was simply incorrect. In part that means there was not quite so much gas at was once believed. And in part it means that the price per unit fell during the extraction period. The SOEP developers indicated that the rate of extraction could be increased by upping the pressure on the line, thus about doubling the daily volume. This would be tied to the existence of markets, which turned out not to be a problem at all – demand remained robust throughout the fourteen

A drilling rig on the Nova Scotia shelf.

years of extraction of the Sable reserves. In the end, though, it has just meant that the project ended early, and – since the pipeline is reversible – we now have the prospect of Nova Scotia importing natural gas from the USA instead of exporting to our neighbor to the south. Shale gas extraction has accelerated in the United States leading, for the foreseeable future, to the existence of a large available supply.

The core political failing, though, is not the exhaustion of the Sable field. That is just what turned out to be the case. The core political failing was in selling the gas too cheaply. Thank you, Liberal government of Russell MacLellan. The reason this occurred has never been made clear. The problem was the royalty regime adopted by the Liberals the day of the 1999 election call. Here are the problems with it:

- Overall, the rate of payments to go to the province was not high enough;
- The regime was structured to allow significant deductions of development costs;
- The tolling for transmission along the pipeline included a price break to domestic users for the first ten years only, exactly the years needed to develop a local market for gas.

Have we become rich through energy projects? Obviously not. My late mother used to say that when rocks become valuable then Nova Scotians will be rich. Should the question be a different one? Is the question, how bad would things have been without the energy royalties? Perhaps so, but the failure of the Liberals to do a good job in terms of securing overall appropriate benefits for Nova Scotia is really the relevant fact, and was the focus of great debate during the years we were the Opposition. This extended not only to the royalty regime, but also to local access to natural gas for use here in Nova Scotia, access to our gas for our homes, businesses, and industries. It is clear that the petroleum companies saw Sable as purely an extraction project, with all of the product to go to markets in the USA. They were surprised to find any interest at all in the Maritimes. It was only through public pressure that they were persuaded to include laterals off the main line to service Nova Scotia Power's Tufts Cove power plant in Dartmouth and the Irving's refinery in Saint John.

Then, for local distribution of the gas, i.e., for a more widespread rollout of gas service, there were many issues around which company would do this, how the lines would be placed, and fees and rates. All of this went on endlessly, with great opportunity for the opposition to snipe at the government. In 1997-98 I represented the Ecology Action Centre during the whole of the year-long National Energy Board export license and environmental assessment process. Steeped in the facts, I was able to engage with all of these issues.

Initially, the public, through a special-purpose entity called Nova Scotia Resources Ltd., owned a share of the offshore. When in power the PCs decided to sell it. One issue remaining from those days is whether it was sold for an appropriate price. The full books have never been made public, and although in opposition we raised this matter, it was not pursued while we were in office. The key question would have been the projections made for the future value of natural gas. The price has fluctuated, although in the northeastern United States market the price has generally been higher. Without specific details, this remains an open question.

Disappointingly, our government subsequently did not alter the royalty regime either. Indeed, despite the point being urged on the Minister of Natural Resources several times internally, no royalty regime for minerals has been changed either. This came up as we discussed possible new sources of revenue. We still offer our resources to all comers for far too little. If there had been a better royalty regime in place, the early windup of SOEP would not have so seriously impacted government revenues. The next field to be developed, Deep Panuke, will be a generator of royalties, and if the royalty regime had been altered, revenues could have been structured to be much better than they will be. Additionally, with British Petroleum (BP) and Shell about to invest heavily in exploration of the waters off Shelburne County in a search for oil, it would have been timely to revisit the old Liberal royalty regime. Thus, in Opposition, we put a lot of effort into critiquing a hugely important matter, only to drop it entirely when in government.

Electricity

The other main aspect of energy issues is electricity. As a political issue, power rates and service have been highly important. Richard Starr's 2011 book *Power Failure?*[1] recalled the September 1978 election that followed UARB approval the previous year of a 47 per cent rate increase, with another 17 per cent approved in summer 1978. Even with a government offer of a three-year subsidy as a plan to freeze rates on basic electricity consumption, the PCs under John Buchanan ousted the Liberals and took a majority. As Starr says, "The damage to the government from years of power rate increases could not be overcome." (p. 110) Political scientist J. Murray Beck[2] set out a wider range of problems for the Regan Liberals, but also singled out power rates: "The only thing that mattered to the public was the prospective increase." (p. 342) [...] "As he [Gerald Regan] knew all too well, his political future depended on how convincing a case he could make on energy. [...] But, try as he might, he could not convince the electors that he could bridge the gap." (p. 344)

Electricity, since it had become widely available at the start of the twentieth century, transformed life. It had become an essential service. In rural areas, refrigeration became possible, changing and giving a real boost to the fishing industry. The availability of light at night changed education, domestic family life, and business. More recently, with the spread of advanced electronics, even further transformations have occurred. By the late 1970s our lives had become thoroughly electricity-based. At the same time, economic conditions, primarily inflation beyond normal rates, had become a major preoccupation, resulting in wage and price controls between 1974–1979. The scheme was widely seen as having held down wages much more than prices. Consumers felt hard done by. It was against this background that Nova Scotia Power obtained its big increases in rates for their essential service, and the Regan Liberals went down to defeat at the polls.

No one in Nova Scotia politics has ever forgotten the 1978 election. Except Darrell Dexter, apparently. The basic lessons of 1978 were that customers of Nova Scotia Power (i.e., everyone) did not like or trust the company, and were very sensitive to increases in rates. So how did it come to be the case that Darrell aligned himself with Nova Scotia Power?

Nova Scotia Power Inc. (NSPI) is a highly political company. To a certain extent it has to rely on legislation – as to its corporate structure, how its rates are set, allowable expenditures, its expropriation powers, its forms of electrical generation, and its obligations as a "public" utility. And to a very significant extent it has to rely on a public hearing process to justify its spending, its rate structure, and its profits. The company has a long history of maintaining close ties to government.

From its formation in 1972 as one province-wide monopoly until its privatization in 1992, the company was simply owned by the provincial government. This led to the public view that the provincial government was responsible for service and rates. And ultimately it was. The Tory decision to privatize NSPI in 1992 did not remove the perception, and the actuality is that the provincial government has a lot to do with rates. As an aside, that 1992 privatization has never been satisfactorily explained. Nor has its sale price been rigorously reviewed. One of the very good things the Tony Blair Labour government did when it first took office in Britain in 1997 was to review the privatization of various companies that had taken place under Margaret Thatcher. Blair concluded that they had been sold off under-value, and required the privatized companies to pay a five billion pound windfall profits tax to compensate the public. The companies paid up without a murmur. One of the initiatives we should have undertaken was a review of the sale price for NSPI.

Even after privatization, the company had to work closely with government since overall energy policy would affect it directly. After 1998 and the initial rise of the NDP, Nova Scotia Power began to cultivate the party through its leaders, first Robert and then Darrell. The presidents of NSPI and their government-relations staff were in and out of the leaders' office on a regular basis, putting forward their views, and seeking potential allies. With Robert, this led to his advocacy of "clean-coal" technology, whatever that is.[3] With Darrell, it led to his willingness to see things from the company perspective. For the company this paid off when Darrell became premier.

It paid off because Darrell took it upon himself to appear to be the official sponsor of the Muskrat Falls/Maritime Link project, even though the provincial government had no money invested in it and no direct role. Once our provincial energy policy set the objective of what percentage of electricity would come from renewables, and we joined with the federal government in looking for caps in Greenhouse Gas (GHG) emissions, there was little for the provincial government to do. It was up to Nova Scotia Power to get on with the job of delivering. Instead, Darrell became the company's front man. He went with them to Labrador to announce the project. He stood up time and time again to proclaim that Muskrat Falls would provide the lowest cost and most secure source of electricity. He fought off alternative suggestions and went so far as to devise an obnoxious anti-Hydro Québec advertising campaign. Why?

The provincial government's role is primarily one of regulation. If there was a convincing case for the customers of NSPI to take on the cost of 20 per cent of building the project, the whole question had to go to the UARB for hearings and a review in any event. There was no necessity for the NDP government to ceaselessly promote the project.

Worse, there was every reason not to get involved. Every time Darrell rose in the Legislature to defend the project – and this happened frequently – he signaled to the public that he and Nova Scotia Power were as one. Coming on top of the overall positioning of our government as generous to big business, this was poison.

One of the problems for the NDP with respect to electricity rates is that we had campaigned in 2009 on a platform of making life more affordable for families. Electricity is not generally a discretionary purchase. To some extent efficiencies are possible for individuals, but typically homes require fridges, lights, television and radio, other electronics such as computers and cell phones, freezers, washing machines, dryers, etc., and hence electricity. Also, some homes have electric heat. Nova Scotia Power had gone to the UARB requesting increases in rates and it had achieved their blessing for a fuel adjustment mechanism (FAM), i.e., automatic increases to take account of increases in the cost of fuel, without separate UARB hearings. But wages have been stagnant. So increases in the cost of electricity have really been visible to everyone and had been a real irritant. An irritant compounded by the high wages of NSPI executives. And the profits paid to Emera shareholders. And the built in rate of return tied to physical infrastructure. Everyone knew there was something highly problematic about Nova Scotia Power's rate structure, and so when it came to the 2013 election an NDP appeal based on, "trust us, we are on your side," and, "who knows what the other fellows will do," was bound to be weak.

To the extent that there might have been a rationale for Darrell's willingness to talk about electricity rates in the House, it was probably so he could remind voters that it was the NDP that had removed the provincial portion of HST from their electricity bills. This showed on household bills as a "Provincial Rebate." It also offered an opportunity to try to scare voters that the McNeil Liberals would reverse that policy. After all, the Liberals had originally called the move poor public policy. Unfortunately, this backfired. McNeil went on record early in 2012 during this exchange in Question Period:

> **THE PREMIER**: Mr. Speaker, what I will say is this. Here we control what it is that we can do with respect to power rates and what we did was we took every single cent of Nova Scotia tax off electricity, something they oppose and something they would reverse if they have the opportunity.

MR. MCNEIL: Madam Speaker, not only would we not reverse the HST cut on electricity bills, we would take off the NDP electricity tax and put it squarely on the backs of the shareholders.[4]

Indeed, McNeil's statement was completely clear. This did not, however, stop the NDP from continuing to assert that the Liberals would put the provincial portion of HST (10 per cent) back on home electricity bills. And though he has now fudged it as Premier, McNeil as Opposition leader was also promising to reduce electricity bills even further by shifting the costs of running Efficiency Nova Scotia to shareholders and away from ratepayers. That is the item he is referring to as, "the NDP electricity tax."

What the Liberals have now done is to attempt to show a reduction in electricity bills to customers effective January 1, 2015 by deferring some $53 million in Efficiency Nova Scotia in DSM (demand side management) costs to 2016. This would have been only a deferral. In any event, this attempt was frustrated by the Utility and Review Board which promptly assigned these deferred 'costs' to paying down under-recovered fuel costs of 2014. As the Board said: "The Province argued strongly that reducing power rates in 2015 via the DSM deferral is government policy. That policy has not been enshrined in legislation or regulations. [...] The Board has a role as an independent regulator to adjudicate utility matters in the best interests of ratepayers. Unfortunately, that obligation and government policy may not always be completely aligned."[5]

For very understandable reasons, the pocketbook issue of electricity rates does resonate with voters. But there are other very serious issues associated with electrical energy, not many of which did we tackle. The main outstanding issues are those of emissions related to the burning of carbon fuels, and the question of public versus private ownership.

Our record on moving away from carbon-based generation of electricity is good, though mixed. The stated goal should be complete de-carbonization. In 2013 the Ecology Action Centre published a detailed study of electricity generation here. It said:

> The long-term health of Nova Scotians and our province depends on our ability to plan for and implement a low-carbon future. In order to avoid the catastrophic health, economic, and ecological impacts of more than 2 degrees C of global warming, the IPCC (2012) estimates that GHG emissions must be reduced by 60 per cent to 80 per cent below 1990 levels by 2050. Nova Scotia must orient its energy planning to this long-term target. Our current targets take us to 2030 and we are on trajectory to meet them. [...] Sealing the deal on coal phase-out can free us up to invest ... in the renewable energy infrastructure we need to carry us into the next decades. [...] We have the singular opportunity to become a leading example in Canada and the world of complete system transformation from near-total reliance on fossil fuels to fossil-free electricity.[6] (Section 6.1, p. 21)

Electricity is only one portion of energy use, the main others being transportation and building heating and cooling, along with manufacturing. However, electricity is very significant since some 46 per cent of the province's carbon emissions come from NSPI, which relies on coal for 55–60 per cent of its capacity. Most of the coal is imported. Because moving off fossil fuels completely is a real possibility in Nova Scotia, it would have been useful to have stated this as a goal.

Still, our targets for use of renewables are trend setting. One step our government took was to define hydro as a renewable, a step clearly associated with the development of a link to Newfoundland's Muskrat Falls project. What inhibits our moving more rapidly to full de-carbonization is the existence of a series of coal-fired generating plants (at Lingan, Point Aconi, Point Tupper, and Trenton) that still have some economic life in them. Early closure, i.e., in advance of their natural decommissioning through old age, would result in them becoming "stranded assets" and thus a financial loss for the company. This, and not substantive technical difficulties, is what keeps carbon being burned in Nova Scotia to generate electricity.

Nova Scotia Power has become a significantly profitable company. Since the 1992 privatization, profits have run at about $100 million per year. That represents some $2 billion that could have remained in the province to reduce government debt, offer better government services, improve the electrical grid infrastructure, hire more maintenance staff, reduce rates – whatever. So on the face of it, the initial policy choice made by the PCs to privatize the company should have been on the table as a current policy issue. It was not. At least not for Darrell. Many inside the NDP – and indeed other voices in the general public – have continued to raise the point. At an NDP policy convention held in 2008 in Wolfville, party members brought the issue forward. Darrell and Graham both spoke against consideration of it. The result was that the point was "referred" to the party executive for consideration, a procedural maneuver designed to move the whole issue away from public view. This was consistent with Darrell's approach to not have the NDP appear to be a socialistic party.

His stated reason was interesting. He claimed that a buy-back of NSPI would be expensive and add ruinously to the provincial debt. In fact, this was bogus. The province would not have to buy-back NSPI; NSPI would buy itself back. What happened in the 1992 privatization is that NSPI sold shares in itself and took the cash and reduced its debt. It swapped debt for equity. In any re-nationalization, the company would run up its debt again to buy back the shares. It would swap equity for debt. But this is not government debt; it is customer-serviced debt, just as existed prior to 1992. It was discouraging that Darrell did not seem to understand that. And debt, in fact, tends to be much less expensive than equity for a company, especially government-guaranteed debt. This is because equity (shareholders) expect dividends and it exists forever; debt can be paid off. Especially in recent years with low interest rates in the bond market, this would have been a good time to look at the question.

If there are reasons to hesitate about re-nationalization of NSPI they are not so much reasons of debt, although the share price has increased quite a bit since 1992. The real issue is whether the public wants to own a series of large coal- and oil-fired power plants at a time when emissions regulations are becoming so strict, and alternative forms of generation, including decentralization, are becoming feasible and economically competitive.

What might be reasonable would be to nationalize the distribution and transmission grids. Public ownership often makes sense for services that are essential, and that are a natural monopoly. Public ownership should not be automatic in these circumstances, since regulation in the public interest can sometimes serve as the appropriate means of control, but where electricity has become so central to our lives and with so much money involved, there is every good reason to consider it. Electricity generation has evolved to the point where its generation is no longer a natural monopoly: many generators of electric power have emerged, and more can be expected. Wind generation will proliferate, as will solar; other technologies will emerge. But a grid remains a necessity, and there is no need for more than one, so it fits the generalized picture of where public ownership might be appropriate. The UARB has already set an Open-Access Transmission Tariff (OATT), i.e., the rate that independent power producers must pay to wheel their electricity along the grid. Public ownership of the grid should be examined, and should have been looked at by our government in an open discussion, but it was not.[7]

An associated point is whether public ownership of tidal power makes sense. This power source has enormous potential, in part for domestic consumption of electricity and in part for export to the USA. With research and experimentation at an early stage it would be opportune to open up this question for debate. Instead we have drifted into a situation in which private-sector entities are apparently being assumed to be the only appropriate owners.

Right now, though, the big project underway is the Maritime Link to Newfoundland's Muskrat Falls development. Does this make sense? What it is, is a regional project and thus represents some degree of co-operation amongst the Atlantic provinces. The underlying thought is to move towards more local independence in energy matters, that is, independence from foreign sources since most of our fuels are imported (coal, oil, and potentially natural gas). The Atlantic Provinces all have our own individual electrical utilities, just like all Canadian provinces. To the extent that regional co-operation has been present previously, it has been in the form of some small movement of excess energy back and forth across the Nova Scotia-New Brunswick border. Regional co-operation has been rudimentary in Atlantic Canada, but is much needed. The populations are too small to continue to ignore the opportunities. Some regional planning for universities has existed for decades through the

The Muskrat Falls hydro installation as it is projected to look when completed.

South Dam   Intake/Powerhouse   Transition Dam   Spillway   North Dam   Rock Knoll

Tailrace

Maritime Province Higher Education Commission (MPHEC), and joint marketing for gambling exists through the Atlantic Lottery Corporation. A next step towards regional co-ordination could well be for electricity.

This is especially so if tidal power becomes technically achievable, though it hardly needs to wait for this. In fact, electricity is so important that a solid argument can be made that it should probably be regulated by the federal government on a unified national basis, like inter-provincial oil/gas pipelines, rather than be left to individual provinces. This would allow for the movement of energy on a national grid, with system planning for the whole country and an end to provincial rivalries such as the one between Newfoundland and Quebec. If a national grid existed, building a Maritime Link would probably not be on the agenda since electricity generated in Labrador could flow through Quebec to the Maritimes to supplement our own sources.

In the absence of a national electricity grid, Muskrat Falls has emerged as a long-term secure supply of electricity for Nova Scotia as we move away from carbon. It will require an undersea link. It was reviewed by the UARB and has been approved[8] though not in the form in which it was initially presented and so vigorously promoted by Darrell.

During the public hearings before the UARB about Muskrat Falls, all participants other than Emera and the Province criticized the project as not a good deal for ratepayers. The Liberals' Andrew Younger pointed this out relentlessly during the spring Legislature session, drawing some ambiguous replies from the Premier and Minister of Energy. But there was no getting around John Merrick, the consumer advocate, or the large power consumers, or the consultants hired by the Board itself all of whom filed critical briefs with the UARB.

And in fact, in the end the UARB did find the original deal not to be in the financial best interest of Nova Scotia ratepayers, although it liked this hydro project and set out changes to the deal that would make it a reasonable one. The core problem was that the Muskrat Falls energy deal negotiated by Nova Scotia Power was at a cost that was only acceptable if blended with other, additional energy at lower cost. It was believed that such energy would be available, but there was no contract for it. What the Board was looking for was a "robust" proposal – not one that was the cheapest under all scenarios (which the Muskrat Falls deal was not) – but that would work best overall in a variety of scenarios. To make Muskrat Falls into the robust deal the Board wanted, there had to be a supplementary guarantee of that extra, market-price energy secured by contract. The Board approved the project subject to securing a contract with Nalcor. This did subsequently happen, but it was not the deal the Premier had relentlessly touted as, "the lowest and best."

Making hydro-generated electricity the reliable, day-to-day backbone of our system, rather than carbon, is sensible. But Muskrat Falls will meet no more than about 10 per cent of Nova Scotia's overall needs. At the same time, it is a move that contemplates a big project, whereas the future will likely be built on renewables that are more decentralized. Already the stated plans are for some 40 per cent of electricity to come from renewables. Virtually 100 per cent is really what makes sense. What that implies is shifting the 60 per cent that now comes from burning fossil fuels to any form of renewable.

Coal is a real problem. And has been a particular problem for the NDP. With our long-standing links to organized labour, and some early electoral strength in Cape Breton where most of the province's coal mining was located, for decades it was unthinkable to be in the NDP and be critical of coal mining. But the industry has died. There is some residual open-pit extraction, but underground mines have been closed since 1997.

Unfortunately, there are those who continue to talk of the possibility of re-opening the Donkin mine. This is highly unlikely to happen, for hard commercial reasons. The coal would be expensive to get at; it is high-sulphur and high-ash which means it is not a good candidate for burning as fuel for electricity generation; NSPI has already said it is not interested in being a purchaser; export markets are not likely to appear; and majority ownership has moved from Xstrata to Glencore to the Cline Group. The former minority owner, Morien Resources, suggested the coal could be exported for coking (making steel) or thermal (generating electricity) purposes. But most parts of the world have their own coal, Canada has a greatly diminished steel industry,[9] and public energy and emissions policy in Canada heavily favours moving to renewables for electricity. So no matter how much new mining jobs would be welcome in Cape Breton, this is not likely to happen.[10]

There is official NDP policy, adopted in 1991, that supports "opening the Donkin Mine," and this was reflected in the comments of Darrell and of Frank Corbett, both of whom have, while being in the Government as Premier and Deputy Premier, continued to mislead Cape Bretoners into thinking that there might be a new underground coal mine in Donkin. Highly unlikely, and not a good option for workers or the environment should it occur.

Energy issues remain central to Nova Scotia politics, and will do so for decades to come. The major accomplishment of our government was to put hard caps on greenhouse gas emissions. Other initiatives were either already in place (the 2007 *Environmental Goals and Sustainability Act*;[11] Efficiency Nova Scotia[12]) or were led by the federal government (emissions rules) or came from Emera (Muskrat Falls) or from other players in electricity generation (independent wind energy developers; tidal power companies). The removal of the provincial portion of the HST from electricity bills, while a big seller with many voters, is highly questionable policy because it was not structured so as to deliver affordability to those most in need of it, nor did it discourage consumption. Plus it has become much more expensive for government in terms of lost revenues than originally planned.

Fracking

Here is an issue where our government completely misread the public, and, in contrast, the McNeil Liberals have been very adroit.

Modern fracking means extraction of natural gas or oil from deposits that are not in convenient pools but in hydrocarbons dispersed within rock formations. Its purpose is to extract them from otherwise unproductive reservoirs. This is done by injecting pressurized water, sand, and various chemicals down a drilled well. Primarily, this is what the oil and gas industry calls a "shale play," i.e., shale is the type of rock formation from which natural gas (i.e., methane) is fracked. North America, especially the United States, has several areas of particular interest to the industry: in Texas (the Barnett, Eagle Ford, and Haynesville plays), Michigan (Collingwood), Arkansas (Fayetteville and Haynesville), Pennsylvania and New York (Marcellus). In Canada, there is serious potential in British Columbia (Horn River/Montney), and in Quebec (Utica).[13] Fields that are in production are becoming a significant part of US efforts to become independent of energy importation.

There are several concerns. First, this is simply further reliance on a carbon fuel, exactly what is undesirable as an overall objective. De-carbonization should be the aim. Second, there are reasons to be cautious because of the potential for contamination of drinking water sources, and increased risk of earthquakes. Third, it is far from clear that Nova Scotia even has much gas to be fracked anyway, so the financial returns are not likely to be significant.

Even advocates of fracking say that it has to be closely monitored. It is far from clear that we have the resources to do so. A useful comparison may be made with aquaculture. There are some forms of aquaculture, in some locations, that might well be carried on safely, with tight, top-grade regulation and monitoring. Community consent, careful selection of locations according to tidal flushing capability, limited open-net pens, moving pens on a rotation, limiting antibiotic and pesticide use, are among the steps that could allow for sustainable fin-fish aquaculture.[14] Not so for fracking. This activity is simply too risky and we should have rejected it immediately. Instead, we opted for the expedient of setting up a task force to study it, with a timeline that put the decision-making off until after the 2013 election. Even that was done only because the negative public opinion was palpable.

Given a choice between public opinion, backed up by the precautionary principle (as stated in the 1992 Rio Declaration on Environment and Development,[15] "where there are threats of serious or irreversible damage, lack of full scientific certainty shall not be used as a reason for postponing cost-effective measures to prevent environmental degradation." [Principle 15]), and the stated desires of the oil and gas industry, our government tended to favour the industry. True to form, the Dexter government would not risk being seen as opposed to business. In a caucus discussion in April 2012, Darrell said that the critics had distorted the information, which angered him because then, "you can't have a reasonable discussion." He cited the Council of Canadians, and the 2010 film *Gasland* that he said was, "over the top." Fracking is, "the same as traditional drilling," he said; the critics, "are not prepared to listen."

The formal study we commissioned, chaired by David Wheeler, has now reported.[16] Overall, it was thoughtful and cautious. With respect to risk, it said: "Although none of the potential negative impacts could be defined as catastrophic, there remain many outstanding questions requiring further research," and cited the need for baseline monitoring, effective regulations, and community consent. On actual potential in the province, it said: "Knowledge of the subsurface ... is extremely limited at the present time. Thus it is difficult to quantify the potential or even to rank various basins in terms of overall prospectivity." While saying this, it nonetheless did put numbers on various possible scenarios, thus clouding the issue. What it called a "low-medium case" of one basin, with 4,000 wells operating over forty years, could offer regional benefits of $1 billion per year. This has been envisioned as a major hope for prosperity, even though the actual potential is an unknown and the only test wells drilled here so far have produced no gas.

Economist Michael Bradfield quite convincingly challenged the potential for financial returns to the province from fracking. In an October 2014 article for the Canadian Centre for Policy Alternatives[17] he wrote:

"A major problem with the Review Panel's report is that the 'benefits' are over-estimated and the costs under-estimated." Bradfield pointed out that jobs and royalties estimates are speculative and underwhelming. The royalty regime calls for a 10 per cent payment to the government, but only after the first two years of production from a lease; most production is in the first year of any lease, so this royalty regime could lead to no royalties at all or only trivial amounts.

The Liberals have been relentlessly criticized by *The Chronicle Herald* for their decision to legislate against fracking, but they have been sticking to their position. They introduced Bill 6 on September 30, 2014 to ban high-volume hydraulic fracturing in shale formations.[18] Bravo for them, and shame on us.

Protestors opposed to fracking march in Halifax in 2013.

10

Poverty and Housing

I n terms of general support inside the caucus, and reflecting opinions inside the party at large, a serious focus on poverty reduction was extremely popular. Unfortunately this was not one of the priorities of the party leadership once in government.

The reason for this was their view that poverty reduction is not a vote getter. This attitude became perfectly clear in discussions about the first budget, which was to include an increase in the HST. Graham Steele's memorable comments on this point have previously been noted in Chapter 5.

The overriding policy concern was to balance the budget as a means of establishing the fiscal credibility of the party. When choices had to be made about which other policy priorities were to receive government attention in its first term, anti-poverty measures did not make the cut.

To some limited extent this was understandable as a short-term policy choice. Because of the overall fiscal crisis dating from 2008, the federal government had put in place a stimulus programme that focused on capital spending. In Nova Scotia, that meant some $128 million to be spent over two years on repairs, renovations, and energy efficiency for public housing. This was an important investment with real benefits in terms of improved quality of accommodations for residents of public housing. But it did not account for the low priority of engaging with long-term anti-poverty planning.

Poverty remains a real problem here. Acadia University sociology professor Lesley Frank has tracked child poverty since 2001. In her latest report, issued November 2013 and covering the period 1989-2011, Frank noted that 29,000 children remain in poverty, some 17.3 per cent of all children, the fifth worst rate in Canada.[1] The significance of 1989 is that it is the date when Parliament pledged to eliminate poverty for children by 2000. Various measures of poverty exist. Statistics Canada primarily uses the LICO (low-income cutoff), the essence of which is that individuals or families are in poverty if they are spending 20 per cent or more than an average family of after-tax income on food, clothing, and shelter.

Other provinces were generating anti-poverty plans through public consultation processes (e.g., *Breaking the Cycle: Ontario's Poverty Reduction Strategy*[2] and Newfoundland's *Reducing Poverty: An Action Plan for Newfoundland and Labrador*[3]). This extended to housing plans. Housing is widely seen as crucial to combating poverty. It is not the only major step, but an essential one. Other resources that would have been truly progressive would have been to call for a Guaranteed Annual Income (GAI) – or even better, a Guaranteed Adequate Annual Income (GAAI) – and also to back the campaign of the Canadian Labour Congress (CLC) for a doubling of the Canada Pension Plan (CPP) benefits over time.

One of the advantages of being a government is the control of the means to communicate: ministers can make statements, policy papers can be put out for discussion, issues can be brought to the regular meetings of other provincial ministers, and the Premier can bring them to the Council of the Federation. It would have been a useful contribution to a national discussion if Nova Scotia under the NDP had done any of this to promote serious anti-poverty measures. It is not always necessary to achieve implementation of policies to achieve success; sometimes it is useful simply to articulate a vision, and indeed, often it is a necessary preliminary to action to have spoken out. Positing a direction serves to stimulate public debate, promotes the search for the best alternatives, and lets the voting public know what it can expect over time. Even by these modest measures, we were poor performers.

It would have been especially useful to have spoken out about steps that the federal government could take. When the Canadian Labour Congress (CLC) started its campaign to double CPP benefits, proposed to be phased in over seven years of increases in contributions, there was little immediate support from Canada's finance ministers. The CPP has been an enormously successful social undertaking since its inception in 1965: it is financially sound and has had an important role in reducing seniors' poverty. Once the CLC's proposal became public in 2010, it was exactly the sort of idea that the NDP should have enthusiastically endorsed and promoted. Instead, the reaction was largely muted. Later, it made it onto the agenda of the finance ministers, but our support was tepid where it should have been enthusiastic. Instead of the finance ministers spending their time discussing a national regulator for stock markets or "pooled registered pension plans," national anti-poverty measures should have been on their agenda.

Pooled registered pension plans (PRPP) were actually mainly in the bailiwick of Labour ministers rather than Finance ministers. But they represented a fake measure to pretend to deal with a real problem. Emanating from the federal government, the idea was to pretend to deal with inadequate retirement savings by many Canadians, not by increasing CPP contributions and benefits, or by making private pension plans mandatory, but by encouraging employees to make additional contributions, although without matching employer contributions and allowing employers to pool their pension plans for investment purposes. Essentially, they are not much different than RRSPs (Registered Retirement Savings Plans). PRPPs would not have been useful contributions to reduction of poverty. Our government wanted to go ahead with legislation facilitating this, but in the end it never happened because of skepticism at caucus. The Liberals have now brought in legislation to implement them.

The province never did produce an overall anti-poverty strategy under our government. We also introduced a silly communications standard for the Department of Community Services instructing employees not to even use the word "poverty" or to speak of "the poor." God forbid we should draw attention to class inequalities. The most we did was to say, in our first Speech From The Throne, and employing a standard cliche, "The strength of any society can be judged on how its most vulnerable are treated."[4] We relied on the Poverty Reduction Strategy produced in 2008 by the Tories, a weak document. We tinkered with the existing system over our four years, no more.

The only advance has been – finally – with respect to housing policy. A public consultation was held and an affordable housing policy document was issued in year four.[5] The delay reflects its overall low priority inside the government. Its content reflects lack of serious innovative thinking. It is a weak document, an embarrassment really.

As it happens, I had the chance to see some of the workings of the Department of Community Services (DCS) over housing matters. One of the features of the NDP government was to create Ministerial Assistants (MAs). Some MLAs not appointed to Cabinet were assigned to Ministers. To some extent this helped ministers with their workload; to some extent the appointments were *pro forma* only. Although legislation was introduced to give a context for the MAs, any duties depended on direction from the Premier along with actual dynamics inside the various departments. My appointment was as MA to the Minister of Community Services, for housing including a particular focus on co-op housing.

At the DCS I was provided with a small office and access to staff for briefings. The Premier's June 29, 2009 press release on MAs said, "Ministerial Assistants will represent ministers and government to build relationships with important stakeholders, and oversee policy and program development that helps government keep commitments."[6] Representing ministers and government apparently did not extend to speaking publicly. In my initial discussion with DCS Minister Denise Peterson-Rafuse and her Deputy Minister Judith Ferguson they made it clear that, "the Minister will continue to be responsible for public comment on housing matters, including speaking with the press and attending formal events; the Ministerial Assistant will not normally speak with the press unless requested by the Minister and will consult with DCS communications staff." And when I attended meetings with external organizations, I should take DCS staff with me if they were available. At the same time my help was being sought to build bridges to non-government organizations (NGOs). Well, there it was and off I went.

The Department of Community Services housing staff were a big help. They knew their topic and had a lot of good ideas, even though it was clear they were both preoccupied with delivering on the federally supported stimulus spending, and were used to generally being neglected

Department of Community Services Minister, Denise Peterson-Rafuse.

inside what was pretty clearly a chaotic and problematic department. I set out to read files and meet with the relevant NGOs. As I met with the NGOs, I briefed the Minister and her senior staff in written memos.

As time went by, it became clear that Denise was not really interested in what I had to say about housing, which had not been chosen as a priority item by the Premier's Office. But because Darrell had expressed specific interest in housing co-ops, I was asked to focus on that. The United Nations' *International Convention on Economics, Social and Cultural Rights*,[7] signed and ratified by Canada, included a right to adequate housing? So what? Respected Dalhousie University nursing professor Jean Hughes, along with everyone else in Nova Scotia who studies poverty, thinks housing is crucial? So what? The Premier thinks slackers in co-ops are the issue, so co-ops are the priority.

And, of course, something that was nowhere near being on our agenda was rent controls. A system that limits increases in rents to some set percentage, and usually requiring a justification from landlords, previously existed in Nova Scotia in the 1990's. Rent controls are a straightforward response to rising costs of living for an essential purpose. Hotly resisted by property owners, the system was abandoned in 1993 by the John Savage Liberals. The NDP has embraced market-driven solutions, i.e., a faith that the private sector will build enough units to meet demand, and that competition will regulate costs to tenants. Especially in HRM, where there has been significant migration into the metro area, it is far from obvious that rents are affordable, even with all of the new construction in recent decades.

So co-ops it was.[8] The Co-operative Housing Federation of Canada, which I consulted, hit the roof. They pointed out that housing co-ops represented only about 1 per cent of housing units in Canada; any move to convert co-ops to private ownership would just reduce what was already only a small niche. Their hope was for expansion of the sector, not its reduction. And they pointed out that they were already engaged on the issue of member participation, but approached it through supports and education, not through undermining the existence of co-op membership.

Housing co-ops have a long history in Nova Scotia including one variant, an association designed to be temporary and to allow a group to assemble so as to increase their creditworthiness, and often to assist each other in construction, the plan being to convert to private ownership of the individual units (houses on separate lots) after construction was complete. These were known as "builders co-ops." By July 2010 I had finished my research on co-op housing and reported to the Minister. [Extracts from this report are available as Appendix 4 in the online appendices.] I pointed out the downsides, especially the political downsides, of converting housing units to private ownership.

The Minister and her deputy were not pleased. They were particularly put out that the memo implied that the Premier's idea was neither practical (How do you account for the interests of former members of a co-op who have contributed "rent" and "sweat-equity" if the units are to be sold?) nor desirable (CHFC opposes reduction in the numbers of co-ops.) "Are you on the same page?" Denise challenged me. The Premier wanted all models to be considered; are there models that fit? It was agreed that a variant of the memo, set out as a PowerPoint, that could be used for a presentation to Cabinet should be produced. It was, though whether it was ever seen by Cabinet I have no idea. No special co-ops consultations took place. No legislation came forward. What did happen was that a low level consultation on housing generally took place, finally resulting in a "Housing Strategy" in 2013.[9] It is a vague document, notable mostly for the appearance in the Minister's opening "message" that, "The Strategy charts a clear course...." marking yet another incorporation of John Hamm policies, style, and phraseology into the NDP government.

There are other aspects of the Housing Strategy. Co-ops did make an appearance: we were told that the province will be, "considering equity or builders co-operatives," apparently in, "new housing co-ops," though how this would occur and whether any money would be on the table was not stated. The other main point was ongoing reliance on the private sector to build "affordable" housing with no details offered, but given the Department's warm embrace of HRM's plans for high rises all over the Halifax North End, it seemed the NDP government wanted to continue Darrell's policy of being good friends with land developers. And when the Housing Strategy talks of "building not just homes, but healthy, diverse neighborhoods," it means something different than many of us would have in mind. What it is actually supporting is a series of ugly, alienating, cash-cow apartment towers that should have gone out of style decades ago – exactly the opposite of healthy neighborhoods.[10]

I was not a part of producing the Housing Strategy, having left the position of Ministerial Assistant to the Minister of DCA in the fall of 2010 – it having become fully apparent after a year or so that the Department was not serious about housing and was happier ignoring my input. The specific project on housing co-ops was never anything more than a make-work project, and not worth putting any more time into. My successor as Ministerial Assistant, Gary Burrill, was never asked for any input on anything. And a poverty reduction strategy, identified in our first Speech From the Throne in 2009, and the subject of work internally by DCS staff, never appeared.

The Highland Housing Co-op in Antigonish, Nova Scotia.

The NDP caucus after our 1998 election victory. (Clockwise from lower left): Don Chard, Howard Epstein, John MacDonell, Helen MacDonald, Maureen MacDonald, Peter Delefes, Robert Chisholm, Reeves Matheson, Charlie Parker, Bill Estabrooks, Kevin Deveaux, Jerry Pye, Frank Corbett, Darrell Dexter, John Deveau. (Center four; left to right): John Holm, Eileen O'Connell, Yvonne Atwell, Rosemary Godin.

The NDP caucus in the Red Room, Province House, after our 2009 election victory.

11

Legislation: It's What We Do

B eing in the Legislature as a place to work is a complete treat. The building is beautiful. Charles Dickens happened to be in Halifax for the opening of the 1842 session of the General Assembly, "... at which ceremonial the forms observed on the commencement of a new Session of Parliament in England were so closely copied, and so gravely presented on a small scale, that it was like looking at Westminster through the wrong end of a telescope." Dickens' comment is about right: everything perfect, but in miniature.[1]

The proportions of the rooms are classic. The desks are comfortable, not lavish but designed for their purpose: to accommodate some papers, bills as introduced, a place to stand and speak. The library is tiered, ornate, and handsome. When I had a small law practice in 1978-81, my office was across Granville Street from the Legislature in a small building owned by the late Grover Cleveland, a building with the old Pace, MacIntosh & Donahoe law firm on the second floor and a well-patronized family-run cafeteria on the ground floor (I was on the third floor walk-up).

The building does not exist now – it is the site of One Government Place (OGP), the Premier's offices, and the locus of the Cabinet, Treasury Board, and Policy and Planning. Running a bare-bones enterprise, I had no photostat machine for a long time and would go across the

The Nova Scotia Legislature.

street to the Legislative Library and pay for making copies. And to try and flirt with Ilga Leja, then Deputy Librarian and later mother of our children, Hannah and Noah. I am a big fan of the Legislative Library and of the Legislature.

One of the frequent experiences of all MLAs is to receive school visits. Many schools arrange trips to the Legislature, to meet with their MLA, to sit in the gallery and watch a bit of the proceedings, Question Period if possible, and to be introduced and welcomed as visitors. What I like especially about these visits of schoolchildren is trying to explain to them what an MLA does for a living. Usually we gather in the Red Chamber, the former chamber of the upper house when one existed, but now used for some committees and for formal receptions. Handing out Nova Scotia flag lapel pins, I explain that an MLA generally does three things: we pass laws; we deal with budgets; and we offer services to families living in our constituencies. All of these can be complicated. Nothing becomes a law unless it is presented to the full Legislature where all members get the opportunity to speak about it, several times as bills go through the process. And the process here includes a mandatory opportunity for the public to speak at a session of the Law Amendments Committee, something quite valuable. I have often learned new aspects of a topic by hearing witnesses at Law Amendments. For budgets, we debate what taxes are to be in place, and how the money is to be spent. This is important because taxes pay for necessary services such as health care, education, environmental protection, and workplace safety inspections. Taxes are about who pays and how much.

As for services to residents, it often happens that people have difficulty understanding how to navigate the system. Thus, they might not understand how to go about obtaining home care or to be considered for admission to a nursing home. They might have trouble with a student loan application, or be having a landlord/tenant difficulty. Anything the provincial government has power over, the MLA can be called upon to try to help with. We cannot obtain for anyone more than they are entitled to but we can try to expedite or explain matters. We all have offices in our constituencies with staff who specialize in these matters, so accessing services is not difficult. There is a fourth function for MLAs whose party is in the Opposition, which is to hold the government accountable. It is part of the democratic process that the Legislature be open; open to the public and the press, and that the government be required to make public what it does. A part of that is the opportunity for Opposition MLAs to ask cabinet ministers questions, which happens three days a week when the House is sitting.

No matter how simply I tried to explain the workings of government, the kids always asked who the people in the big paintings were (King George III and Queen Caroline) and were the frames really made of gold (No).

Legislation, as important as it is, is only one aspect of governing. Existing legislation allows government to adopt regulations; a budget allows spending according to chosen priorities; contracts may be signed; appointments made. These are examples of how governing may continue and adhere to the particular preferences of the government in power without needing to adopt new laws. Still, it will often be the case that governments will want to bring in legislation either to signal in a very public way its priorities, or will find that some new initiatives do require changes in the law, or good governance will call for some cleaning up of old rules and appropriate modernization. For any of this, an organized process is needed and is in place.

The formal system works like this. Departments are given two dates each year for putting forward RFLs, Requests For Legislation. The dates that have made sense to us have been early August and early January. These dates are tied to the requirement of holding two legislative sessions per year, one in the fall and one in the spring. The RFLs follow a set format. A memorandum is prepared and is sent to the Executive Council, with the effective body being the Legislation Committee. It shows the subject, the originating Minister, and bears the names and signatures of those who prepared and reviewed the submission. After the short initial summary of what the proposed bill does, there is a section giving background, the key issues, and including a comparison with other jurisdictions if relevant. Alternatives and their consequences are set out. There are sections on timing, financial impact, government-wide implications, consultations held or planned, how the measure fits with government priorities, efficiencies, legal implications, and policy lenses. They are structured to be thorough documents, and are a great help to the Legislation Committee. Sometimes draft bills are attached, or outlines of drafting instructions to go to the Legislative Counsel. And although departments are the main source of RFLs, they might also come from individual MLAs or from the Premier's Office. All RFLs go to an internal government committee known as the Legislation Committee. Composition is of both Cabinet and backbench MLAs, with a variety of staff in attendance.

The Legislation Committee reviews all proposals for bills. I served on this committee from its inception. Dave A. Wilson was its initial chair. After Dave was appointed to Cabinet, Leonard Preyra chaired, and after he went into Cabinet, I chaired. Because the committee composition included both Ministers and backbenchers, both Dave and Leonard remained on the committee and its overall composition was quite stable. The Deputy Premier as House Leader (and therefore the main person organizing the formal movement of bills through the House and as link to Treasury Board) is a member, as is the Justice Minister. Other members have been Mat Whynot, Becky Kent, Pam Birdsall, Clarrie MacKinnon, and Gary Burrill. Gordon Hebb QC chief Legislative Counsel, whose office drafts the bills, attends. Lawyers from the Justice Department who are assigned to the Privy Council attend. As do staff from Policy and Priorities, the group inside the Premier's Office who advise on policy. There is never any shortage of staff in the room.

There is a standard joke that there are two things you never want to see close up: how sausages are made and how laws are made. Too true. But to some extent the system works reasonably well. It could be much improved by better choices of initial proposals, but once in the works, the review process is reasonably effective. Proposals have certainly been rejected. Others have been modified. Some, for which no consensus emerged at the Committee, were moved to caucus for a fuller debate. A lot turns on how well informed MLAs are on the actual subject before them. It is very easy to be led astray by taking a proposal at its surface worth. Often, what looks to be something of a housekeeping measure can have serious policy implications not identified in the RFL. And sometimes, we have found ourselves deep into the process to the extent of having a bill before the House before problems become apparent. Here are a few examples, all from 2010:

Bill 89 – Personal Health Information. This bill was amended after the Law Amendments Committee hearings to incorporate changes suggested by a Journalism professor from the University of King's College who was concerned over some conflicts with the existing Freedom of Information and Protection of Privacy (FOIPOP) legislation. This bill was developed over a long time (years) including formal consultation with the specialist informed community, and still this valid point did not emerge until an advanced stage of the legislative process.

Bill 99 – Conflict of Interest. In reviewing this bill, which amended existing legislation, the Liberals pointed out that one clause in the existing statute allowed a commissioner to deter frivolous complaints by both an award of costs against the complainant and an award of "damages." They argued convincingly that this is not appropriate. The government consulted legal counsel who agreed. The change was made, in Committee of the Whole House.

Bill 100 – Unified Labour Board. This bill came forward without having been identified as likely to lead to the extensive debate and controversy it ultimately did involve. This misunderstanding of consequences has to be seen as something of a failure of our political sensitivity. It is also the case that the "contracting out" clause was not sufficiently analyzed in the RFL. Both Opposition parties used the bill to try to generate a positioning of the government as beholden to unionized labour, especially the public service, and as unfriendly to business, especially small business. They focused on the purpose section, the title, the possible impact on non-unionized workplaces, successor rights (contracting out), and consultation. In the end, their filibustering did not seem to gain much traction, yet there were a lot of communications from umbrella groups for the business community. The government's willingness to clarify the bill was the correct response. It is not clear why it took so long to make the changes, though.

Bill 125 – Heritage Property. This bill in its original form was rejected by caucus, one of two for which caucus called for important changes
(along with Bill 119 on Residential Tenancies). When the changes were
incorporated, the bill still was shown, by presenters during the Law
Amendments process, to need a small, one-word tweak. Unfortunately
many bills were then moving through the House all together as the session drew to a close, and the Minister was unable to fully consult his staff
about the proposed change in a timely fashion. This raises the question
of why there were no department officials present in the Legislature
throughout the whole process to monitor their bill and be available for
just this sort of last-minute question. (There was a promise made to the
House to try to deal with the point through regulation, though it is unlikely this could actually be done.)

In addition to the examples cited, some other bills showed less than
rigorous adherence to an organized process. There were bills where
caucus thought changes should be made, after hearing presentations at
Law Amendments, but the leadership showed a marked reluctance to be
flexible. Sealing on Hay Island is an example; this became highly controversial at caucus because the proposal was to allow the hunt, a commercial activity, in a designated wilderness area,[2] but the Minister refused
to change his view in favour of the sealing, on the basis that the fishing
community throughout the province would see this as very negative, and
the bill went ahead. There were bills that came in on a supposedly urgent
basis and that received no formal review and only last-minute briefing
of caucus, for example the binding arbitration bill for paramedics in the
summer of 2013.

A particularly unfortunate experience had to do with an amendment to
the *Liquor Control Act* promoted by Graham Steele as Minister of Finance
in 2011. The Department had been involved in a dispute with vendors of
wine making kits who also offered a fermentation service, the business
known as "U-Vint" or on-site wine making. The concern of the Department was that it might be missing out on tax revenue, and that while
genuine at-home, personal winemaking is not a concern, when a store
does the fermentation then that ought to be seen as something different.

Threats of prosecution had been made to some stores. The Department wanted to be able to seek an injunction as a quicker measure than prosecution, but there was no provision for this in the existing *Act*. The Legislation Committee considered this proposal twice, during spring and fall sessions, and turned it down both times. The Committee doubted that the revenue loss would be very great, saw the measure as heavy-handed, and also likely to bring adverse public reaction. The RFLs included statements that the whole of the *Liquor Control Act* was due to be reviewed, and the view was taken by the Committee that any such amendment could and should be brought forward during public consultation about the *Act* as a whole.

The reason the Committee considered the RFL twice is that Graham, for no clear reason, became committed to this amendment and asked to present the proposal personally to the Committee after it was rejected the first time. When it was rejected a second time he took the proposal to caucus and argued for it there, managing to convince enough members that it was an urgently needed amendment to the statute for it to go ahead. As predicted, it was controversial, and drew adverse public reaction. At Law Amendments, U-Vint operators expressed their objections. The best that Leonard Pryera and I, as members of that Committee, could do was to point out that a full review of the *Act* was going to take place soon, and they could then argue for repeal of the measure.

A few days after the Law Amendments Committee hearings, Graham approached me to ask why Leonard and I thought the *Act* was going to be reviewed. I pointed out that this was stated in both of the RFLs he had signed. He then said that he had not been aware of this statement in the RFLs and that in any event no review of the *Liquor Control Act* was planned. (Nor was one held.) Of course it is not appropriate for a Minister not to know the contents of an RFL he has signed. It is not appropriate for an RFL to include misleading statements. And it is not appropriate, and embarrassing, for MLAs to be put in the position of misleading the public based on inaccurate information provided to them. Finally, on this measure, the public reaction was so adverse that the Government had to back off of it after media editorials tore a strip off us.[3]

There were also instances of bills that were highly controversial in caucus. An example was the 2010 Bill 55, the *Internal Trade Agreement Implementation Amendment Act*. Internal trade means trade among the provinces. A detailed agreement dating from 1994 set a framework for removal of barriers to open trade among the provinces, similar to NAFTA and other international trade agreements among nations. The essence of the Agreement, though, was that it amounted to a political promise. That is, there was no legally binding enforcement mechanism. If one province wanted to object to anything it saw as a barrier to open trade it could file a complaint or make a public issue of the matter. But it would be up to the home province to decide whether it would remove the alleged barrier or not. What Bill 55 did was to convert the political promise into a legal obligation. It allowed for the filing of disputes before arbitrators that could result in an order penalizing the province monetarily. Many of us did not like this exposure to potential, unknown claims. But the bill went ahead.[4]

After I took over chairing the committee, I looked back over the six or so legislative sessions we had presided over, to assess what had been accomplished. A pattern of sorts emerged.

The key point about legislation is not just the orderly preparation of it, but what is chosen to go forward at all. At a minimum, orderliness means less likelihood of discovering some flaw in the proposal late in the process, or being surprised by opposition shown by some interested segment of the population, or realizing that a group should have been formally consulted. At its best it means mature consideration has been given to the proposal. So there are significant virtues to an orderly and measured process. Still, our focus should be on the policy content of the measures brought forward.

In the time the NDP was in Opposition a lot of bills were presented. Some came forward multiple times in different sessions as the older bills on the Order Paper lapsed. Taken together they indicated the sort of measures an NDP government would be expected to favour. I have had a look back through all of the legislative sessions from 1998 on to remind myself of these.

Here are various significant legislative proposals made by the NDP in Opposition that never made it onto the NDP agenda while in government:

1. Public automobile insurance.

Bill 4, fall 2003, as introduced by Darrell Dexter, would have created a commission to outline options for legislation to create a publicly owned automobile insurance corporation.

2. Four weeks of vacation.

Bill 53, spring 2001, as introduced by Darrell Dexter, would have amended the *Labour Standards Code* to provide for increases in the minimum amount of paid vacation from the current two weeks to three or four weeks, depending on length of employment. It would have granted eligibility for benefits for some part-time employees comparable to full-time employees.

3. No privatization of public services.

Bill 14, spring 1998, as introduced by Helen MacDonald, would have protected public sector functions and positions from privatization. It would have required an, "open and independent review," to see if privatization would, "improve services for the public without unreasonable cost to the individuals or communities affected." The same protection would apply to the sale of major assets.

4. Audit of grants and loans.

Bill 76, fall 1998, as introduced by Darrell Dexter, would have required a value-for-money audit by the Auditor General of government assistance to business and imposed a moratorium on grants or forgivable loans, "to a large corporation," pending the audit results.

5. Stronger environmental assessments for underground mines.

Bill 126, spring 2002, as introduced by myself, would have made mandatory a Class II environmental impact assessment, which involves a public hearing before a panel, prior to any approval of an underground mine. Bill 127 would have applied the same provision to the grant of an offshore exploration license by the Canada-Nova Scotia Offshore Petroleum Board (CNSOPB).

6. Review of municipal amalgamation.

Bill 42, fall 1998, as introduced by Robert Chisholm, would have directed the UARB to review the appropriateness of the creation of HRM.

7. No toll highways.

Bill 46, fall 1998, as introduced by Bill Estabrooks, would have prohibited toll highways.

8. Tuition freeze.

Bill 150, fall 2002, as introduced by Darrell Dexter, would have implemented a tuition freeze for university students and required a stable financing plan to be generated. He reintroduced this proposal as Bill 5, spring 2003.

9. Africville apology.

Bill 123, spring 2005, as introduced by Maureen MacDonald, would have offered a formal apology to the former residents of Africville, required meetings and a report, and established a development trust. She reintroduced this as Bill 8, spring 2006.

10. Expedited certification of unions.

Bill 60, spring 2001, as introduced by Frank Corbett, would have mandated quick certification of unions where they could show 50 per cent or more of the proposed bargaining unit had joined the union. (Also proposed was first contract arbitration, banning the use of scabs, and some clarification of successor rights.) Expedited certification was reintroduced by Frank Corbett as Bill 220, spring 2005, where the required percentage was proposed to increase to 60 per cent.

11. Commission on Resources and the Environment.

Bill 63, spring 2001, as introduced by John MacDonell would have established a commission to convene round tables on large land use issues so as to try to sort out differences (modeled on a Commission of Resources and Environment that operated in British Columbia during the 1990s.) He reintroduced the proposal as Bill 25, spring 2003, Bill 28, fall 2003, and as Bill 103, spring 2006.

12. Expand standing in challenges to municipal land use decisions.

Bill 67, spring 2001, as introduced by Graham Steele, would have changed the *Municipal Government Act* to change the test for standing to take appeals to the UARB from being an "aggrieved" to being an "interested" person.

13. Limit "SLAPP" suits.

Bill 61, spring 2001, as introduced by Graham Steele, would have created a quick mechanism for courts to determine if certain law suits (such as for alleged defamation) are really, "Strategic Law-suits Against Public Participation" (SLAPP), and allow them to be dismissed early in the process as an abuse of process.

14. No loan forgiveness.

Bill 114, spring 1999, as introduced by myself, would have limited a government's ability to forgive a loan unless it obtained a resolution by the Legislature.

15. Improve presentation of the Public Accounts.

A series of measures were introduced to strengthen openness in the presentation of the finances of the province in budget documents: Bill 27, fall 1998, would have required listing the foregone revenues for all the expenditures (i.e., deductions) as well as the debt of municipalities, universities, schools and hospitals. Bill 37, spring 2001, would have required a listing of all user fees. Bill 65, spring 2001, would have added the measuring of well being following the methodology of GPI Atlantic. The fees list was reintroduced as Bill 139, spring 2002, by Graham Steele, who also introduced Bill 140 to require prompt public filing of a list of warrants and additional expenditures. Bill 37, fall 2003, would have required an accounting for federal transfers for health; Bill 154, spring 2005, would have required an accounting of how all federal transfers are spent. And Bill 184, spring 2005, would have required disclosure of all bonuses paid to civil servants.

16. Increase public participation in the Legislature.

Bill 81, fall 2001, as introduced by Darrell Dexter, would have required bills referred to the Law Amendments Committee or any other standing committee to be held for seven days to give the public notice, thus seeking, "the widest possible public input on the bill and giving the public an opportunity to appear before the committees and to comment on the bill."

17. Miscellaneous environmental protections

Bill 126, fall 2004, as introduced by Joan Massey, would have required a Class II environmental assessment for new quarries. Bill 66, spring 2001, as introduced by John MacDonell, would have required sustainability to be a principle in forestry management. Bill 194, spring 2005, as introduced by Frank Corbett, would have imposed a moratorium on new strip mines pending a study. Bill 89, fall 2007, as introduced by Graham Steele, would have created a voluntary fund for carbon offsets.

18. Coastal access

Bill 104, spring 1999, as introduced by Bill Estabrooks, would have mandated a study to facilitate public access to the coasts.

19. HST off funerals

Bill 17, fall 2007, as introduced by Darrell Dexter, would have removed the provincial portion of the HST for funerals, as a basic necessity of everyone's life.

This list speaks for itself. We introduced bills in Opposition that we never touched while in Government. Some of them are in stark contrast to how we behaved. Probably the leading example is Darrell's Bill 76 from 1998 expressing profound skepticism about grants and forgivable loans to large corporations and calling for a value-for-money audit by the Auditor General.

Darrell, in his election-time comments on the Liberals and PCs has been fond of saying that the best predictor of future behavior is actual past behavior and past policies. Surely this test applies to the NDP as well; that is, voters should have been able to rely on the NDP to follow through on policy positions set out by the party while in Opposition. As this list illustrates, this has not always been the case.

To be fair, there were many proposals made by the party in Opposition that were adopted either by the NDP in government or by the Liberals and Tories, partly in response to pressure from the NDP. The list of such proposals includes: removal of the provincial portion of the HST for home heating and from essentials; the registration of lobbyists; closing up the Liberals' trust funds; expansion of the applicability of FOIPOP laws; change in the rules for school closures; a consumer advocate at UARB rate hearings; objective criteria for road work; automatic assumption for firefighters eligibility for workers compensation for certain diseases; upper limits on assessment changes for residential properties; the reestablishing an independent, arm's-length Arts Council; banning handheld cellphone use while driving; and the regulation of gasoline prices at the pump.

Taken together, the list of items implemented is an impressive and worthwhile set of accomplishments. And other legislation has been adopted that had not been prefigured by Opposition bills. Yet at the same time it is an incomplete agenda, one that is at variance from the party's traditions, and signals sent during long years in Opposition. What happened to those items that simply disappeared? Like the "disappeared" in some authoritarian countries, the facts have been plain to see but have usually not been mentioned. Either Darrell never believed in the proposals (though he never said so in caucus) or he was just prepared to jettison them in pursuit of how he thought he could achieve electoral success.

Some things are striking in reviewing the party's legislative proposals in Opposition. First is that as we moved from 1998 when we first became the Opposition, to 2009 and the election in which we won government, the number of bills that we introduced tended to stay steady at 20 to 30, but then diminished after 2007. The second striking fact is that the progressiveness of the proposals tended to diminish along with their numbers. Repetition of bills from previous years was common. So, too, was a move to examples of novelty, trivial, or small focused bills: the Sable Island Horse as the Provincial Horse; put rumble strips in highways; exempt Canadian Forces members posted here temporarily from obtaining a driver's license; eliminate expiry dates on gift cards, and so on.

More importantly, Darrell regularly began to signal his accommodation of a business-class agenda as a way – it was explicitly stated internally – to "immunize" the party from any claim it is inherently anti-business. He signaled his eager alliance with the local establishment in other ways in addition to legislation. Supporting the HRM bid for the 2014 Commonwealth Games stands out, since the 2006–2007 process was a complete waste of money. It was Rodney MacDonald's Tories who finally popped this bubble when it became overwhelmingly obvious that it was going to be ruinously expensive.[5]

The two first legislative examples of Darrell's going on record as a new business-friendly NDP leader were his support for the "Atlantic Gateway" initiative in 2007 (Bill 139) and for changing the land use planning law framework for the Halifax downtown so as to allow the HRM By Design process to go ahead. Darrell himself introduced bills to create a "Small Business Service Agency" (Bill 153, spring 2007; and Bill 40, fall 2007) and to create a Manufacturers and Processing tax credit as the last NDP bill immediately prior to the 2009 Election (Bill 257, spring 2009).

The Atlantic Gateway was always a bogus idea. Nothing has ever happened about it. It was a free-floating idea that tried to promote a transportation corridor for the Atlantic Provinces through Maine and New Hampshire to connect us with the big New England markets. It depended heavily on the willingness of the USA government to build a major new highway system, though there was never any explanation of why it would be interested in doing that since the corridor would overwhelmingly benefit some small Canadian provinces rather than the USA itself. The idea survives only as a few paragraphs on the Internet.[6] But at the time it was heavily hyped. Darrell got on board.

So, too, was HRM By Design. The essence of this initiative was to do two things. It severely reduced the opportunities for public participation in planning decisions for the Halifax downtown. And it dramatically increased the as-of-right heights for new buildings. This change in the legal framework for land-use planning decisions profoundly offended many traditional NDP supporters in Halifax. The PC government brought in the bill at the request of HRM Council. The Council originally pressed for this set of changes in the legal framework to be applicable throughout HRM, or at least for the whole of the Halifax Peninsula and central Dartmouth inside the Circumferential Highway (bounded by Routes 111, 118, and 102). Ultimately the PCs (in a minority government) proposed Bill 181 only for the Halifax downtown, which was put forward as a special case. Maureen MacDonald, as MLA for north-end Halifax, said in discussion,

"I would not want this for my area," an opinion I certainly shared. But she and the rest of caucus at Darrell's urging supported the measure not because they thought it to be good (or bad) policy, but on the basis that it was being strongly supported by the Halifax business community. What this represented was the emergence of a prevailing caucus dynamic in which many measures were analyzed not so much as to whether they were good or bad for Nova Scotians, but whether they were thought to be good or bad for the NDP. I voted against the bill.[7]

My award for virtuous persistence in pursuit of a decent legislative proposal goes to Michèle Raymond. In 2005, she proposed that health insurance plans be made portable (Bill 212). The proposal was that individual and group insurance plans be required to take on individuals previously insured under another plan, "on the same terms and conditions as the preceding policy." The result would be no interruption in coverage for employees who change jobs. Importantly, the bill would also have required coverage for any pre-existing medical conditions to continue. Michèle's notes on her proposal said:

> "They [i.e., insured persons] have paid into health plans and should be able to collect benefits when needed (usually needed more later than early in life …). Health insurers are reaping windfalls every time divorce/death of uninsured spouse/loss of job takes away an insured who has been paying into the plan. Often, the province ends up paying the tab, if medications for now-excluded conditions are too expensive. Another alternative would be to say that all plans offered in Nova Scotia must have buy-in provisions (i.e., when insured leaves group plan, has option of continuing coverage in group at own expense.) This has been debated in House at least twice, with Liberal support."

She proposed it again twice in 2006 (Bill 40, spring and Bill 73, fall) in 2007 (Bill 20) and again internally after we formed government, but then found no support for it. By then a more elaborate mechanism was in place for review of legislative proposals and this one disappeared inside whatever department reviewed it.

Once in government, the process for consideration of proposals for legislation became somewhat more elaborate than a discussion at caucus. For the most part, individual MLAs, or groups of us, were not encouraged to propose serious measures. We were asked to think about proposals for small items that might respond to a particular interest in the community or garner a headline. It was especially good if the proposals involved no expenditure. The main fount of serious legislative proposals became the departments and the Premier's Office. The overall agenda was set by the list of proposals that had been made during the 2009 election.

Many of these were good ideas that disappeared into the maw of day to day governance, the drive to balance the budget, sheer ignorance of NDP history on the part of new Cabinet Ministers, or Ministers being driven by bureaucracies rather than having, or researching, NDP policy ideas or having their own. Ministers who had been in caucus since the 1998 election, as well as senior staff, should have known different.

In August 2012, I wrote a retrospective piece for caucus on our Legislative record, with a look forward to what was likely to be the last year of government prior to an election, and included some suggestions for items that could be introduced to advance the public interest and our positioning as ongoing champions for our traditional supporters. The actual array of bills bought forward in the last year of the government was mixed as judged against these proposals.

Few of the suggestions emerged as items adopted during the 2012-13 legislative sessions. The government did introduce consumer protection items such as allowing for early termination of tenancies where there was domestic abuse. Nova Scotia Power issues were advanced by a small rates freeze and by requiring shareholders to bear the cost of excessive raises for executives. There were bills dealing with bullying. Transgendered persons were included in categories protected under the *Human Rights Code*. Many bills were relatively routine – good administration, but routine. Nothing to protect the principles of the *Canada Health Act*. Noth-

ing much to help labour. Much of the agenda renamed constituencies or declared the Nova Scotia tartan to be "official." The last year of legislation was a manifestation of the momentum the government had around the idea of being "incremental."

Province House

12

Putting Neighbourhoods at Risk

A s former US Speaker of the House, Tip O'Neill, observed, "all politics is local." I don't take that as a fundamental principle, but it does get at something real. People often more easily understand an issue that affects their day-to-day lives. What their neighbourhood looks like is one of those issues.

Halifax is a wonderful city, but it has been abused by a combination of shortsightedness at city hall plus a rapacious land development industry. It is the responsibility of the province to oversee all municipalities, but this rarely happens. Very little effective oversight happened on our watch; indeed quite the opposite. The result is going to be the ruination of most of our comfortable residential and mixed-use neighbourhoods, starting with the North End of peninsular Halifax. Dartmouth is next.

Let's step back for a moment since this requires some legal and historical context. I have enormous respect for local government. Municipalities have been assigned an important range of powers and have the potential to influence our day-to-day lives and long-term futures. They deal with water, sewage, garbage, local transportation, and, of course, overall land-use designations like residential, industrial, or commercial.

The key word is "assigned." Municipalities have no inherent powers. In fact they have no inherent (Constitutional) right to exist – hence amalgamations happen if a provincial government passes legislation. Municipalities have only those powers assigned to them by the provincial government. Whatever they want to do, municipal councils have to be able to anchor it in some statute setting out their powers. I taught Land-use Planning Law at Dalhousie University's Law School for seventeen years and regularly published legal articles on the subject. This lack of Constitutional status and the necessity of relying on specific grants of power from the province is a starting point in what had to be taught, and can lead to various complexities.

The basic way municipalities control land use is through planning and zoning. Our *Municipal Government Act*[1] (and for Halifax Regional Municipality, its *Charter*[2]) encourages municipalities to go through a public process of deciding what their entire local area ought to be and what it hopes to accomplish in the future, and to write it down in the Municipal Planning Strategy (MPS). At the same time, they are asked to adopt zoning designations that are consistent with the MPS. Zoning tells an owner what they can and cannot do with their land. A proposed use that is allowed by the existing zoning is often called an 'as-of-right' development.

So far, pretty clear. Of course zoning has become much more than a simple type-of-use control instrument. Zoning now typically deals with percentage of lot cover, height of buildings, number of buildings, setbacks from lot lines, and much more. So, although zoning has become more sophisticated over time, it is still regarded as somewhat inflexible – with limited ability to respond to special circumstances or to respond to innovative proposals. To allow councils to consider such proposals, legislation typically includes some measure of flexibility. One example is rules around subdivisions: they allow consideration of multiple lots at the same time. Another example is Development Agreements (DAs). DAs are the classic flexibility tool for municipalities faced with a proposal for departure from what the applicable zoning would allow as-of-right.

A DA is like a contract between the municipality and the landowner. It allows the zoning restrictions to be lifted from some piece of land. In exchange for this special treatment, land use planners say there should be some public benefit, although the controlling legislation here in Nova Scotia has not been clear about the nature and extent of that public benefit.

DAs have been available in Nova Scotia for many decades. And, they have been successful. As with all land use powers of local government, the rules around DAs are set out in provincial legislation. The statute requires that the MPS identify where a DA may be applied for; that the MPS indentify what detailed rules apply; that there be a public hearing before a DA is signed; that any DA be recorded at the Registry of Deeds so it binds future owners of the land; and that an appeal to the Utility and Review Board (UARB) is available whether the DA is granted or refused. Most major projects, especially in Metro, have come forward as applications for a DA.

There is a long-running history of contention around major development proposals in Halifax. The ugly, concrete 33-storey Fenwick Tower apartment building in the south end of Halifax, an intrusive eyesore from pretty well any vantage point, went up in the 1960s along with several other developments all of which had the effect of pushing the city to write comprehensive land use planning strategies.

Fenwick Tower in Halifax's south end.

Scotia Square was another example. It involved street closures, demolition of a residential neighbourhood adjacent to the downtown, and creation of a big office (two 16-storey towers) and retail complex, which put huge stress on other existing downtown enterprises. The Royal Bank (13 storeys) and Bank of Montreal (16 storeys) both were allowed as was local developer Ralph Medjuck with the Centennial Properties office building (12 storeys). Ultimately, the issues came to be seen as a mix of the desirability of continued development in the downtown, along with preservation of the traditional low-rise character of Halifax, especially through its heritage buildings, plus the specific concern over views from Citadel Hill. A somewhat reform-minded city council adopted a "view planes by-law" in 1974[3] and subsequently a comprehensive official plan, predecessor to the MPS and then called the Municipal Development Plan, was adopted in 1978.

So things stood for forty years until HRM by Design. Anyone even remotely familiar with land use issues in Nova Scotia will doubt that last statement. Of course a great deal did go on during the intervening forty years. The accuracy of my statement relates primarily to the legal framework for local governments, as set by the Province. The basic tools (an official plan, a zoning by-law, and some flexibility devices, all bound up with significant public participation) remained basically the same for forty years even with the evolution of the original *Planning Act* into the *Municipal Government Act* in 1998.

A lot did happen both on the ground and in terms of public debate. Two big industrial parks were developed, one in Burnside in north Dartmouth, and the other in Bayers Lake to the west of Halifax along Highway 102. Both of these included office and commercial space that very effectively competed with the downtowns, thus undermining what continued to be a stated objective of support for a vibrant Central Business District (CBD).

Sprawl, through big and intensive housing developments became a fact of life, putting stress on the roads system along with other hard infrastructure such as water and sewer lines as well as soft infrastructure such as schools, parks, and libraries. In the Halifax CBD and elsewhere, developers continued to come forward with proposals for intensive buildings that ran up against the desires of residents in their neighbourhoods. Dalhousie's sports centre Dalplex was one example. Others were the Quinpool Centre (a much more intensive proposal than what was built) for the former Roman Catholic Episcopal Corporation monastery and orphanage lands. MT&T, the predecessor of Bell Aliant, built the 22-storey office tower at the foot of Spring Garden Road. Two more bank towers went up on Barrington Street. The Purdy's Wharf office buildings were erected. Condo towers were built along Summer Street adjacent to the Public Gardens, which involved the demolition of a registered heritage building.

Large-scale amalgamations were imposed for both the Sydney area and in Halifax in 1995.[4] The preceding year I had been elected to what turned out to be the last City of Halifax council, and then was elected to the first council of the Halifax Regional Municipality (HRM), which officially took power in 1996. Thus, I had a close-up view of the local government process at work to supplement my work as a lawyer taking land use cases to the UARB and the courts.

Every one of those development proposals was controversial. But there was room in the system for active public debate and formal involvement. The most intense fights happened over downtown Halifax projects. The city controlled development there through a restrictive as-of-right height limit, along with policies to favour maintaining views from Citadel Hill, views down streets to Halifax Harbour, compatibility with existing heritage buildings, maintaining street grid, compatibility of scale, keeping shadows off public open space, etc. The height limit was forty feet, and twenty-five feet along the harbour. Since most proposals were for buildings in excess of that, developers had to apply for a DA, making CBD land development proposals matters for public input. Several tough fights took place, especially for land adjacent to or near Citadel Hill, or impacting the view or nearby smaller buildings: the Cambridge Suites lands proposal, the Homburg Building, the Midtown Tavern land proposal, and the so-called 'Twisted Sisters" proposal are all examples.

The development community started to complain about delays in proceeding with their projects, and

Artist's rendering of the proposed "Twisted Sisters" (a.k.a. Skye Halifax) project (not built).

focused especially on residents' appeals to the UARB. In fact, there was no evidence that our process is any more time consuming than anywhere else. Nine of the ten provinces have provincial planning appeal boards to oversee municipal land use decisions, and ours is the most restrictive as to how hard it is to take or to win an appeal (it is not easy to qualify as an appellant, plus the statute in effect presumes that whatever decision a municipal council made was correct and puts a heavy burden of proof on any appellant). Nevertheless, the PC government was prevailed upon to impose time limits on the processing of appeals, and the UARB was given a power to impose some limited costs against an appellant.[5]

In the meantime, HRM was struggling with its official vision for the future of overall development. In 2006 a new Regional Plan was adopted. This plan was characterized by its recognition of the negative impacts of sprawl. It called for more development in what was termed the Regional Centre Area: the Halifax Peninsula plus Dartmouth inside the Circumferential Highway. That target area was to have more residential growth and more office space. We know now that this has not happened. Targets for growth in the Regional Centre have not been met, not by a long shot.[6] Mostly this has been because HRM Council has ignored the stated objective of restricting sprawl and has enthusiastically approved a huge number of residential and commercial buildings outside the central area. This is obvious to anyone driving into Metro: growth in the suburbs has been enormous. But in 2006, a planning approach to dealing with the HRM central area came forward, known as HRM By Design.

It is crucial to note that HRM By Design was originally to deal with all of the Regional Centre area. Initial studies started to look at the various components, the CBDs of both Halifax and Dartmouth, and the various residential areas of R-1[7] and R-2[8] housing that predominate around those CBDs. A Toronto design and planning consulting company, the Office for Urbanism, was brought in to assist HRM staff. HRM staff were led by planners Andy Fillmore and Jennifer Keesmaat (now the Chief Planner for Toronto) who came from Ontario. They led public consultations and started to look at the residential neighbourhoods. One day I was asked to take Fillmore and Keesmaat for a walking tour around my neighbourhood so as to show them its features and to make suggestions as to what was needed.

Very quickly, though, the idea of looking at the whole of the central HRM area was abandoned. HRM By Design came to focus exclusively on the Halifax CBD, and references to HRM By Design came to mean only the questions associated with development there. So the term was used and so the public came to understand it. Revised planning for the residential neighbourhoods was put off for another day. This was a very bad idea. Planning works best when it looks at the same time at larger areas that are connected. In carving out the Halifax CBD, HRM was showing itself to be responsive mostly to the calls and noise of the development community rather than to the community at large. Developers saw this as an opportunity to change the way planning happened in the CBD. And my colleagues latched onto this as a great chance to show that the Nova Scotia NDP under Darrell Dexter was not anti-business.

What HRM proposed to the Province was this: change the land use planning laws for the HRM central area so that most development would take place as-of-right, though subject to review by a Design Review Committee which would apply standards set by Council; any appeal would be to Council, and could be taken only by the developer if turned down or by landowners in the immediate area. There would be no public hearings for the individual proposals as they came forward, nor would there be any appeals available to the UARB. This request came forward at the same time as HRM Council was considering changing the as-of-right allowable heights for the CBD from the prevailing 25 and 40 feet to a patchwork ranging from six storeys to twenty-two storeys – essentially a shift to a preference for high-rises. Thus, supporting the legislation meant supporting both a reduction in public participation in the land use process and also supporting high-rises as the general mode for the CBD.

The PCs brought in two bills, 179[9] and 181[10] in the fall session of 2008, to amend the HRM *Charter*. Initially, the legislation was to apply to the full HRM central area, but the government changed it so that it would apply only to the Halifax CBD. As a supporter of full public participation in land use matters, I opposed the idea of our caucus voting for the bills. At caucus, Maureen MacDonald said she certainly would not want this type of land use laws to be applicable in her constituency (Needham, which is North End Halifax). But she did see that there was a lot of demand for streamlining the development process in the CBD.

Our party membership, however, did not see it that way. Many Halifax NDP members supported the preservation of small-scale buildings, especially the protection of heritage buildings, and saw the new as-of-right heights as incompatible with this. But Darrell signaled that he wanted to support the bill. In the end, I spoke and voted against Bill 181, the only member of our caucus to do so.[11]

Fast forward to 2012. HRM again came to the Province with a request for a change to its governing legislation. This time it wanted to expand the ambit of what had been in Bill 181, which was limited to the Halifax CBD, to the whole of HRM. This became a fascinating story and was no longer a mere signal of not being anti-business – by this time the NDP government had made itself into the best friend business had for quite some years. In line with a scramble to obtain jobs at any price (Daewoo, the Irving Shipyard, Michelin, the Stern Group, Bowater, etc.), Darrell was prepared to follow HRM Council in its thralldom to developers – yet again.

The issue was known as "density bonusing." Density bonusing means just what is available through a DA: greater height than would otherwise be allowable in exchange for some public benefit. It had been a feature of Bill 181, although with all the public participation rights stripped away. HRM had asked the Department of Municipal Affairs at least twice to be allowed to extend Bill 181 to the whole of HRM. But the Minister, John MacDonell, had consulted me each time and HRM was told no, either at the Department level or after discussion by our internal Legislation Committee. This time, they had figured out that the way to get what they wanted was to bypass the Minister and deal directly with the Premier. Darrell was very amenable.

HRM started a campaign to find support. It made a presentation to caucus. It held talks with the Department of Community Services (DCS). The stated rationale employed now was that the density bonusing tool would facilitate negotiating for affordable housing (hence the connection to DCS), something the province wanted to promote.

As a former Ministerial Assistant in DCS for housing issues I certainly supported ways to facilitate affordable housing. So what was wrong here?

First, the whole mechanism still had at its core the removal of public participation, and so remained anti-democratic. That had not gone away. Next, a viable alternative did exist, the DA. I told the ministers and my colleagues a number of times that if development agreements needed to be strengthened we should do that instead. Make it clear in the legislation that HRM is obligated to negotiate for a public benefit in exchange for any DA. Worst of all, the affordable housing benefit was amorphous and discretionary. Standards for what constituted affordable housing were not being defined, and if they were to be tied to income, which would make sense, there was no monitoring or enforcement power. And under HRM's proposal, a density bonus could be given to a developer in exchange for a piece of public art outside the building. Public art is great, but it is not affordable housing. Finally, just as with Bill 181 and HRM By Design for the CBD, the stage was being set to facilitate tall towers, especially in the North End.

North End Halifax is mostly a low-rise area of mixed uses: residential (gems like the Hydrostone district), commercial (along Gottingen St or Agricola St), and industrial (the Oland Brewery, the Shipyards). To some extent it has been blighted. Many businesses and services fled Gottingen St (there being no supermarket or bank). Much of the housing stock was allowed to fall into disrepair (for example in the Creighton-Gerrish area). With the dismantling of Africville, a community was set adrift and has been slow to overcome its dislocation in the face of persistent racism. At the same time this is an area of real strengths. Community organizations are active (the North End Community Health Centre, the Ecology Action Centre, the Mi'kmaq Friendship Centre, Stepping Stone, Dalhousie Legal Aid, The Bus Stop Theatre, etc.) There is significant gentrification, resulting in some renewal of the housing stock. Arts and culture are thriving. There are new cafes and restaurants. Being on the peninsula and adjacent to the downtown, the generally affordable housing in the area has allowed a diverse mix of persons the chance to live here.

Shops in Halifax's Hydrostone district.

Having dealt with the Central Business District (CBD), HRM was turning its attention to the rest of the Regional Centre area, but it was doing this in a very particular and peculiar way, a way designed to maximize benefits for developers and not to put the local residential communities first. What Council, led by its staff, had decided to do was to designate some eleven special, "growth corridors that are experiencing development pressures and need to be dealt with urgently."

Not in my opinion. In a memo to caucus on November 22, 2012, I pointed out:

> The reason HRM planning staff have been pressing for this new planning law tool, is that their vision for achieving densification in the Regional Centre area ... is through tall buildings. [...] The future of what are mainly residential areas was put on hold. This has now led to pressure to allow intense development of the commercial corridors, because the targets for population increase in the Regional Centre have not nearly been met. But there is an alternative to highrises in the corridors. This is to allow R-1 and R-2 homes to add basement and attic apartments and to build on more of their lots. Experience in other cities, especially Toronto and Vancouver, shows that the uptake is generally very good. Younger families especially

like the opportunity to have some income from their homes. But developers do not own all the individual homes; they own the commercial properties, and HRM staff have moved so as to accommodate the developers in preference to accommodating homeowners. Increasing density through concentrating on the existing residential neighbourhoods means that the look and feel of neighbourhoods is maintained. High-rises are ugly and socially isolating places to live. Why would we want to facilitate the building of an ugly and socially alienating capital city?

I see that architect Tom Emodi has recently been saying that the municipal rules around adding apartments to R-2 housing need to be changed to make it easier for owners to add units to their homes, and *Chronicle-Herald* business columnist Roger Taylor seems to agree: "If there were minor changes to zoning regulations ... the municipality could easily accommodate all of the targeted density," Emodi is quoted as saying.[12] About time *The Chronicle Herald* understood this, though the newspaper still fails to understand its relation to overall patterns of land development.

There was a blizzard of memos and meetings. It was obvious that the file was being managed out of the Premier's Office rather than the Department of Municipal Affairs. At one point, when we were down to the last day or so of the spring 2013 session, Darrell and his Chief of Staff were in the caucus room reading and editing the final bill.[13] Apart from how striking this was, the various debates at caucus were also illuminating. Maureen, who had said in 2008 that she would not want this type of planning tool in her constituency, was now a strong advocate for it. There had to be towers in the corridors, she said, because private homeowners would charge too much for their basement or attic apartments, and so this would not end up being affordable housing. Needless to say, there is absolutely no evidence for such an assertion.

In any event, developers are simply not interested in building affordable housing. This whole story was a fantasy, designed to lure the province into approving the new legal land use mechanism that would just allow HRM to ease the way for tall towers to be built with minimal opportunity for the public to object. Plus, there are ways for developers to abandon the affordable housing promise. For one, the Province is asking only for fifteen years of affordable housing, though the life expectancy of buildings is 75 to 100 years. For another, the affordable housing is secured through a mortgage. An owner could refinance, pay off the provincial mortgage and put an end to the affordable housing. Overall, this potential scam will not likely do much that is useful for anyone except the building owners.

Thus, in acquiescing to this HRM proposal we have facilitated what will be a major adverse change to the North End. There will be high-rise apartment buildings on Robie, Young, and Gottingen streets, all putting pressure on the adjacent residential areas. And all this is simply unnecessary. On Young Street the proposed maximum height is 85 m or 24 storeys. On Almon Street it is 43 m or 12 storeys. The Robie Street heights include the adjacent side streets, Demone, Russell, Macara, and Bilby at 43 m and 64 m.[14] Darrell once lived on Macara Street as a teen. He seems to have lost touch with his oft-mentioned humble origins.

And for Dartmouth, the designated corridors include portions of Portland Street and Windmill Road. There will be many more high rises to come, thanks to the "people's NDP government." Terrible canyons will be created along streets that certainly do not need them, reducing light and creating wind tunnels.

Is this judgment fair? Doesn't the Province simply facilitate the actual detailed planning by the local municipalities? Is it not primarily up to the municipal councils to make these decisions? Is that not what they are for?

We started out noting that municipalities have only those powers over land use, or indeed over anything else, that the Province chooses to grant them. Provinces control municipalities under our Constitution, to the point of being able to create, merge, or abolish them. All provincial statutes governing municipalities are full of provisions limiting what the municipalities can do. It is a part of the duty of provincial governments to take a reasonably detailed interest in what our municipal delegates are up to. Effective and democratic oversight requires this. But we really failed here. In the end, and only because I made a huge fuss, Bill 160 did include affordable housing as a required rather than just an optional bonus to be provided by developers getting any special deal.

In addition, the provincial government has the power to define affordable housing. These are improvements (which HRM neither proposed nor wanted) but the basic flaws of this new set of legal tools are still the main point. And we provided that.

Land use planning is a wonderful undertaking. But it was a blind spot for our government. There are many weaknesses in the *Municipal Government Act* and the HRM *Charter*, but at no time was there any attempt to have a thorough formal review of the legislation, though I did suggest it. Nor did we lead by providing planners for those municipalities that do not have any MPS. Adopting an official plan is optional under our laws, a great flaw. The Department of Municipal Affairs could have created a small team of planners to send to those municipalities that have pleaded poverty or have been uninterested in formal planning. Or they could have put a formal planning process in place for regions of the province, involving multiple municipalities. I also suggested this. The whole of Cape Breton would have been a good place to start.

The one time the Department of Municipal Affairs did act seriously had to do with protection of agricultural land in Kings County.[15] That was an entirely appropriate initiative and the Minister got it right, but it stands out as the one time we became involved in the necessary details of land-use planning, except for the major financial support for the Convention Centre, and for which we also rewrote policies so as to go the extra mile for the benefit of that boondoggle. And the party leadership complains that the membership failed to support them in 2013. What a surprise.

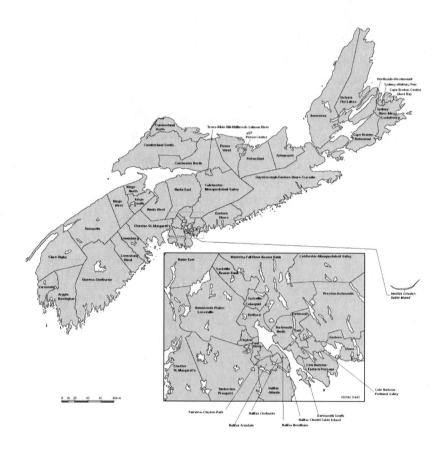

Nova Scotia's 2013 electoral boundaries

13

Electoral Boundaries

By statute, electoral boundaries are revised in Nova Scotia every ten years, the year after the regular federal census so the revision is based on reasonably current population data. The last revision had been in 2002[1] and an independent Electoral Boundaries Commission (EBC) was to be established in 2012.

The system had not always been this. For a long time the Legislature itself set the boundaries. Clearly this can quickly lead to the partisan drawing of lines and classic gerrymandering attempts. (Gerrymandering is the system in which instead of the voters choosing their representatives, the representatives choose their voters.) In 1991 it was finally agreed by all parties that an arm's length body should take charge of this crucial function. The point was to try to support the credibility of the electoral process. At the same time, some degree of political interaction is inherently necessary in that the terms of reference for the EBC are set by the Legislature.

Because I had been involved in the 2002 process, I wrote to my colleagues early on to make some suggestions about how the 2012 process should be approached.

The full Memo is available as Appendix 5. Its main points were that we should try to establish constituencies with as near as possible equal numbers of voters; that we should do so even if that meant giving up on the so-called 'protected seats;' and that we should initiate a process to promote proportional representation. The only part of this that occurred was some redrawing of the boundaries of three 'Acadian' seats, and since the results of the 2012 redistribution process will govern elections for the next decade, all of the Electoral Boundaries Commission work has to count as a major missed opportunity for the NDP.

The way to try to achieve constituencies with almost equal numbers of voters is to set a target of plus or minus 10 per cent of the average. This is the standard that mostly prevails in the country for federal ridings and in most seats in most provinces.[2] It is also the standard that the UARB has set for municipal districts in Nova Scotia. Any tolerance of a greater variation leads to vote dilution, i.e., inequalities of citizens as voters. The Supreme Court of Canada has said that it is permissible, but not required, to take into account other factors besides parity of voting power, such as geography and history. Nova Scotia has had a large shift of population to the Metro area, which over the last forty years has been consistently under-represented in the Legislature. There have been wide variations between the voting populations of some of the largest and smallest of seats.

As for proportional representation, this has been NDP policy for years, and the existing first-past-the-post system has frequently meant fewer NDP seats than the overall votes have indicated as the measure of public support. If any party should have been alert to the opportunity for voting reform it should have been the NDP. There are different systems of proportional representation, and I did not have in mind that an Electoral Boundaries Commission should adopt a particular new system, just that its mandate should include an initial examination of how such a system might work in Nova Scotia, and initiate a public debate on this issue. But this proposal found no takers.

At the Premier's Office, the electoral boundaries file seems to have been primarily the responsibility of Matt Hebb. An adherence to strict voter parity (one person, one vote – equal number of voters in each constituency) would have nudged about three or four seats to HRM, the NDP voting base. Voter parity is not what was put to caucus, however. It was pointed out that the more closely the terms of reference for the EBC relied on voter parity, the greater the number of constituencies that would have to have boundaries redrawn. There was some resistance to that at caucus, and although Matt suggested we look at a permissible variance of plus or minus 15 or 20 per cent, caucus balked and most members favoured 20 or 25 per cent. Even this proved to be highly problematic when it came to drawing the new boundary lines. And those new boundaries will govern elections for a decade.

There were two other aspects of the EBC that proved to be problematic. One was the implication in the set limit of +/- 25 per cent that there was to be no exception, not even for those constituencies that had previously been set below the 25 per cent number that prevailed for all other constituencies, to try to achieve election of persons from the Acadian and Black communities. This became a hotly contested point.

The other aspect was the composition of the Commission. Whoever had responsibility for vetting the members did not seem to do a very good job. One of the people I had suggested, the planning professor Jill Grant, did prove to be a reliable member, adhering to the terms of reference, and resigning when the others did not want to hold to them. It is often difficult to manage such things – and I am certainly not suggesting that the members ought to have been partisan to the government; that would simply undermine the credibility that an EBC must have for a democracy to function properly – but an appreciation of the principle of voter parity should have been the first qualification, along with respect for the formal terms of reference as set by the Legislature.

Instead, the EBC in its first interim report simply ignored the terms of reference and tried to reestablish the so-called 'protected' constituencies. This resulted in a prolonged process, a confrontation with the government, which correctly rejected the interim report as not fulfilling the set mandate, thus making the government the focus of the Acadian community's concerns. The terms of reference required no more than a +/- 25 per cent variance from the average population.

On behalf of the government, the Minister of Justice, Ross Landry, rejected the interim report and instructed the Commission to rewrite its interim report. This was all very public and led to allegations of improper political interference. I certainly did not see matters that way.

The 2012 ECB revised interim report[3] then did something quite peculiar as the EBC wrestled with the same problem: it recommended splitting the Yarmouth constituency so as to put part of it with the adjacent Acadian area of Argyle and the rest with the other southwest Acadian constituency of Claire. This provoked massive outrage in Yarmouth, and was dropped from the final report.[4]

Many of us had thought that the EBC would merge those two small constituencies to create one appropriately sized constituency that would then be overwhelmingly Acadian. It did not do that and the opposition of the Fédération Acadienne d'Nouvelle Écosse (FANE) might have been the reason. In a meeting I had with FANE's executive director she dismissed the merger possibility on the basis that the residents of the two areas had differing cultural traditions and spoke different variants of French. It may well be, but the result of not merging the two is some dilution of the Acadian factor in both constituencies (which continue to exist, as does Richmond) plus a promise of a law suit, which was eventually filed in June 2013. For a full year the law suit was mired in procedural wrangling, but has now been referred to the Court of Appeal for a ruling

Following the final EBC report, a special Legislature committee to focus especially on the EBC-proposed merger of most of Shelburne with Queens county held hearings in Shelburne. Representatives of the Acadian community also came to speak and said that their preferred position is that no reduction in their boundaries at all should take place, even if that put them even further at variance from the provincial average than they already were. It is very hard to see the logic of such a position.

Overall, the 2012 EBC produced mixed results for all political parties. For the NDP, we failed to secure an increase in constituencies in Metro, and two seats we held, Cape Breton Nova and Shelburne, were redrawn in ways that made holding them a serious challenge. For the Liberals, there was a reduction in seats in Cape Breton, one of their traditional strongholds, but also some potential problems with the redrawing of boundaries for Clayton Park. And for the PCs there were small changes making it harder for them to win in Truro but perhaps easier to run in Antigonish.

The main points about the whole exercise are that it was not well planned, it missed an opportunity to adhere more closely to the principle of voter parity, which is the preferred policy and would have at the same time favoured the NDP, and there was serious alienation of the Acadian community. One more on the list of missed opportunities. It was not a good basis for the election that was soon to come.

A demonstration in Halifax protesting against voter supression and urging respect for democracy.

With pioneering Canadian pacifist, feminist, and social activist, Muriel Duckworth.

14

Real Accomplishments

There were of course real accomplishments during the four-year term of the NDP government. And while many of them are more in the realm of competent general administration, others do show some adherence to a traditional NDP agenda. Even competent administration is a step forward and is not to be minimized. Yet both the public and the party membership were looking for more and different.

With some regularity, the party would issue lists of "the top twenty accomplishments" or even "the top fifty accomplishments" of our government. They were useful summaries. To some extent they were designed to inform party members and consolidate support; to some extent they gave MLAs speaking points. One of the better summations of the government's own view of its accomplishments was given in the Legislature by Maureen MacDonald, then Finance Minister, on December 5, 2012.[1] Her statement glosses over much, but does aggressively state the case. She praises, "living within our means," a key phrase for the Back-to-Balance exercise, although it omits the sheer ignorance or duplicity of having made the balanced budget promise in the first place. She emphasizes attention to the poorest in society through removal of the HST from daily necessities, improving social assistance rates, and raising the minimum wage.

Here are some examples of more or less successful struggles with tough issues.

The H1N1 Virus

One of the few real joys of our time in office was the performance of Maureen MacDonald as Health Minister. She did a wonderful job. On all occasions she was organized, calm, clear, in charge, informed, logical, and reassuring. For the H1N1 influenza epidemic all of this was necessary. We should all be extremely grateful.

The internationalization of virus diseases is a modern phenomenon, even with such precedents as the Spanish Influenza of the post-World War I era. A *New York Times* article suggests that causes and vectors for the spread of serious virus infections have to do with, "population growth, deforestation, antibiotic overuse, factory farming, live animal markets, bush meat hunting, and jet travel."[2] In fact, this is a globalization of disease. It is a phenomenon that was known prior to its arrival in Nova Scotia. The SARS outbreak had occurred in 2002-2003. Mad Cow disease was another example of how easily health problems can move around the world. Thus, pandemic preparedness was expected to be a standard feature of a province's health system. And indeed it was. Nova Scotia was the first province to have a lab-confirmed case of the H1N1 virus. When the first human Swine Flu case appeared in Nova Scotia in April 2009, plans were in place to deal with a major outbreak. The first

Health Minister Maureen MacDonald.

plan was adopted and made public in June 2007 with an updated version from January 2008.

Pandemics in the form of both bacterial (bubonic plague, cholera, typhoid, tuberculosis, diphtheria) and viral (influenza) infections have been identified and fought with varying degrees of accurate medical knowledge for well over 100 years. A serious bacterial pandemic existed from 1894 through 1918, preceding the better-known influenza pandemic during and after World War I. By 1947, the World Health Organization (WHO) had been formed and physicians had realized that annual updates in vaccines were needed because of ongoing mutations of the bacterial or viral agents. In 1957 the H2N2 virus originated in China, spreading overland and causing some 2 million deaths. In 1968 the H3N2 outbreak causing almost one million deaths. In 2003 SARS (Severe Acute Respiratory Syndrome) was a major concern in Canada. Later that year 30 million chickens were slaughtered in Holland to contain an outbreak of H7N7. So by the time H1N1 hit, there was every reason to have expected such an occurrence.

As it happened, the Auditor General had done a special review of pandemic preparedness in the spring of 2009 and made it public in July. In his typical blunt manner the Auditor General pointed out that:

> "There is no entity in place that can exercise joint executive leadership to provide overall command and coordination of government's pandemic response efforts in a severe pandemic situation. [...] We believe the Emergency Management Office ... is the logical agency to ensure both government and non-government entities have plans to deal with a pandemic emergency. Adequate emergency plans are necessary to ensure critical services such as power, water, snow clearing, policing and fire response continue during a time when absenteeism may be high."[3] (p. 3)

In other words, the Department of Health was treating an illness that spread rapidly as a pure medical matter, whereas there were other, more general consequences. It was a very good point, and was accepted by the government without reservation.

As the flu spread, a campaign to vaccinate as much of the general population as possible was put into place. As this was rolled out, Maureen was subject to non-stop questioning in the House. How many people are in Intensive Care Units (ICU)? Have there been more deaths? Why are there delays in obtaining the vaccine? How many health personnel are off work, ill? Who are priority patients? Why were prisoners vaccinated so quickly? Are there risks associated with vaccination itself? For all of these Maureen was an inspiration. She was on top of the material. She was calm and reassuring. She did not evade. She was clear.

Collaborative Emergency Centres

The creation of collaborative emergency centres had some virtues, but represented a backing away from a specific election promise to keep rural emergency departments open, and diverged from what could have been a more community-based model, namely health clinics. As usual, there is a history.

In recent years, the PCs had commissioned a wide-ranging review of the province's health system, the so-called "Corpus Sanchez Report" (named after the consultancy company that prepared it) the full title of which is "Changing Nova Scotia's Healthcare System: Creating Sustainability Through Transformation."[4] In a response to the report sent to the NDP caucus, the Canadian Union of Public Employees (CUPE) identified an overwhelming concern with finances: "The smokescreen in the report is, 'improving the overall health of Nova Scotians.' The real goal of the report is "financial sustainability." Integration and consolidation of services, as one of their three broad goals, is a clear example of this." In health matters, concern over money is so tightly bound up with concern over quality and effectiveness that it is often hard to disentangle.

Corpus Sanchez (2007) identified a need for a "rural health strategy" to, "define a baseline set of services that should be available as close to home as possible, to reduce the further erosion of programs and services in rural Nova Scotia" (p. 27). With about 50 per cent of the provincial population residing in rural areas (including small towns) the availability of effective services is crucial. Corpus Sanchez (2007) noted, "the special case of small community emergency departments," and summed up: "With the possible exception of obstetrics, Emergency Departments (EDs) are considered the most defining element of a local hospital by the population it serves. From the public's perspective, the availability of a local emergency department around the clock represents not just medical services, but a degree of comfort that local help is available. Unfortunately, while Nova Scotians maintain their emotional ties to EDs in their local hospitals, it is not because EDs are used for their stated purpose. Instead, as elsewhere in Canada and beyond, EDs are used as substitutes for primary healthcare clinics and doctors' offices." (p. 37)

This gets at the heart of the matter. Darrell's choice to promise keeping rural Emergency Rooms (ERs, a.k.a., EDs) open was contrary to the evidence of what was needed. To get out of the promise, our government commissioned a report by Dr. John Ross, an ER specialist. Dr. Ross suggested creating collaborative emergency centres in his report, "The Patient Journey through Emergency Care in Nova Scotia."[5] His recommendations were adopted by our government in December 2010 in the "Better Care Sooner"[6] document.

What was offered were ERs staffed by doctors from 8:00 am to 10:00 pm, with nurses on-site overnight. Undoubtedly this makes a lot of sense, especially when combined with the 811 nurse phone line for health advice, and the ability of the overnight nurses to access advice from physicians, including specialists in Halifax. This "collaborative emergency centre" model is being adopted by some other provinces, and to that extent it has been something of a success, even though the detailed breakdown of open hours shows that unavailability of staff remains a problem.

Public Sector Negotiations

One of the major problems for the Bob Rae government was its inability to manage negotiations with public sector workers in a time of restraint. This led to a serious erosion of support by the many thousands of public sector workers who had tended to vote NDP, along with their unions, which had donated to the party. It was a classic clash between a government determined to deal with deficits brought on by a recession through expenditure reductions, and unions not interested in wage concessions or unpaid days off.[7]

Faced with the stark reality of the province's fiscal constraints, our government looked to the public sector wage package as a place to save money. The sensible decision was made not to attempt to roll back compensation or to legislate freezes. Negotiations were successful in establishing a two-year (2010-2012) pattern of 1 per cent and 1 per cent increases. This was acceptable to all unions involved. It had the virtue of having been negotiated, of providing employees with some offset for inflation, and not straining the province's ability to pay.

As a way to help get the province through the recession years, that round of negotiations has to be counted as a success. Recently, much has been said criticizing staff in the Premier's Office who had previously worked at the NSGEU (Nova Scotia Government and General Employees Union) as being involved in labour negotiations. The criticism comes from Graham Steele's book *What I Learned About Politics*[8] but has been taken up by Bill Black in *The Chronicle Herald* newspaper as illustrating the undue influence of unions on an NDP government.[9] If only.

Unions are often progressive organizations with sensible policies to advance on important social issues. Listening to unions (though not being directed by them – that is simply a myth) should be expected of an NDP government. But if anyone had outstanding influence over the Dexter government it was big business, not unions.

The criticism is focused on the results of the next round of negotiations (2012–2015), which was resolved through arbitration with a government offer of 5.1 per cent over three years as a starting point. The criticism is overblown. It is certainly true that having Shawn Fuller, who came from the NSGEU to the Premier's Office where he was the lead in negotiations, and who then returned to the NSGEU after the government's defeat, can be seen as problematic. The problem is one of perception, more than reality. More serious is the fact that Graham's account of the episode is not entierly accurate. What caucus agreed was that everything should be done to settle the negotiations, and most consented to legislation if all else failed. No one else seems to think that a caucus decision was overturned by staff. As a basis for resignation from Cabinet, the episode is not persuasive; indeed it is very puzzling.

First Contract Arbitration

NSGEU President Joan Jessome

First contract arbitration was the most significant legislative measure supportive of organized labour brought in by the government. Other useful steps included a change in rules about what constitutes a union member in good standing, wider powers for arbitrators including for civil service matters, and a stronger preamble to the *Trade Union Act*. The first contract arbitration change was relatively trivial, though you would not know that from the chorus of business-led denunciation. All our bill did was bring Nova Scotia labour laws in line with the prevailing model elsewhere in Canada. Where a workplace has been unionized, and the employer and the union are not making progress towards setting the terms of the first collective agreement, either of the parties may move the process to binding arbitration. This reflects the known reality that it is often the first collective agreement that is hardest to establish. Frequently this is due to lingering employer resentment at having to deal with a union at all. After there is experience of negotiations, and then of administering a collective agreement, the unease tends to go away. Hence the need for binding arbitration to put in place a first collective agreement. That was it. Nothing much. But the whining went on endlessly. In my view, this illustrated how off-base the party leadership's view was, that by being business-friendly, businesses would either support the government wholeheartedly or be very moderate in its criticisms.

United Labour Board

We merged several labour relations boards into one, and had the good sense to appoint Douglas Ruck as its chair. Doug Ruck is a smart, experienced, gracious lawyer from Nova Scotia's Black community, who has been working for years in Ontario. Bringing him home was a very good idea. He is doing a good job, just as he did years ago as chair of the Labour Standards Tribunal, one of the entities now merged into the new Labour Board.

Douglas Ruck

EGSPA Updates

The *Environmental Goals and Sustainability Act* (EGSPA),[10] brought in by the Tories in 2007 and passed with all-party support, sets out goals but is essentially aspirational. It provides a framework for policy analysis so specific sustainability measures can then be further framed in law. It was a very good initiative of the PCs. After its first five years we updated it.

EGSPA can be critiqued as being mostly without specific regulatory rules. And while it is true that it is more of a policy document, and governments still have to choose which specific implementation tool to use (regulations; incentives; research and development; supports; market-based mechanisms), its mere existence is a good thing. It helps benchmark what is on the agenda. It helps to hold governments accountable.

The 2012 changes included adding goals with respect to local food. It included specifics about sulphur dioxide, nitrogen oxide, and mercury emissions. It prompted development of a "Greener Economy" strategy. And there was more. And again, even though the updates can be critiqued, EGSPA is a serious accomplishment.

Bought Land

One of the aspirational goals set out in EGSPA is to increase protected area to 12 per cent of the province's landmass. We changed the goal to be *at least* 12 per cent. This goal has been on the record as an international standard since the Rio Declaration of 1992.[11] Nova Scotia had been somewhat slow in moving towards this. We did have a head-start in having two large national parks, Cape Breton Highlands and Kejimkujik, which total about 2 per cent of the province. Unlike many of the other provinces, in which a majority of the land is owned by the provincial government, in Nova Scotia only some 23 per cent is publicly owned. This implied setting aside a lot of the province's landholdings to reach the 12 per cent goal. But it has happened. Indeed, it has even been slightly exceeded. This occurred through land purchases that were part of the supports offered to the failing or struggling pulp and paper mills.

BUY BACK THE MERSEY!

Now that they have closed the Liverpool mill, current Bowater-Mersey owners Resolute Forest Products of Quebec, Nova Scotia's single largest private land owner, wants to sell their entire 220,000 hectares of forest lands! But to whom? To foreign interests who will clearcut ruthlessly and then chop up the remains for the highest bidders? No way!! Nova Scotians are rallying - these lands are our birthright! For a hundred and fifty years large corporations have made money off our forest. Now suddenly with pulp prices down, they are headed for greener pastures. Well, their misfortune can be our gain. With grit and determination we can take back what was always ours. Let's BUY BACK THE MERSEY!

PROTECT YOUR BIRTHRIGHT!

Greener Energy

There is a simple line of thought that should have driven policy on energy: burning carbon results in emissions that cause global climate change. Climate Change is a destabilizing and potentially highly dangerous phenomenon. It is a pressing issue. We can and must do something about it.

Energy use in Nova Scotia is about equally divided between electricity generation, transportation, and the operation of buildings, including their heating and cooling. Thus, policy initiatives towards de-carbonization should deal with all of these. In reality, most of the government efforts have been directed at the electricity sector.

To some extent this is understandable. Transportation is a matter that is mostly about type of vehicle and thus is something for "Detroit" to deal with, and regulation is probably better handled at the national or international level, although there are aspects that can come under local control such as investing in public transit and design of cities to promote alternatives to motor vehicles. We did not do much about transportation. As for buildings and manufacturing processes, much of the conservation efforts are driven by private sector attempts to control their energy costs. Still, serious improvements to the energy aspects of the Building Code would have been helpful. Some have been put in place, but not nearly enough. And, of course, we did nothing about introducing carbon taxes. Indeed, the universal elimination of provincial sales tax from home heating has been widely seen as a retrograde measure in terms of any inducement towards energy efficiency. It would have been possible to structure the measure to be both an affordability item and an energy-savings item, but that was not the choice made. So, the record is mixed.

However, in terms of electricity generation, there were significant progressive steps. We increased the target for percentage of electricity to be generated by renewables from 25 per cent by 2015 to 40 per cent by 2020. We encouraged the development of wind energy through the Community Feed-In Tariffs (COMFIT). We advanced research into the potential for tidal power, including by issuing a Marine Renewable Energy Strategy.[12] Bioenergy is being investigated at the Innovacorp dem-

Wind turbines on Dalhousie Mountain in Pictou County, Nova Scotia.

onstration facility in Liverpool. Greenhouse gas (GHG) emissions limits were imposed on Nova Scotia Power. An agreement was reached with Nalcor (the Newfoundland and Labrador electricity utility) for purchase of hydro-electricity (the Maritime Link to access Muskrat Falls). Each of these initiatives can be critiqued (some like biomass, are highly dubious), but overall the trend was in the right direction.

Capital Spending

Although it increased the public debt, significant spending on capital projects helped the province to get through the recession. This was very important. What is more, for some of that spending, we had fifty-cent dollars. This means that the federal government was cost-sharing the projects. The feds were also looking to finance capital projects, and were looking for what quickly became known as "shovel-ready projects." The global fiscal crisis was seen as so serious a matter that immediate government spending was promoted. We took the opportunity to put improvements into all publicly owned housing. Repairs were made and insulation was added to houses. This was a major preoccupation of the Housing Commission for at least two years.

We introduced the public announcement of an annual capital plan. This sets out the intentions and past performance for capital spending.

Historically, the provincial government spends about $400 million per year on capital projects. This is for buildings (mostly schools, but also significantly, for health), for highways including bridges, for vehicles and other equipment, for information technology, and for land. Over the five fiscal years 2009-2010 through 2013-2014 we spent $3.275 billion on capital projects. Against the historical background of normal yearly capital spending, this was an additional $1.275 billion over five years to help the province weather the recession.[13]

Capital spending by governments is an important public policy tool. And while I was not happy with some specific projects, I thoroughly approved of this step. In lean years governments have to step in.

Five-year Paving Schedule

A longtime matter involving allegations of patronage or political interference (more paving done in constituencies held by government MLAs) was addressed by the publication of a "5-Year Highway Improvement Plan." Bill Estabrooks, as Minister of Transportation, put out this document in an effort to be transparent, and to assist construction companies in their planning. Criteria for getting on the priority list were set out, and because there was a five-year plan, residents could know what was coming in their area.

Although the Liberals sold the asphalt paving equipment we purchased as a way to improve competitive bidding for jobs, they have kept the 5-Year Plan. Criteria are traffic volume, safety studies, collision statistics, road condition (cracking and other deterioration), and the presence of nearby development. It remains a matter for judgment as to what amounts are put into the various categories of roads (e.g., twinning a 100-series highway at $3 million per km or repaving a secondary road at $300 thousand per km.) And while it is, of course, possible to manipulate any system, this published plan does offer some objectivity and transparency, something that had been absent from the department's approach previously.

Schools Closure Process

The potential closure of any school is a fraught matter. Given the shift of population away from rural areas, and also the overall fall in number of births, school boards have been faced with difficult choices. The province sets the legal framework for the school boards to approach this question. Since the high water of the baby boom, many schools have been closed. Sometimes this involves consolidation, with a new school being built [e.g., in Halifax where the two high schools, Queen Elizabeth High School (QEHS) and Saint Patrick's High School, were closed and merged in a new structure as Citadel High School.] Sometimes it means busing students to another school, as was proposed for the elementary schools in River John, Maitland, and Wentworth by the Chignecto Central School Board. There is always resistance. And often for good reason. In larger communities, small neighbourhood schools have many virtues. And in smaller communities, the presence of a school is an attraction to families with children – and it functions as a community centre.

Politically, the provincial level is often seen as responsible for school closures. Partly this is because the province sets the overall budgets; partly it is because the province sets the rules.

In 2010 we adjusted the rules so as to require school boards identifying schools for review to prepare a report, which has to be made public. The board must then strike a study committee to review and respond to a closure proposal. The study committee's report must also be made public. Then a public hearing must be held. The whole point was to try to make the process open and extended.

Citadel High School in Halifax.

In the context of changes in funding for the school boards, an improved process for assessing schools for closure – however necessary – did not help the government. Indeed, school closures remained a big irritant throughout the province.

George's Bank / Uranium Mining

During our term in office, one ban and one moratorium were enacted. In 2009 (Bill 39) we prohibited the exploration for or mining of uranium. This had been a long time in coming. There is no clear indication that there are commercially exploitable amounts of uranium in Nova Scotia, although there had been sporadic exploration prior to 1976, and then more intense exploration between 1976 and 1982.[14] Kidd Creek Mines Ltd. explored in Hants County, and seemed to be serious about moving to the next stage, bulk sampling. This occasioned a large negative public reaction.[15] The fuss was such that the provincial government imposed a moratorium and then appointed a commissioner, Robert McCleave (a former Tory MP and a provincial judge) to examine the issue. His hearings became a mess. Instead of quietly solving a problem, the commission of inquiry process simply stirred up more negative publicity. Mr. Mc-Cleave was apparently under a great deal of personal strain and seemed to suffer a nervous collapse during the hearing process, abusing a *Toronto Star* reporter and others along the way. After a long pause, his report was issued in 1985 and recommended a five-year continuation of the moratorium and further public review before any lifting of it.[16] When the moratorium expired it was treated as though still in effect for the two decades until we brought in a legislated ban.

The uranium mining ban was followed by Bill 82 in 2010, a moratorium on exploration for oil and gas on George's Bank. The moratorium is to last until 2022. This was a popular step. Fishing on the George's Bank is very productive, and the fishing community in the south-west of the province had been concerned for some time about the possibility of damage to the grounds if there were ever a hydrocarbon spill.

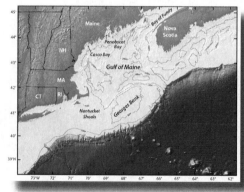

Pesticides Regulation

In 2010 (Bill 61) we brought in a framework for the regulation of non-essential use of pesticides. This too had been a long time in coming. The 1994–1995 *Environment Act*[17] mentioned pesticides as something requiring regulation, but the extent of action had been to license sprayers and limit spraying times according to wind conditions. This is very far from the reduction or elimination of the cosmetic use of pesticides. (Their use in forestry and agriculture is a different matter, though one also requiring more scrutiny and regulation.)

The legal jurisdiction with respect to pesticides is shared among the three levels of government. The federal government regulates what pesticides may be used in Canada at all. The provincial and municipal governments then deal with matters such as sale, licensing, application, and notice. Municipal governments in Nova Scotia started out by being reluctant to deal with pesticide use. When, in 1998, a specific power to deal with them was being added to the *Municipal Government Act*, representatives of the Union of Nova Scotia Municipalities (UNSM) said they did not really want to get involved in the debates that would ensue. HRM, having been pushed by residents, was prepared, and subsequently did adopt a by-law. The *Municipal Government Act* and a Supreme Court of Canada decision[18] made it clear that municipalities may regulate cosmetic pesticide use, and indeed may go beyond provincial rues as to stringency. In recent years, some municipalities outside HRM have adopted regulatory by-laws, while HRM has considered stepping away from this responsibility.

What is desirable is that there be some uniformity of rules, at least as a base. Hence the importance of provincial legislation. Our bill unfortunately exempted golf courses, and said nothing about advance notice of spraying through the placing of signage. But it was nonetheless a step forward.

Arts Nova Scotia

There was at least some acknowledgement of the significant place of arts and culture in the province by the re-establishment of an arms-length arts council in 2011. The original had been summarily eliminated by the Tories in 2002, to the extensive dismay of the arts and culture community around the province.

The Nova Scotia Arts Council had been established in 1996 so as to deliver funding to organizations and projects on a peer-reviewed basis. The idea, based on the sort of principles that tend to prevail in research grants for academic undertakings, makes a lot of sense. Not least because it tends to remove politicians from the process of arts funding. Governments would still set financial envelopes but allocation of grants would be by peer committees. The system had worked rather well, having the virtues of independence and transparency. But with no stated rationale beyond the assertion that, "the government is restructuring the way arts and culture investments are made," the Arts Council was eliminated.

Re-establishing an Arts Council was a good step, though the arts and culture community has a wider agenda, including its support for NSCAD and a wish to see some set percentage of the provincial budget assigned to its support. While canvassing I regularly met at the door with people concerned with the arts and culture sector. They are close observers of the political scene, and a very productive and talented segment of Nova Scotia's knowledge-workers.

Opposition leader, Darrell Dexter, addresses the "Save Our Arts Council" rally on April 18, 2002 on the steps of the Legislature in Halifax. Dexter promised that the re-establishment of an arm's-length arts council was only, "one election day away."

15

A Taste of Bitterness: Internal Dissent

As the party entered its third year in power, many long time NDP members became agitated. Resignations started. Complaints were common. Where were serious anti-poverty measures? Why had we adopted the tax policies of the Tories? Why were we not being clear with respect to fracking? Why were fish farms being approved? Why the support for the Convention Centre? Pick an issue, and the government had its critics. And the critics were especially sharp from inside the party. Cliff White, a long-time activist (Ecology Action Centre, Council of Canadians) resigned. Donna Parker, a long-time Halifax Chebucto volunteer, and latterly my constituency assistant, resigned. Later on Margie MacDonald a NDP stalwart and executive assistant to the Minister of Community Services, reduced her monetary contributions to the party to a minimum. At some point "used to be NDP" buttons were printed and worn. Mary MacLachlan (an art history professor at NSCAD) wrote a critical letter because of the government's position on NSCAD. Leonard Preyra's constituency executive members, David and Jodi Asbell-Clark, resigned.

In fact, well before 2012 the caucus itself had become uneasy. At various meetings starting in early 2010 caucus members identified two main problems; one was a lack of wider involvement for caucus in decision-making, and the other was insufficient emphasis on traditional NDP policies. "We are not part of a team; we are just on the bench," said Jim Boudreau (MLA for Guysborough) at a March 2010 discussion of the budget.

Gary Burrill noted that the distressing cynicism about all politicians that had surfaced during the Expenses Scandal over the previous few months made it all the more important that the NDP show itself as different. It was a tough situation. Any government faces a wide range of difficult issues and it is easy to be distracted and swamped. The reaction of some Cabinet members was a mixture of clichés ("We are family"), criticism ("You need a thicker skin. It's not a cakewalk. If you can't take it, maybe you're in the wrong business"), and reassurance ("We are defining ourselves. We are moving ahead in a limited way. If Nova Scotia had a Liberal or PC government you would see a major attack on the public sector. We do have a different set of values.")

A group of about ten backbench MLAs began meeting in the caucus room to talk amongst ourselves. This made the Premier's Office nervous. Staffers were sent to monitor the talks. Conversation initially focused on anti-poverty issues. But requests for data to help the discussions were ignored or were slow to be answered. The group moved out of the caucus office for its meetings, then held them without staff being present. There was acknowledgement that better communication internally was desirable. Darrell held some stilted meetings with backbenchers that accomplished little. Caucus started to be given "Issues Summaries" that previously had circulated only to Cabinet. But all of this did little to deal with the core problems.

In the summer of 2011 three of the MLAs (not including me) wrote to Darrell to again urge some change in direction. I have these letters. The authors wish to remain anonymous; however, here are some extracts: **MLA "A"** wrote: "There are two years left in this mandate. We have the time to come up with a distinct and unique NDP initiative, which will be a beacon to rally the grassroots troops and energize those of us who need to see the advancement of the NDP principle of greater social equality. To date, our initiative has been to balance the budget. This will not be enough to get us re-elected." **MLA "B"** wrote: "We have indeed honoured our careful election commitments by making a point of ticking them off one-by-one. But despite our central principles ... social justice issues and poverty concerns appear to have been considered only after considerable backbench effort. In my view, our business-focus and our careful incremental approach are helping traditional foes ... while our neglect of a social justice agenda ... discourages our traditional political base." **MLA "C"** wrote: "Speaking for myself, I find our present mode of operation, in which we are constantly called on to defend various expenditure restraints, etc., simply not adequately worthy. This malaise of morale is much in evidence amongst party activists, and more in evidence in our caucus than [the Premier] may be aware. The undertow force in our situation is the unique way in which collective negativity functions in Nova Scotian political culture. [Voters are] poised to say 'See, we told you; those guys are no good either.' This deadly cultural propensity to the negative is not very amenable to incrementalism. Small measures, with scattered focus, are not capable to re-direct it."

There was a mantra that emanated from the Premier's Office: "Don't let the perfect get in the way of the good." This message came regularly. Joining it was a message from long-time Manitoba cabinet minister Gord Mackintosh who was invited to give caucus a pep-talk in January 2012. The Nova Scotia NDP has had a close relationship with Manitoba Dippers. Dan O'Connor worked there for a while. He brought two talented Premier's Office staff from there – Shawna Martin and Wade Dirksen. And of course the NDP has won four elections in a row in Manitoba, something our planners aspired to. Mackintosh told us, "The most effective change is incremental change. It takes a long time to make real change. One term is not enough." In a way this appears to set up a contrast with what critics inside the party were saying, but it is not necessarily the case. Party stalwarts were not opposed to incrementalism. What troubled critics were that the wrong priorities were favoured, and that no clear long-term vision appeared that would inspire members.

In the summer of 2012 a group of fifty NDP supporters, long time members who had worked hard to support the party to the point of gaining government, signed a letter written primarily by economist Lars Osberg. The main point was that in proposing to reduce the HST revenues, and in reverting to the *status quo*, the government was heading down a path of not being able to afford new social spending, and in effect we would be simply adopting Tory tax structure and policy instead of crafting our own.

Internal criticism had tended to be ig-nored by the party centre on the theory that when it came down to an election, party members would have to support the NDP no matter what. But the group of fifty finally did get some attention. At the instigation of Leonard Preyra, two meet-ings were held, the second addressed by Rick Williams, to try to explain what the government had been up to. The first was a round table, and was quite lively. Both Leonard and I spoke, and there was serious engagement. Here is what their letter said:

Economist Lars Osberg

Subject: Letter from supporters
Date: Sunday, 24 June 2012
From: Molly Hurd and Lars Osberg
To: [various recipients]

Dear NDP Caucus Member,

We are writing this letter – as supporters who have worked for, and donated to, the NDP through many past elections – because we would like to support the NDP in the next Nova Scotia provincial election, but we are now trying to see the point.

We supported the NDP, through many years, because we think Nova Scotia needs changes. Although in many ways this is a won-derful place to live, Nova Scotia could do better. For many years, while in opposition, the NDP spoke to the values of social justice, equality of opportunity and environmental sustainability that we think to be important. One can only imagine what the NDP, when in op-position, would have said about the priorities of a provincial budget which:

• Gave (via forgivable loan) $304 million to the Irvings;
• Cut the tax rate for large corporations;
• Forced spending cuts on health care, and primary, secondary and post-secondary education.

We recognize that building a fairer, more sustainable and more beautiful province will take resources. However, even before the provincial budget was presented, the Premier announced that the government's over-riding priority, once budget balance is achieved, will be to cut the HST and reinstate the rates of provincial income and sales taxation established by the previous Conservative government.

One cannot expect to receive public services without paying for them. The Dexter pledge to restore the previous Conservative government's tax rate policy will tie the hands of a re-elected NDP government for the long-term. If the over-riding priority of an NDP government on the tax side is to reinstate the tax rates of the previous Conservative government, then budget balance implies that on the expenditure side one cannot expect that Nova Scotians will ever receive better public services than those provided under previous Conservative and Liberal governments.

Indeed, in addition to the revenue from income and sales taxes, the previous Conservative government could, and did, spend the money from temporary increases in revenue from offshore natural gas and equalization – revenues which are now gone. And this NDP government has also chosen to forego over $90 million per year in revenue by exempting home heating fuel from sales taxation (a policy choice which provides the biggest benefits to those with the largest houses, least insulation and highest thermostat settings).

So when the NDP now promises to return to the previous Conservative government's tax rates, one cannot expect that this will provide enough revenue to pay for the level of public services actually provided by the previous Conservative government, let alone honoring long-standing NDP commitments to reduce poverty and improve healthcare and education.

We recognize that government must pay its bills. We know that if tax rates on Nova Scotia's more fortunate citizens increase, to pay for the services, which will benefit all members of the community, then we personally will pay more taxes. We think that it is only fair that those of us who have received greater financial benefits from the community should also pay more to support the community – and in past elections, we worked for, and donated to, a party that we thought shared these values of social justice and would change Nova Scotia for the better.

However, a party whose principal taxation pledge is to bring back the tax rates of the previous government is not a party of change. And there is nothing new about the expenditure priorities of the last NDP budget – indeed there is a long tradition of Nova Scotia governments throwing millions of taxpayer dollars at large industrial employers, from Clairtone to Sydney Steel, in attempts to maintain blue collar jobs, while starving education and social services. So if the NDP now actually stands for anything fundamentally different, for any change from previous governments, it is hard to see what it is. And if the NDP is not a party of change in Nova Scotia, why should those who want change support it.

Yours sincerely,
Lars Osberg and Molly Hurd

Jackie Barkley	Winifred Kwak
Carl Boyd	Heather MacDonald
Helen Castonguay	Innis MacDonald
Milton Chew	Margie Macdonald
Theresa Chu	Sheila MacDonald
Joeanne Coffey	Jane MacMillan
Blanche and Tom Creighton	Leanne MacMillan
Michael Cross	Ann Manicom
Gwen Davies	Carol Millett
Patricia De Meo	Wayne Mundle
Dick Evans	Paul O'Hara
Anne Marie Foote	Brian O'Neill
Heather Frenette	Donna Parker
Ruth and Herb Gamberg	David Roback
Jim Guild	Olga Scibior
Judy and Larry Haiven	Linda Scherzinger
Jane and Steve Hart	Wendy Watson Smith
Patricia Hawes	Linda Snyder
Barb Keddy	Sarah Wakely
Marie Kettle	Cliff White
Pat Kipping	Rita Wilson
Carole Woodhall	James Wolford

Originally, Osberg and Hurd intended to send the letter on their own. They consulted a few friends about their draft and found a lot of volunteers asking to sign on. They had tapped into a strongly-held view inside the party. Inevitably, the letter found its way out into the public via email exchanges; columnist Ralph Surette made a reference to it, then other news outlets asked for interviews, which the authors declined, wanting to keep the exchange internal. Amazingly, even after the hard evidence of the facts around the 2013 election loss, the view of the party leadership is that the government was done in by this group of fifty.

A couple of points about this letter: first, it was internal to the party and not circulated publicly. Second, it was written well in advance of the expected timing of an election, so there was opportunity for the government to act on it. In both of these points, the letter differs from the one sent to Ontario NDP leader Andrea Horwath in the midst of their 2014 provincial election and widely circulated.[1] That letter said, "You are running to the right of the Liberals in an attempt to win Conservative votes. It is not clear whether you have given up on progressive voters or you are taking them for granted. [...] Please reconsider or you will lose not only our support but also the support of thousands of others who will turn to other parties or not vote at all. As for those of us who sign this letter, our only loyalty deeper than that which we feel for our party is our loyalty to the principles on which that party was built." The Ontario letter was signed by several dozen core NDP members such as Michele Landsberg (journalist, author, and spouse of Stephen Lewis), Judy Rebick (journalist, rabble.ca), Winnie Ng (Canadian Labour Congress), Geoff Bickerton (CUPW), and Mary Morison (formerly the Nova Scotia provincial secretary, and staff member in Ontario Premier Bob Rae's office). These are people with the backgrounds and stature similar to the NDP members who signed the Nova Scotia letter.

David Wallbridge, party president, and also MLA Mat Whynot wrote replies that listed many of the accomplishments of the NDP in office. The party seemed to take the letter seriously – at least in the sense that they wanted to attempt to control this negative reaction because the potential loss of support by longtime members could be devastating in the next election. Plus, if they could be persuaded to be articulate supporters they would stiffen the support of others.

Leonard and I organized a meeting for the group at the seniors' drop in place, Spencer House. About nineteen of the signatories attended. At the meeting, Lars Osberg made the point that the membership, the base, feels no real consultation is going on. Michael Cross, retired from the History Department at Dalhousie said the response to the letter was condescending and dismissive; he did not expect to have elected a very progressive Conservative government. Jim Guild, retired from the staff of the NSGEU pointed out that the polls showed that the general public was rejecting our government. Margie MacDonald, retired from Health Canada and who had served initially as Executive Assistant to Community Services Minister, Denise Peterson-Rafuse, said there was little opportunity inside the party to have a discussion about what is going on; that members were offered scripted commentaries; that she had lost faith that anyone cared, and members offering different views became labeled as not just wrong but disloyal.

The discussion became testy. Dick Evans intervened to calm things down, saying he felt no need to vent. Dick is retired from teaching Law at Dalhousie University. He is a former director of Dalhousie Legal Aid, and was national chair of Oxfam. He is a quintessential Nova Scotia New Democrat. If Dick Evans has a problem, we all have a problem. He said he agreed with all the comments, and feared we were setting ourselves up to be a one-term government. In the end, he saw too much spin from the government and not enough intelligent analysis. The discussion went on, with points being made about the contracting out of the SAP (Systems, Applications, and Products in Data Processing) function, the tarnishing of Darrell Dexter during the MLA Expenses Scandal, the over-emphasis in the jobsHere program on heavy industry, and the apparent failure to recognize that rural Nova Scotia is in a long-term decline.

David Wallbridge was in attendance, and summed up the discussion by saying that the letter had been considered, and that although there might not be agreement on all points, the party was a democratic one with room for debate; that the objective has been to do things the other parties would never do and to make a difference in people's lives. We ended the evening by promising a follow-up meeting.

This second meeting took place later in October in the Cabinet room. This time Maureen also attended. The discussion was led by Rick Williams. Again, some nineteen of the signatories attended. It was not a happy event. Rick was brought in to offer an overview of the thinking of the government as to its long range strategy, to show that a lot of planning had been going on, and perhaps because he knew a lot of the people who had expressed concerns and came from the same background. But the presentation took over an hour and those in attendance did not really see it as responsive. Rick explained that a lot of time had been put into the Core Policy Priorities exercise, that over almost a full year it had involved examination of health, the economy, the province's demographics, and its fiscal situation. The objective was to focus on a few or limited number of priorities, and that the long-range strategy was to achieve fiscal discipline. Then, over two or three terms as government, to nudge the province towards effective transformation, and to do so avoiding the Bob Rae and John Savage fights with the public service.

Advances had been made in fiscal management, health care, growing the economy, energy, social policy, and education and training. But the government found itself in a tough situation, that spending was hard to reduce, in part because three-quarters of it was in the control of arm's length agencies (health boards, school boards, municipalities, and universities), and revenue growth was uncertain, though it had certainly helped Liberal and Tory governments in the past. But the growth in revenues was not due to tax changes, but due to overall increases in GDP; Nova Scotia, he said, just does not have enough rich people to make it worthwhile to look to tax revenue to make a difference.

It took a long time to get to the point that the best bet for a change in the demographics and an increase in government revenues was to keep young people here by creating jobs in the province. The economists took issue with the presentation and no one seemed convinced about the tax system. Retired Dalhousie sociologist Herb Gamberg said, "We are doing what the PCs and Liberals wanted to do but are doing it better. This does not reflect what a social democratic government should look like." Saint Mary's University business professor Larry Haiven said that Tommy Douglas had engaged in belt tightening, but also laid out a vision of the future. We had been effective at balancing the budget he said, but where was the vision, the promise? Cliff White agreed, and pointed out that missing was how to get to the future. Dick Evans said that the core problem of declining revenues, resulting in an inability to spend, remains. Specific issues associated with Cooke Aquaculture, the contracting out of the SAP function, and the Convention Centre were also raised.

The meeting ended with the general observation that there are cumulative frustrations inside the party, but also agreement that some useful things had been accomplished by the government, although communications needed to be much improved.

I saw the fact that these meetings had been organized at all as an indication that the party leadership was starting to pay some attention to the membership, and to be a bit worried about possible loss of support from traditional voters. In fact, there was every reason to worry. Moreover, the session did not go down well. A flurry of follow-up email included comments such as:

> "If I had realized that we were being invited to a two-hour lecture, I would not have come. I had the perhaps naive belief that the objective was to engage in dialogue. I would have been quite prepared to hear, briefly, about factors influencing policy direction. But I would have then expected that you, as representatives of the NDP establishment, would have wanted to hear and understand the concerns that prompted us to sign our letter to the NDP caucus. I believe that Leonard attempted on a number of occasions to make this dialogue happen, but it did not. And so I am left feeling dismissed."

Another participant wrote:

> "Rick, I did not find [the session] helpful. Nor do I find it helpful to be dismissive of people who are struggling to find a rationale to continue support of the provincial NDP. Your note [Williams had exchanged email with another participant], like earlier responses to the June letter, illustrates the gulf that has opened between social democrats and the current government."

A third participant observed:

> "Instead of our concerns being taken seriously, we were treated to a long, implicit defense of the very policies that we consider problematic. The point that was repeatedly raised by people around the table about the direction, principles and vision of social democracy was basically ignored."

What was fascinating about this entire process was the persistence of the conviction among the central planners that NDP supporters would, in the end, have to vote NDP because they had nowhere else to go. Several of us in caucus saw this as an error, and said so. They could vote Green. They could decide not to vote. They could vote NDP but not take signs, not give money, or not work in their local campaigns. Any of these protest options would hurt the party. And options there certainly were.

Internal discontents were ignored on the theory that core supporters would come around in the end. This continued with the usual slighting comments about individuals. When Tony Tracey and Kyle Buott, leading labour activists, organized the annual Labour Day parade and carried a banner saying, "Capitalism isn't working for the workers," Darrell said, "What is that, some kind of nineteenth-century slogan?" About the "group of fifty" signatories his view was, "All our critics live together within five blocks of one another," in other words a small clique of little account.

A contrast between dissenting Dippers who had problems with Darrell's direction, and said so, is with how Finance Minister Graham Steele approached his discontent. As he says in his book, "As I understand the principle, a Cabinet minister who has misgivings about a major decision or policy direction of the government must resign."[2] Quite right. It is a quasi-constitutional convention, anchored in the idea of collective ministerial responsibility. But there is another aspect to that tradition. Which is that a resigning cabinet minister says publicly why he has resigned. If a minister resigns over a scandal, or allegations of impropriety, this goes on the record as well. This happened to

Kyle Buott (with megaphone) at a rally.

Rollie Thornhill in 1988. It happens frequently in the UK, where cabinet ministers seem to have interesting and indiscreet sex lives. But on matters of principle, principled cabinet ministers state their views. In 2005 Joe Comuzzi left Paul Martin's government because he opposed same-sex marriage, and said so. In 2006 Michael Chong left Stephen Harper's government because he was Intergovernmental Affairs minister but was sidestepped over Québec policy, and he made his reasons for leaving public. In the summer of 2014 Baroness Sayeeda Warsi left David Cameron's cabinet in the UK because she disagreed with the government's policy on Gaza, and posted her resignation letter online. Other British luminaries such as Harold Wilson and Michael Heseltine have resigned from cabinets, and have stated their reasons for doing so.

When Graham resigned in May 2012 it was major news. The stated reason was that he had decided not to run again and it was necessary to put in place a new minister right away so they could learn the job. I happened to be out of the province when the resignation was announced. As soon as I returned, I asked around extensively about the resignation. No one knew any more than the official story; and no-one believed the official story. And, indeed, Graham now tells us that the official reason given was not true.

As for his now-stated reason, I disagree with it. He tells us he was so opposed to a potential financial settlement with health care workers that he had to leave. An alternative to that was to retain the two per cent HST increase, but Graham apparently had no problem with giving up some $380 million in revenues, just a problem with paying wages to keep up with inflation. All of this was an active issue within caucus. If Graham was not prepared to go public, it would at a minimum have been very useful for caucus to hear from him as to why he was leaving. But not a word.

Graham is aware of the tradition of a cabinet minister stating publicly the reasons for a resignation. His book includes the speech he prepared but never gave. This failure to be frank – even to be forthright with his caucus colleagues – is greatly regrettable, but all too typical of the party leadership's propensity to avoid serious, open debate inside the party. As for the 2 per cent HST, Darrell put an end to discussion by announcing its scheduled termination.

16

Air War, Ground War:
Year Four – Into the Election

Our election slogans evolved over the years. In 1998 it was, "Priorities for people," followed by, "It's time to elect a government that's on the side of ordinary Nova Scotians," in 1999. In 2003 we proclaimed, "A better deal for today's families." "A better deal – a plan you can count on," is what we ran under in 2006. Then, "Genuine leadership for today's families," in 2009 and finally, "The future starts here," in 2013. Opposition taunts across the floor in the Legislature picked up on our slogans and promises: "A promise made, a promise broken," "Back To Deficit," and "A Bitter Deal," came back to heckle us. It was much easier to be in opposition rather than in government.

The game plan for re-election was made up of a variety of elements: rely on the popularity of Darrell Dexter, and if that was somewhat eroded, stress that he is better than the other two leaders, certainly more experienced. Deliver a balanced budget, as promised. Reduce the HST increase, as promised. Point out that all 2009 election promises had been delivered. Keep on mentioning the good economic news that was about to appear with the federal Ships Start Here jobs, plus other initiatives that had been supported by the government. Claim credit for Muskrat Falls as the best way to long-term lower (lower than with fossil fuels) electricity rates. Successfully redraw electoral boundaries. Get incumbents to work their constituencies. Avoid any messes. Find some new benefits to offer, especially to seniors. And relentlessly remind voters of all the problems the previous Liberal and Tory governments had made or failed to solve. Plus, attack Stephen McNeil, or "define him" as it was termed, as inexperienced, unqualified, a flip-flopper, angry, and not up to the job.

In many respects, this is not a poor plan. But it certainly backfired. Political columnist Lysiane Gagnon wrote: "There's an old saying; Opposition parties don't win elections, governments lose them. Usually it takes a few years for governments to beat themselves – typically more than one term in office. As time goes by, they accumulate mistakes, disappoint people, and end up looking stale."[1] Gagnon was writing about Quebec, but the observations are widely applicable. Starting in the summer of 2012, I wrote a series of three memos to caucus pointing out the perils with our electoral positioning. They are included as Appendicies 6, 7, and 8.

The main fact was that jobsHere had not actually materialized here as advertised, at least not outside HRM. The unemployment rate remained stubbornly at 9 per cent (or higher), and very high, even double that, in Cape Breton. Basically, Cape Breton unemployment numbers were Depression era numbers. Any hope of improving the seat count through gains on the Island disappeared with that. The best hope had been for the newly reconfigured Richmond seat. It was expanded so as to include Port Hawkesbury, where the big cash infusion for NewPage/Stern was being relied on to deliver the seat to Bert Lewis. He ran third, worse than he had done as our candidate in 2006. Michel Samson was reelected for the Liberals. Despite having had some adverse publicity about whether he really lived in the constituency or had effectively moved his family to Halifax, Samson was a prominent member of the Liberal caucus. Highly unpopular with the NDP leadership, he was nonetheless effective in the House, articulate, and their caucus's only lawyer. He was a valuable player for the Liberals, and well entrenched in his constituency. The other main Cape Breton target was Manning MacDonald's old seat, Cape Breton South. After twenty years as an MLA, Manning was retiring. When Manning took his usual winter vacation in Florida and was absent from the House for a longer period than usual, Darrell Dexter tried quite successfully to stir up public criticism and to tag McNeil with the issue since the Liberal leader defended Manning. *The Chronicle Herald* ran a biting cartoon showing Manning as "tanned" and a voter as "steamed." The NDP focus on his seat was, however, frustrated by the redrawn boundaries, which were no help, along with the stubborn lack of jobs.

Cape Breton is a wonderful place to live – beautiful and a cultural treasure. But almost without exception, hardcore Liberal. And where not Liberal, then Tory. Frank Corbett and Gordie Gosse have been elected time and again for the NDP because of their personal popularity. But they are exceptions. The phenomenon of indifferent NDP success in Cape Breton defies class logic. As the home of some of the most prominent industrial working class in the province, voters there should see the NDP as their natural allies. Over the years this has hardly ever happened. In his 1976 book on unionization in Cape Breton's heavy industries, *Miners and Steelworkers*,[2] Paul MacEwan commented on the political situation in the 1960s: "The situation in Cape Breton could well have been ideal for a party of protest, had some local leadership existed." (p. 341) Not much has changed. I tend to ascribe it to the party's failures in basic organizing. In constituency after constituency there is just no political infrastructure: no functioning executive, no membership drives, no youth recruiting, no sizzle to attract participation.

So, the *status quo* prevailed on Cape Breton. And a slew of losses in rural and small town seats where we had won for the first time in 2009: Brian Skabar in Cumberland North, Ross Landry in Pictou West, Jim Boudreau in Guysborough, Ramona Jennex in Kings South, Pam Birdsall and Gary Ramey in the Lunenburg seats. Or losses where there were no incumbents running, or where the boundaries had been redrawn. So, the new Halifax Fairview was lost. And so were Halifax Atlantic, Halifax Chebucto, Timberlea-Prospect, Armdale, and Dartmouth South.

As the election grew closer, there were two inconsistent messages emerging. One was that the objective was to gain seats, to do this by holding all incumbents and then taking certain target growth seats (the two in Cape Breton previously mentioned, Dartmouth North, Preston, Clare–Digby, the new Armdale.) The other was that the polls – both the public and the NDP's internal ones – showed the Liberals as ten points ahead, including an erosion of support in the longtime base of HRM, especially in Dartmouth and in the suburbs. It was up to each MLA, we were told, to get themselves re-elected. There would be an air war waged by the central campaign, aimed mostly at the Liberals, but the ground war had to be fought seat-by-seat by the candidates and their organizations. This latter message was tantamount to saying that the party and the leader offered no tailcoats this time.

It seems always to have been assumed that the election would be sometime in year four or early in year five of the mandate, i.e., between spring and fall 2013, with running out the full mandate not really a serious possibility. There was no explicit discussion of this, but the intensity of pre-election preparations during year four made it clear. What limits a government's time in office is a specific provision in the Constitution that limits Parliaments and provincial legislatures to five-year terms. Some provinces have abandoned the flexible option that allows a majority government to call an election according to their best sense of timing – generally good economic news, or fear of pending poor economic news – that favours it. Where there is legislation, the timing chosen tends to be of four years, with set dates. But running out the full constitutional mandate does have some logic to it. It certainly maximizes the opportunity to govern. It maximizes the period before invoking the uncertainty of an election. It does not happen often that governments do go that long since the exercise of judgment as to timing is too tempting. Also, such a long delay exposes a government to allegations that it is afraid to hold an election.

That ten point spread was a killer. The numbers during the late 2012 and early 2013 indicated the Liberals at 41 or 42 per cent, NDP 31 to 33 per cent. The important thing about these numbers is that the NDP was ten points behind the percentage needed to form a *minority* government, never mind receiving a second majority.

In a first-past-the-post system, a party needs about 45 per cent of the overall votes to be in a majority position. Percentages between 38 and 42 usually mean a minority. There are of course exceptions: with the vote splits, Stephen Harper's Conservatives took a majority in the federal election of 2011 with only 39 per cent of the vote. The splits in each seat are always crucial. In a three-party arrangement, and with a close vote, it is in theory possible for an MLA to be elected with a bare 34 per cent of the vote if there were a 33/33/34 split. But this is highly unusual. (Although it is almost exactly how I myself was first elected to city council in 1994. The highly popular and very effective incumbent, Nick Meagher, decided not to run again. About seven candidates ran, three of us as serious contenders. They each received about 32 per cent and I took about 34 per cent and was elected.) Other splits that could lead to a candidate being elected with less than a majority of the votes are patterns like 30/34/36 or 20/39/40. But these very slim numbers are only pertinent constituency by constituency. Parties considering the province-wide picture need to seek that 45 per cent number. Where someone like Frank Corbett or Bill Estabrooks takes 70 or 80 per cent of the vote in their constituency, the additional votes over 50 per cent do not elect extra members.

Analysis of the polling numbers in various presentations to caucus were always the same: core NDP support was holding; the target had to be the soft NDP supporters, those who had either voted NDP for the first time in 2009 or who saw themselves as open to persuasion by any party, but did like the NDP. A particular focus was seniors since so many of those who actually vote are over the age of 55.

When the first public polls appeared that showed the Liberal lead, initially the senior staff generally dismissed them. Dan O'Connor pointed to the margin of error in polling. Later on he pointed out that coming from behind just spurs us on. Finally, in June 2013 with the Liberals leading in the CRA (Corporate Research Associates) poll at 45 per cent, O'Connor said to just ignore the polls.

When internal polling confirmed the trend, there was an especially fascinating presentation to a caucus retreat in Membertou, Sydney, in March 2013. This was Matt Hebb's last presentation, as he pointed out. Darrell Dexter sat in stony silence as Matt presented. He never said one word to caucus about the departure of his Principal Secretary, then or ever. It was left to Matt to note his own departure and to say his own farewell. He said the NDP had been his life's work, ever since he first helped his mother Tessa who had been a candidate, but especially since 1997-1998 when he left a PhD programme at York University to work with Darrell. He said he was leaving the government with tremendously mixed emotions, and would have preferred different timing, but that it was just time for him to move on. But he had optimism for the future, knowing that, "this bus is headed for great future things." He offered his thanks especially to Darrell Dexter and to all of us. Matt appeared in the gallery of the House the next week in his last days in the Premier's Office, but was not introduced. Was he pushed out, or was his choice of another job seen as a betrayal, so close to an election? It is unknown. Certainly, being the party's most experienced election planner and manager, his departure in an election year was a great loss.

Matt Hebb

The target Matt set for us to achieve was 165,000 votes – fewer by fifteen thousand than in 2009, and only 37 per cent of the likely voter turnout; however, Matt projected a majority of 27 seats (a bare majority plus one) could be won with this. It certainly pushed the normal understanding of what was needed to gain a majority. Like the bogus statistic that was put to us as a caucus and to the party in 2006, that a shift of only 500 votes would have delivered the election to us – bogus because it assumed that only those 500 votes that would affect the particular seats where we ran a close second would be the ones to shift, and not others. Such bogus numbers focused on gaining the votes in particular target seats, something that is always highly unlikely. Matt's analysis said that we could get to 100,000 votes by holding our core voters plus those generally favorable to us. The key then became to bring back 65,000 voters now parked elsewhere; i.e., people who voted NDP in 2009 but now thought they would vote for another party.

Joined by his successor Paul Black, the briefing noted that unless the polling numbers changed, the result would be 29 seats for the Liberals and only 13 for the NDP. The ballot question had to be managed so that it became, "keep on looking forward to a better future," "don't get stuck in a rut," and "the future is looking brighter;" basically, "don't go back to the past." The opposition parties could be expected to try to make the election about the NDP's four years in government, which would be highly problematic. Problematic because it would leave un-scrutinized the opposition party agendas, the implied standard would be perfection, and some government decisions are always divisive.

The claim to be advanced to the electorate would not be that the NDP deserved to be rewarded for achievements like getting the budget back to balance, but that it had the best plan for the future. And that the opposition parties had a terrible record when they had been in power.

The opposition parties had a few themes. "Take away the cheque book," was one – the notion that too much money was being spent on big companies that did not need it (big bucks for big business), and not to much positive effect. That money had been taken out of the education system. That power rates were going up to unaffordable levels, bills included an "NDP electricity tax," (i.e., funding for Efficiency Nova Scotia programmes) and the Muskrat Falls project would increase rates still farther. That the HST had been increased. That the experiment of an NDP government had not been a success. Most of this was Liberal talk. To the extent Jamie Baillie said anything different he also pointed to increased debt and talked frequently about lowering tax rates. All of these were powerful themes that appealed to anyone inclined to be critical, which of course, is generally exactly what people are inclined to be as their basic attitude to any government.

The points of difference on the economy were instructive. Darrell was a strong interventionist. He defended the government's support of business opportunities such as the Irving bid for federal ship work, or pulp and paper plants in communities with few other opportunities, on the basis that these investments secured jobs, and would ultimately generate tax revenues that would support social programmes such as health care and education. He denounced the opposition parties' preparedness to not intervene as the true scandal.

As the election drew closer Darrell tried to smooth out any problems, but was showing the strain. There were hints that the prevailing view inside One Government Place (OGP) was that the coming election was likely to be lost. During the final Legislature session Darrell brought in a bill to deal with the pension of former NDP MLA Trevor Zinck. On the face of it – a penalty of the loss of earned pension in the event of a conviction for a serious crime – could apply to any sitting MLA (and there was a process underway that might have caught Michel Samson in the net), but really this was about punishing Zinck. It was highly obnoxious legislation, partly because taking away any earned pension is wrong, partly because it could affect spouses and other family members, partly because it changes the rules under which a person first ran for office, and partly because it pandered to those who hold politicians in contempt. But Darrell wanted to try to gain any electoral advantage possible, and to avoid any criticism that he failed to deal with the situation.

Further rare glimpses into his inner workings arrived a few days later in a small rant he gave about Tony Smith, a litigant in the Nova Scotia Home for Coloured Children (NSHCC) case. On the day *The Chronicle Herald* ran yet another story about the Home, Darrell called Smith a sociopath. Darrell's inner tension was palpable in the unusually emphatic way he allowed his taste for personal abuse to overwhelm him that day. It was not unusual for him to make slighting personal remarks about critics, but there was something extra here. This prompted John MacDonell to say to him, "Darrell, I am worried. I have known you a long time. What are you going to do after we get out of here [i.e., after the caucus meeting]? You usually can keep it all contained." By the time Question Period rolled around a couple of hours later Darrell had regained control and dealt with the three questions posed about the Home for Coloured Children with some measure of calm.

It must have been a generally tense time because that same day Percy Paris, the MLA from Waverley-Fall River–Beaverbank, grabbed Liberal Keith Colwell outside the Legislature washroom and almost got into a fight with him.[3] Percy had been put on edge having heard the Preston MLA, who is white, refer to the Preston populace as, "my residents," which Percy took to imply an attitude of ownership reminiscent of slavery. Percy Paris losing his temper with Keith Colwell ended up with the police charging him with

Percy Paris

assault. Percy had to resign from Cabinet. Graham Steele was tapped to return as the substitute Minister of Economic Development. The whole event was a huge embarrassment at the end of the session and just before an election. Caucus was called together for an early morning meeting in the Cabinet room. Darrell Dexter spoke about adopting a calm attitude. He announced Graham's return to Cabinet. He told us that the Liberals would present a motion to refer the matter to the Internal Affairs Committee. Any end of session strategy to focus on Liberal misbehavior over helicopter rides, and Manning's absence from the House for an extended period, went by the board.

The interaction at the early morning caucus meeting was particularly interesting. After Darrell introduced the matter of Percy's resignation with an emphasis on calm and regret, he seemed at a loss at what else to say. Graham Steele smoothly stepped in and took over directing the meeting ("I have a few things to say. When the Premier calls, you say yes, whether it is for a few weeks or for a year. This does not change the fact that I am not running again. It does not open the question of why I left Cabinet."), expressed measured concern for Percy, and called for those who were close to him to offer their support in the weeks ahead. His usual manner of logical calm and order and command came across strongly. I do not imagine I was the only one present who saw the moment as one strongly in his favour should he later choose to return to political life.

At the same time, newspapers were carrying the story that Jane and Gordon Earle had resigned from the NDP over the government's refusal to appoint a public inquiry into the NSHCC.[4] Gordon, an African Nova Scotian had been an NDP MP elected in 1997. Jane had been director of the NSHCC years after the time of the damaging events to the children had taken place. She had publicly expressed concerns about the past history of the Home. They joined a lengthening list of NDP members who had resigned over one issue or another.

Gordon Earle

A strong part of what was problematic was that caucus was learning of this in the press, and not from the Premier or the party office. The Earles had resigned and were reported in the newspaper to have told the Premier a week earlier.

By the time caucus met for its next retreat in June, things had not changed much in terms of polling and focus group results. The spring session had just ended, and election preparations were at an advanced stage. The party secretary, Jill Marzetti, was to be the overall campaign manger. Eugene Kostyra had arrived from Manitoba to join others from out of province and local staff who had already been at work for weeks. Kostyra was a former Manitoba MLA and cabinet minister under Manitoba Premier, Howard Pawley, including having been Finance Minister; Kostyra's roots are in CUPE (Canadian Union of Public Employees).

A draft platform had been generated. Candidates had been nominated where incumbents were not running again. Drafts of literature were being vetted. Pre-election communication literature was being distributed. Phoning was going on to supporters who had voted NDP in 2009 to test their thoughts. Campaign managers were being sought. Voting patterns were being analyzed. Message boards were being drafted. Other elections such as the USA presidential election as well as the recent Canadian provincial elections were all being sifted through for ideas, lessons, and slogans. Social media were being monitored and a social media communications team was in place. Everything was in gear. The moment was upon us, though no exact date had been announced. Darrell had passed on calling a spring election – the poll numbers were still not strong enough, the Legislature session had not been positive enough, there were still some weaknesses in the economy, and there was some doubt about what the UARB would do with respect to the Muskrat Falls proposal, but also an ongoing hope that the result would be positive, or could be spun as positive. More and more it was looking as though the election call would be in August for September or late August, or early September for October.

Then the June CRA poll[5] came out, showing the Liberals in majority territory, with 45 per cent of decided voters. Very bad news. We were at 26 per cent, tied with the PCs for third place. Not good. Don Mills, the principal of CRA, said it would be "suicidal" for the NDP to call an election

CORPORATE RESEARCH ASSOCIATES

MEDIA RELEASE: June 10, 2013

For Immediate Release

NS Liberals Widen Lead Although Many Voters Still Undecided

HALIFAX: The provincial Liberals have widened their lead ahead of the NDP and PC Party in terms of voter support this quarter, according to the most recent survey conducted by **Corporate Research Associates Inc.** Support for the Liberal Party has increased over the past three months (45%, up from 39% in February 2013), while support for the NDP has declined (26%, down from 32%). Support among decided voters for the PC Party is stable at 26 percent (compared with 24% three months ago). Three percent prefer the Green Party (compared with 5%). Over one-half are undecided, do not plan to vote, or do not offer a response (55%, up from 48%), an unusually high number at this junction in the electoral cycle.

over the next few months. But Dan O'Connor sent out a memo saying: "When the NDP hit new highs in the CRA quarterly over the last five-six years, I advised caucus and candidates that it was a good day to ignore polls. Today is another good day to ignore polls. Why? Six days ago at Dundee, caucus saw polling numbers that were much more recent and more accurate than the CRA polling. [...] The numbers you saw at Dundee show a relatively close race. [...] The best professional analysis we have is that the NDP has begun to turn around the trend against us, most notably in the areas of core strength where the election will be decided. CRA shows an extraordinary undecided/don't know level of 55 per cent." He went on to mention Justin Trudeau as accounting for a big burst of Liberal support. And so on. Overall, this was messaging that was designed to try to keep everyone from becoming any more discouraged than they already were. In fact, our own internal polling showed us at exactly the same percentage as did the CRA, 26 per cent; the differences were in the undecided votes, which we showed as only 15 per cent, and in the Liberal support, which we had at 33 per cent.

"The areas of core strength where the election will be decided." What on earth could that possibly mean? Geographic areas? Does that mean HRM or does it mean rural Nova Scotia? There was nothing in the numbers to show that. Maybe policy areas? Which ones? Jobs and the economy? That was clearly the lead issue among all voters and also the swing voters. How exactly were we beginning to turn around what even Dan called, "the trend against us," on jobs and the economy?

On this, our core message to voters was to have faith that prosperity was just around the corner and a return to the old parties would lead nowhere. Unfortunately for us, the jobs that had actually materialized were all in Metro where we already had strong (but eroding) support. Outside Metro jobs were just not being created. Think tourism in Southwest Nova Scotia; think the closure of Bowater; think the lack of success of the old TrentonWorks morphed under Daewoo to manufacture wind turbines; think of the closing or downsizing of call-centres; think of the Stern takeover of the paper plant in Port Hawkesbury with half the workers laid-off. If not jobs and the economy, maybe Dan had in mind electricity rates, another hard sell. In 2009 we had removed the HST from home electricity, a big cost item. But in terms of cash left in customers' pockets, we had nothing else on the table, whereas the Liberals did: their promise to remove from customers the $43 million per year cost of Efficiency Nova Scotia. This was nonsense, of course, but glittery, shiny, attractive nonsense. We were being outbid.

The Dundee Resort caucus retreat was also full of positive, but magical thinking. Darrell spoke of there being various routes to victory, and encouraged all candidates to get out on the doorstep and deliver the message personally (we were joined at the retreat by seven of the new nominated candidates), "in a way people understand." He emphasized that what counts now is the actual campaign itself and not the advance polls. He referred to British Columbia, Alberta, and Manitoba as examples of governments coming from behind. In a friendly gesture to the new candidates he said, "we see ourselves reflected in you," to which Frank Corbett reposted, "does that mean they see in us what they will become?" No doubt a sobering thought for the newbies. Eugene Kostyra emphasized persuading swing voters. He pointed out that core supporters may have priorities that are just not election issues, for example increases in minimum wage or Income Assistance rates. Supporters and others have to be told of the negative consequences of not having an NDP government. The ballot question has to have wide appeal. And defining the opposition in negative ways is important. Stay on message. The lesson of the British Columbia election was that the incumbent Liberals had used the strategies Kostyra was outlining and that had been used successfully by the Manitoba NDP to win five consecutive elections. Ignore the noise from the media and from party activists, he said. People are not looking for change; just give them a reason to stay with you.

Electricity

For entirely understandable reasons, overall energy policy is always a very important public policy issue. It has repercussions for all aspects of personal and commercial life. Consumers are generally very aware of its cost. Energy policy often serves as a proxy for overall concerns about the economy.

In terms of electricity, there was a clash of positions between the NDP and the Liberals, with the PCs having a go at the topic, but not really being in the fight. Our argument was that moving to reliance on renewables was a necessity because of federal policy that impacted CO_2 emissions, and also because of the general upward trend in the marketplace cost of fossil fuels. So we could not promise lower rates, but we held out the promise of lower rates than they would otherwise be. The support for the Muskrat Falls project added a core supply of electricity from a renewable source, with the hope in the future of a real economic advantage. In addition, with the removal of the HST from electricity, there was a direct benefit to customers now. The Liberals were, somewhat dishonestly, portrayed by us as supporting putting the HST back on electricity. In fact, although McNeil had avoided this point for a while, he went on record a year before in the Legislature during Question Period saying that he would not do so. Instead, he said he would remove what he called the "NDP electricity tax," namely the amount added to power bills to support Efficiency Nova Scotia. The Liberals expressed skepticism about Muskrat Falls, and spoke in favour of breaking Nova Scotia Power Inc's (NSPI) monopoly by allowing competition. The Tories just said freeze the rates.

Recall the Question Period exchange between the Premier and Stephen McNeil on May 16, 2012, cited in Chapter 9. As of that date, it was entirely clear that the Liberals were not going to put the HST back on electricity. This did not stop us from saying they would, or that they had voted many times to put it on (i.e., by opposing our budgets), or that no one knows where they stand on the issue. All innuendo and not honest. On removal of the designated surcharge for Efficiency Nova Scotia, the Liberals were off-base. The agency has been doing good work, and although not all of its focus is on efficiency in electricity, if not paid for one way it has to be paid for in another. Thus, its costs could just come out of the general tax base or they could stay as a surcharge on electricity bills. It does not make much difference. Nor does it make sense to talk about shifting its costs from ratepayers to shareholders. This may provide some sense of satisfaction by appearing to shift it to shareholders, but in the end all expenditures by NSPI of any sort come only from bills sent to ratepayers so shifting items around on the balance sheet has no effect on those bills.

As for the competition issue, again the Liberals were off-base and a decade out of date. Their proposal for what is called retail wheeling, dated from the 2002 study of the electricity marketplace done for the Tories by Dalhousie University oceanography professor, Bob Fournier.[6] At the time, he was looking for ways to introduce more renewables into the grid but not to create instability in the overall system. One of the ways he suggested this be done was by retail wheeling, i.e., allowing an independent power producer to generate power and then sell it to some customer by sending the power over NSPI's lines, though paying for that use. At the time this might have made sense. But in the interim, there had been a shift to general endorsement of renewables, plus the adoption of a system of feed-in tariffs (COMFIT) that encouraged independent power producers to generate from renewable sources, and NSPI would buy that power. Wheeling might be useful as a marketing device for independent power producers, but was no longer necessary as a way to establish more renewables capacity, since a new system was in place. Nor would wheeling 'break the monopoly' of NSPI. So what the Liberals were proposing with respect to electricity had no serious substance, though they were effective as critics of what the NDP was doing. They raised doubts. There were serious responses that could have been made, but were not; the party leadership having chosen instead to run a negative campaign around electricity, connecting the Liberals to, "the big monopoly Hydro Québec," and suggesting the Liberals were against developing Atlantic Canada's economy, ultimately leading to the slogan "Stephen McNeil, not the right guy for Nova Scotia." In earlier versions of the ads, the association was with "Québec" and not "Hydro Québec" and the ads had quite an anti-Québec flavour, not very palatable, and certainly questionable for a party where our federal counterparts had achieved a significant number of seats in Québec, and who hope to use that base to form a national government. Critics in caucus, such as Gary Burrill, were ignored and slighted.

Own Goals

If you've never been knocked down, you've never been in a fight. No one expects perfection in politics. You win some but also lose some. Yet one of the peculiarities of our time in office was the extent to which we brought trouble upon ourselves, publicly and internally. There are various examples. There was the fight with Dalhousie Legal Aid over a change in the rules for welfare recipients in special circumstances. There was the refusal to call a public inquiry over the events at the Nova Scotia Home for Coloured Children (NSHCC). There was the fight with Talbot House in Sydney over its ability to carry out its mandate. There was the assault of Keith Colwell by Percy Paris. There was the largely internal mess over my defence of the government on the issue of debt, and involving the Auditor General. There was the dubious record of Nova Scotia Business Inc. (NSBI) in creating jobs. There was the reversal of policy on sex change operations. There was inaction about the grounded vessel, MV Miner. All of these were peculiar episodes. There are examples from earlier in the mandate, but these are features of year four.

To expand on a few of these: early in 2012 the Department of Community Services announced a change in rules governing special payments for clients on Income Assistance. "Special needs support," is a flexibility element of the income assistance system. About two-thirds of the Department's clients receive some form of special needs allowance. Most of these are people with disabilities. It covers additional expenses related to disability or health maintenance. What is covered is listed, but the Employment Supports and Income Assistance Policy Manual also allows coverage of anything deemed "essential." This would usually be shown by physicians' letters. What the Department did was to eliminate the residual category of "deemed essential" items.

The core issue was that a client of the Department had applied to Health Canada for permission to treat pain by smoking marijuana. This medical marijuana programme had been in effect since July, 2001 and generally had the blessing of the medical community as an effective analgesic for certain medical conditions. Litigation had confirmed the validity of clinics offering the service. What happened was that the client applied for Income Assistance to cover the cost of purchasing this prescribed medicine, and although the Department refused, the request fit the criteria of the rules and an appeal overruled the Department and ruled that the client could have this cost covered. For no clear reason, Denise Peterson-Rafuse fastened on to this and changed the rules. Her position was that this is not what the special circumstances fund was for, and that to have the government paying to support smoking dope was bad public relations and could lead to supporting grow-ops.

This all ended up with Denise Peterson-Rafuse making rude remarks about the staff at Dalhousie Legal Aid, especially Claire McNeil, the staff lawyer who was the lead on the matter. This was particularly odd because Dalhousie Legal Aid had a long history of progressive activity of exactly the sort the NDP had traditionally been a part. So what was Denise Peterson-Rafuse doing squaring off against them?

It was actually a ridiculous position.[7] The amount of money at issue was no more than about $25 thousand per year. What Denise thought she was doing was never obvious. It alienated traditional allies, some of whom were party members (Claire McNeil was a member of my constituency executive). It puzzled caucus members to the point that a group of us met with Denise over lunch at a caucus retreat, basically scolded her for her sharp remarks, and urged her to mend fences. Later on, labour lawyer Ray Larkin was brought in to mediate a settlement between the department and challengers who were getting ready to take a *Charter of Rights* case to court.

While at least some of this episode was somewhat private, the dispute with Talbot House was all too public. Again, Denise Peterson-Rafuse took a leading role. Journalist Parker Donham wrote several columns attacking Denise for her intransigence. It was never completely clear what was going on. Talbot House is an addictions treatment centre in Cape Breton. It has been in operation for upwards of fifty years. It is operated as a non-profit with a Board of Directors. As the only such centre on Cape Breton, it receives provincial government funding through the Department of Community Services. A departmental review led to suspension of the funding, and a report full of innuendo about the centre's director, a priest with a good reputation. Talbot House had to close. There was back and forth with the Board, accompanied by community outrage and evasive answers by the Minister during Question Period. *The Cape Breton Post* published a letter by long time New Democrat John Hugh Edwards, a former federal candidate for the party:

"For decades, the staff and volunteers at Talbot House have provided Cape Breton with incredible service to those among us who have suffered from the ravages of addiction. Now it appears that the good work of these dedicated people, and the legacy of many years of service to our community, are to be thrown aside because of little more than false allegations, innuendo, and a tissue of technical and picayune complaints by nameless bureaucrats."[8]

The minister never officially backed down or apologized, and neither did the Premier who also steadfastly resisted opposition calls for Denise Peterson-Rafuse to be fired, but in October responsibility for oversight of addiction recovery centres was moved from the Department of Community Services to the Department of Health. And provincial funding to Talbot House was restored. However, as Parker Donham quite correctly observed, for years in opposition the NDP had been a harsh critic of DCS bureaucracy, but in power the party through its minister gave every sign of being completely captive to that same bureaucracy. In the end, the whole episode was an embarrassment, and of exactly the sort we should never have found ourselves in. It reflected poorly on all of us.

My little heart-to-heart chat with the Auditor General (AG) early in 2012 was another example of a lot of fuss, both internal and public, that we could quite easily have lived without. What happened is that the Premier's Office received an advance copy of one of the AG's regular reports, and found that he had included an introductory essay on the province's debt, setting out his view that increasing the debt was immoral. As the senior NDP member of the Public Accounts Committee, I was asked by staff to take on the AG and defend the government. Which I did.[9] I pointed out that the essay about the debt problem was flawed in several ways: debt has always to be considered in a context that looks at taxation, spending priorities, and the state of the economy, but this had not been done by the AG. That the debt of the province by any measure was not out of control, was well below that of many jurisdictions, and was in fact being reduced in comparison with GDP, the traditional measure. And, finally, that in offering a flawed analysis the AG had strayed into the overt political realm, which he ought not to do. I assured the public that Nova Scotia was not about to go bankrupt.

It was a spirited session, during which I lectured the AG using all of the NDP's allotted time at the committee. Essentially, I did what the Premier's Office had asked me to do. The problem seemed to be that I did it too effectively. Some sympathy was generated for the AG, and in the face of that both the Premier and the Minister of Finance made very unhelpful critical comments. Graham Steele called the AG's remarks a, "thoughtful essay," and – much worse – Darrell said, as reported in *The Chronicle Herald,* "Howard always expresses his opinion. It's just a part of his character and his participation in all his political activities."[10] Well, screw that.

Although a few times I had come close to resigning from caucus, this was the moment I came closest. I am not interested in being publicly disrespected by the Premier. And clearly he should not have done it. This was profoundly offensive. Although it did not lead to me resigning, it did determine, when considered cumulatively with other discontents I had with the direction of the party in government, that I would not run again. When nothing happened either publicly or privately to alter the record, I sent this letter to Frank Corbett:

Hon. Frank Corbett, Deputy Premier
Government House Leader
Halifax, Nova Scotia

February 3, 2012

Dear Frank:

I am writing to you in your capacity as House Leader.

You will know that on January 18th the Public Accounts Committee (PAC) received a report from the Auditor General, which dealt with the broad topic of Government financial reporting, and included a preliminary, "Message from the Auditor General," on the subject of debt. Apparently the Premier's Office had seen or been advised in advance of the public release of the report, about its contents. I say this because research staff in the caucus office so advised me a day or two prior to the January 18th meeting. They relayed the request that I, on behalf of the Government caucus, resist and critique the "Message" chapter; concern was particularly focused on the Auditor's use of language that said debt, "raises ethical questions." I was also asked to make it clear that the main accumulation of debt took place under PC and Liberal governments.

I myself did not see the report until the morning of January 18th but had prepared some thoughts for addressing the general subject and did so in consultation with the caucus researchers. On the day, I spoke in blunt terms to the Auditor. I was also clear about the sources of debt being the opposition parties. During the session of the PAC, all other Government members of the committee were enthusiastically supportive of the approach taken.

Later in the day and the next day the Minister of Finance and the Premier publicly undermined what I had said. The Minister of Finance said the Auditor's "Message" was, "a thoughtful essay." [CBC] The Premier said that, "Members are entitled to their own opinions," [Metro] and, "Howard always expresses his opinion ... It's just part of his character." [Chronicle-Herald]

I repeat that I was specifically asked to resist and critique the Auditor's "Message." His "Message" was not a thoughtful essay, it was a piece of junk that deserved exactly the criticism it was given. He inappropriately inserted himself into the political process, leading predictably to the PC press release issued later in the day that cited the Auditor as calling our Government unethical for adding to debt.

Also, in no way was the critique of the Auditor a matter of personal opinion; quite the contrary – a message was being conveyed at the request of the Premier's Office.

We are regularly told in caucus that we must support one another. This current episode conveys just the opposite message to me. Since January 18th, I have had no communication from the Premier or the Minister of Finance. The only contact has been from the Premier's Communication Director who called to tell me I should not be concerned about the Premier's statements because no one in the Premier's Office was mad at me, a point that is, to say the least, entirely irrelevant.

In the circumstances, I am resigning from all committees on which I serve, except for Public Accounts. I shall remain on Public Accounts so as not to draw public attention to this overall matter, and because the PCs called for the Government to remove me from the committee.

Please, therefore remove me from: Law Amendments Committee, Legislation Committee, Resources Committee, and the Veterans' Committee.

Yours truly,

Howard Epstein

cc. Hon. Darrell Dexter, Premier
Hon. Graham Steele, Minister of Finance
Hon. Ross Landry, Chair, Law Amendments Committee
Leonard Preyra, Chair Legislation Committee
Syd Prest, Chair, Resources Committee
Gary Burrill, Chair, Veterans' Committee

Basically, I went into work-to-rule mode. I would do my job, but no more. I do know that some staff in the Premier's Office pointed out that it would diminish the effectiveness of some committees, especially Legislation and Law Amendments, if I were not there. Leonard wrote to Darrell in support of me, and spoke to the matter at caucus to say that caucus members have to be backed up by Cabinet when asked to do things for the government. After a few weeks, Darrell asked me to a meeting. He did not apologize. In fact he tried to say that he had not intended to indicate I was on my own on this, a patently unacceptable thing to say, and I rejected that characterization. I pointed out that with the time that had gone by it was too late to apologize publicly or correct the record, but I did want him to state to caucus that I had taken on the AG at his request. He agreed, and did so at the next meeting on March 20, 2012. He said I was "justifyably upset not to get support. [...] The Auditor General deserved criticism. [...] Howard did what he was asked to do. I want to set the record straight." This garnered a round of applause, for which I thank my colleagues. They do know when something untoward has occurred.

Year four saw several examples of attempts to correct the course of policy choices that had proven to be problematic. School closures were an important example.

As I've previously mentioned, the education portfolio had not been well handled. Putting policy in the context of funding and demographics ran against the fundamental importance Nova Scotia families place on education. We had adjusted the legal framework for considering school closures, but some closures that were highly controversial had still moved through the system and were imminent. Education Minister Ramona Jennex called for the boards to halt their processes, pending a formal review of the overall process used to assess closures.[11] Not all boards complied. But this did signal some concern over the impact of school closures. It signaled that the financial imperative was not the only factor of concern to the government. But it was also very late in the electoral cycle to be doing this. And although the focus was on school closures, the point was not so much this particular issue, as that the government was appearing to listen to communities and was placing some value on the quality of the education experience. This was quite a different message than had been implied by the initial two years of actions that emanated from the department.

One item illustrates the extent to which the government became sensitive to public

Ramona Jennex

criticism, at least in some quarters. In the Autumn 2012 legislative session we changed the Human Rights Code to put discrimination against a person because of gender identity on an equal basis with other forms of prohibited discrimination. This was seen as being responsive to the LGBTQQ community (lesbian, gay, bisexual, transgender, queer, quest/questioning). Several of our MLAs made good speeches in the House in support of the legislation.

It was understood at the time that one likely consequence would be a push for Medical Services Insurance (MSI) to fund gender reassignment operations when medically appropriate, i.e., for well-considered cases and not on a whim. And indeed, a request for this occurred very promptly. But the position of the Department of Health as announced by Health Minister Dave A. Wilson was that, "there was a lack of high-quality research about the effectiveness and long-term outcomes of the surgery and the province would not pay for it." In a written exchange with the Rainbow Action Project of Nova Scotia, the Department rejected making funding available. Public criticism came in the form of a radio interview by lawyer Kevin Kindred. He was interviewed on the CBC on the morning of June 12, 2013. By the afternoon, the Minister was saying he had changed his mind, and a review of what was in place in other provinces and of the material supplied had led to the change of policy.[12] A change of mind is no embarrassment, especially in response to new evidence. Kindred was quoted in the *Halifax Metro* newspaper as estimating that perhaps six or eight people per year might be approved for surgery. "There has to be patient-by-patient assessment that it is medically necessary, so it's not simply a matter of demand, just like you and I can't insist on having heart surgery."[13] What this had the appearance of, however, was not a new understanding of new evidence, but just a flip-flop based on public pressure, especially in the context of a week of bad polling numbers.

· N · S · R · A · P ·

NOVA SCOTIA RAINBOW ACTION PROJECT

Equality for All

The Election

On the fourth anniversary of the 2009 election, there was a lot of press chatter about what had been accomplished, and of course when the election would be held. The *Chronicle Herald* quoted Cape Breton University political scientist David Johnson saying he had seen, "far more continuity than change. I don't see profound change. Most Nova Scotian governments always tend to govern from this broad, mushy, liberal centre."[14] The Premier made the puzzling statement that, "Really, the odd thing is that the kind of change people will generally want is stability. ... They don't want upset." His core message seemed to be that with the fiscal situation of the province under control, it would be possible to start making positive changes like dental care for children. And he warned about putting the province on the wrong track, as would happen with PC or Liberal governments: it would be a return to failed policies of the past. At the same time the press was holding reviews of the performance of the NDP in government, the June CRA poll showed the Liberals as significantly ahead, even in majority territory. *Chronicle Herald* columnist Marilla Stephenson wrote that the question of Darrell Dexter's leadership had to be asked: "Is it time for Nova Scotia's New Democrats to consider dumping Premier Darrell Dexter in an attempt to stave off defeat in the next election?"[15] Some in the press seemed to be writing-off the NDP's chances of winning the election. Brian Flinn of *AllNovaScotia.com* who is a very seasoned analyst, was suggesting the NDP might as well just put the election off so as to enjoy government for as long as possible while it still had it. The implication, though not explicitly stated, was that he believed the party was headed for defeat. But no one in the NDP was going to dump Darrell in

Darrell Dexter greeting a supporter.

advance of an election. Too much had been invested in identifying the party with him. Plus, he was widely seen inside the party as competent and a good campaigner.

For a full year the parties had been in election mode. The pressure became more intense the closer we came to the four year mark, and as small and large events occurred to make the timing of an election call dubious, there was an air of unreality. An election should have been happening, but it was not. Why not? Big picture: the polls were against the NDP. The Legislature session was lackluster. Jobs outside of Metro were not being created. Wages remained flat. Power rates were going up. Population size remained flat, which was bad news both for the dynamism of the economy overall, and for federal transfer payments. Construction, except residential in Metro, was sluggish. Consumer confidence edged up slightly, but home sales were decidedly very slow. Royalties from the offshore continued to decline as the Sable Offshore Energy Project (SOEP) moved towards closure, and Deep Panuke (a smaller field) was not yet producing. The major economic hopes, Ships Start Here and the Maritime Link, were years away from creating major employment. Beyond that, the Rehteah Parsons case demonstrated weakness in our earlier response to the cyberbullying report. The paramedics threatened to strike and were legislated to binding arbitration instead. The Bluenose was not in the water, and the bills for restoration rose to $17 million. (How can you spend $17 million on a sailboat?) There was still no Yarmouth ferry, a point emphasized – not that any emphasis was needed – by the federal government's promise for a new Digby ferry. The spring was long and wet and cold. Summer was slow in arriving. What had been a fairly successful strategy for John Hamm – a summer election with voters in a good mood – did not materialize.

The big hope the party had was the election itself. The hope was that during the campaign we would outperform the Liberals, and that the Tories would remain distinctly in third place. This was bolstered by faith that Darrell would appeal to voters more than McNeil; that Darrell would again be friendly and avuncular, but Stephen McNeil would appear angry and without any clear direction. ("We don't know much about Stephen McNeil.") It was bolstered by hope that Darrell would debate well. It was bolstered by hope that voters were still focused on the future, that the ballot question would be whether you had faith in the NDP to deliver, rather than whether we had delivered.

But the polls continued to be bad. The party spent the summer trying to organize, to nail down irritants so they would not pop up (notably, the Yarmouth ferry: finally a partner, STM Quest, to negotiate with and government money on the table for a projected 2014 restart), celebrating the Irving shipyard and Stern paper mill deals, and reinforcing the balanced budget by offering the September interim financial update early. Overall, the core message as stated by Graham Steele, was that, "The province's finances are in good hands and they're in good shape."[16] But Éric Grenier of *ThreeHundredEight.com*,[17] a national political and polling organization, was along with others, offering very bleak news. By mid-August, though based on end-of-May polling, it was suggesting the likelihood of a Liberal majority of 28 seats with 45 per cent of the vote, with the NDP falling to 13 seats with 26 per cent of the vote. Since *ThreeHundredEight.com* was widely seen as trustworthy and credible, this was bad news indeed.

The *ThreeHundredEight.com* breakdown of individual seat projections was less convincing. I thought Grenier called it wrong in about thirteen seats, and in the end my projections were more accurate. No one, however, thought for a moment that the election would be anything but hard fought and personal. We were leading the way in this: "Stephen McNeil, not worth the risk," said the new literature. To some extent exchanges in the Legislature and internal talking points showed what was to come in the election.

We were given notes with documentation to deliver the message that, "the Liberals are stuck in the past." And we heard, starting in 2011, that the two opposition parties had given the province, "twenty years of the worst economic performance,"[18] a theme repeated by the Premier, the Minister of Finance,[19] backbenchers,[20] and in the Speech From the Throne of March 2013.[21] The Liberals would let Nova Scotia's energy future, "be held hostage by Hydro Québec;" they would, "cut hundreds of rural [health] jobs and centralize health decision making in Halifax;" they failed to balance the budget; they still relied on their, "tainted trust fund dollars;" they, "spoke out against the shipbuilding bid and new high tech jobs;" they would put the provincial portion of the HST back on home heating; they cut dental services to children; they, "would eliminate the energy efficiency program." While most of these items were true, some stretched a point or were wrong. McNeil did flip-flop on the HST on electricity but in 2012 had made it clear he would not put it back on. It was not the energy efficiency program he opposed, but who paid for it. And what is so problematic about Hydro Québec?

Across the Legislature floor the opposition called taunts of, "A bitter deal," for Nova Scotians, an ironic reference to the NDP's 2009 election slogan to make, "A better deal," for Nova Scotians.

The main point about the 2013 election is that it was boring. None of the parties had anything much interesting to say. This was especially true on jobs and the economy, which was ultimately the chief vote determinant along with the issue of trust. The NDP wanted to deliver one main message: look forward. With the budget in balance, better times could be expected and benefits, such as expanded child dental care, would flow. The Liberals doubted the budged was balanced and, in essence, were promising to repeat what the NDP had been focused on during 2009-2013 – fiscal discipline of government. They offered the Darrell Dexter plan: do what the previous government had done, but do it better. The Tories focused more on taxes and the debt, issues that did not resonate

Nova Scotia Liberal leader Stephen McNeil with federal Liberal leader Justin Trudeau.

with most voters, so long as neither was so very onerous as to be a serious problem. Much was missing from the campaign.

In the debate over jobs, the NDP was forced to defend its record, however much it wanted to have voters look forward. The NDP claim was that more than 6,000 jobs had been created during its term. It turned out, however, that 2,000 full-time jobs had been lost, and 8,000 part-time jobs had been created. This hard reality was not lost on the public, especially in areas of high unemployment, i.e., pretty well everywhere outside HRM. What had been accomplished was a small reduction in poverty levels. But this was not something the NDP saw as a big vote winner.

What we have been suffering from is a stagnation of the middle class. It is hardly specific to Nova Scotia. This has been the story of North America for a generation. GDP is up. Productivity per person is up. But middle class family incomes are not up. Instead wealth has become increasingly concentrated in the hands of those who are already wealthy. This growing inequality was not something any of the parties were prepared to talk about, because they were not seriously prepared to try to do anything about it.

The nitty-gritty of this should have been a part of the public debate, but our leaders are not used to initiating a back-and-forth discussion with a public that is well-informed and productive. Mostly, they prefer "voters" to "citizens." They prefer some level of docility to active engagement. They prefer slogans and sales techniques to the messiness of an open democracy.

Just before the election, long-time political commentator Ralph Surette described the election as "shallow" and as having been "infantilized." Too true. By that time, all polls showed the Liberals as maintaining their 20 per cent lead and some polls showed the lead as high as 30 per cent, an extraordinary and unlikely number as Parker Donham pointed out. Since 1960, he wrote, "Only three times has the winning party won more than 50 per cent of the vote," and only once did it take more than 55 per cent.[22] There was now open speculation that both Dexter and Baillie could lose their seats to Liberal challenges. Why this big a swing?

Inside the NDP, the party leadership were blaming the party membership. This did not go down well. Their narrative was that the core supporters asked for too much, were not supportive, and thus undermined the whole enterprise. It is entirely true that long-time supporters were disappointed. This showed itself in many campaigns where the usual enthusiastic hustle and bustle were completely absent; in NDP campaign offices, it was pretty dead; volunteers were just not showing up; it was hard to raise money. In the end most of those long-time supporters voted for the party, and others took signs, but the enthusiasm was not there, and enthusiasm makes all the difference. That the NDP could be virtually shut out in HRM, and one of the survivors, Maureen MacDonald, have come to within 300 votes of a loss is quite astonishing. But Darrell brought this on, not the party membership.

Protesters carrying a "Puppet Premier" figure of Darrell Dexter during the Council of the Federation meetings in Halifax, July 29, 2012.

17

Picking Up The Pieces

I started this narrative with an apology. I repeat it. I apologize to the Nova Scotia public for the performance of my government. As I hope to have shown, there was serious internal dissent, but for the most part, the party leadership remained undeterred. Indeed for the most part the party leadership still seem to be in denial.

There has been no apology from anyone else. They apparently persist in the view that everything they did was right. The night of the election, Darrell accepted responsibility and *The Chronicle-Herald* ran a story under a headline, "Dexter takes full blame," writing: "Afterward, Dexter said if the party's poor showing was the result of ineffective communication with voters, he bears the responsibility. 'I'm the person who carries the message on behalf of the party. I'm willing to take every bit of responsibility for the decisions we made. We made thoughtful, compassionate decisions.'"[1]

But such statements are *pro forma*. Boiled down, it says that the party offered good government but did not communicate it well (as if that were simply a minor point). However, during the campaign and in the year leading up to it, it was obvious that the public was not satisfied; their view was not that thoughtful, compassionate decisions had been made.

During the campaign Darrell tried to show some awareness that mistakes had been made. In a letter to party supporters he said, "We have made some mistakes. We have learned from them." This sounded promising in terms of self-awareness but the hard fact is that Darrell only ad-

mitted to one mistake, the Yarmouth ferry cancellation. Not one other item has ever been conceded to have been anything except, "thoughtful and compassionate."

So what explanation has been offered by the party leadership for the melting away of 75,000 votes between 2009 and 2013? Poor communication. Anything else? Having had some opportunity to reflect Darrell went on record in an interview with the *Globe and Mail* two weeks after the election. "Dexter doles out blame after stunning election loss," said the headline. "Darrell Dexter is blaming his election loss on Nova Scotians who misread or refused to believe what his government was trying to achieve, and the media for misinterpreting his message. [...] Mr. Dexter defended his record as a premier running an activist government. The NDP was the first party in 131 years in Nova Scotia that was not re-elected to a second term. [...] 'There is a point at which you could say ... what more do you have to do? What more do you have to do in order to demonstrate, if not exceptional management skills, at least acceptable management skills and a certain level of vision?'" Then, with respect to the forgivable loan to Irving: "'It seems to this day like a no-brainer,' he said. 'What government in its right mind would not do that when the returns are so great?' [...] He said he doesn't have a single regret – that to regret would cheapen his accomplishments. 'I am completely satisfied with the decisions I made. I made them because I believed they were in the best interests of my province. I'll live with that.'"[2]

It is hard to boil this down into anything other than a statement that the voters are dumb, too dumb even to understand what is in front of their eyes. A far cry from, "taking every bit of responsibility." And nowhere in the same universe as an apology.

At caucus, the one post-election meeting of the MLAs held a week after the election, Darrell picked up on his election night theme that we had a lot to be proud of: "It has been an enormous honor to serve. It has been a tumultuous four years. We never backed down from a challenge. It was thrilling, exciting. It may not feel like it today but the future will see the basic changes we made in all policy areas as being to the good. People said they did not know what we accomplished, and that's not our fault either. You can do a lot with negativity, and it came not just from our opponents, some came from our own people: they stayed home. I have no regrets over a thing. That would cheapen our accomplishments. To the 'Seven Samurai' left behind: you have an enormous job ahead; you can be all things to all people. Sometimes politics is compared to the practice of law – but in law there needs to be a foundation for your positions; not so in politics. I shall consider my own future. This is a time for some self-reflection; we should look forward, not backward. A lot of young people came out to work on the campaign. The young are our future and our path back to government. The party executive meets in November. There will be a process of evaluation of the campaign, if it is like previous times. Discussion in the party needs not to be just about us, but about what the province needs, not just our machinations."

After Party secretary and Campaign Director Jill Marzetti spoke briefly Darrell continued: "It was a good campaign. My thanks to Jill and all staff. Halifax is thriving, just look around: anyone with a vision can get going on their projects. Look at our better bond rating, construction, jobs. We just couldn't catch a break. Last week we were holding an event outdoors beside some of the new construction and an Irving oil truck pulls up behind us and just stayed there, so it was in the photos; it was noisy and chugging: it was funny in a way. Every constituency organized good teams. There were "1s" [i.e., supporters] identified who never voted, you just could not pull them out to vote. A shame, but a reality of political life. The Liberals spent four years pouring poison into the well – some misrepresentations, some lies. But the press just would not go after them. It was not the fault of our campaign, our staff, or the party apparatus: they all worked their butts off for us. Be thankful for that, and say it. Things will turn around. Even now we can identify seats that are vulnerable. This is a point of departure. Even as the Liberals take their first steps into office they are taking steps towards defeat. We have to try to be the ones who benefit, though we will have competition. Nova Scotia is a province of moderates. The campaign was good work. Thanks."

A fellow who is out of a job, unexpectedly and in a very public flame-out, can be forgiven for rambling a bit, even a week after the event. But the content, what was said and what was not said, jump out. Instead of, "we made some mistakes," we heard "I have no regrets over a thing." Instead of, "we failed to communicate," we heard that the press would not go after the Liberals and it is not our fault people did not know what we accomplished. Instead of, "I am willing to take every bit of responsibility," we heard that it all had to do with the negativity of our own supporters who stayed home. In 2009 the NDP received 186,556 votes; in 2013 we received 111,380, with virtually exactly the same overall turnout of voters. So the party lost 75,176 votes. By no stretch of anyone's imagination does this represent party members staying home. I do not think party membership has ever exceeded about 7,000 – and even that number was a temporary high around 1997–1999. About a decade ago it had been at 4,000, dwindling to circa 2,000 at about the time of the 2009 election win. Following the 2013 election, numbers went below 1500. There are simply not 75,000 party members or even core supporters. This is a widespread and general drop in support for the Dexter NDP by a large number of the general population.

During the election much was said about recent elections in other provinces. This came up when commentators were wondering about the reliability of poll numbers. British Columbia was discussed in particular. Its example was discussed internally as well, not just with respect to polls, but also in terms of the general electoral approach. Now we can add another comparison. In British Columbia, NDP leader Adrian Dix frankly admitted to his mistakes and resigned: "...that we fell short on Election

Day is my responsibility as Leader. It has become clear to me that the best interests of our party mean that I need to step aside...."[3]

Internally, the NDP will be focused on the future. But no future can be mapped out without an honest, hard look at the past. The ethos of Darrell and his inner circle can be illustrated by a mocking statement that came from them several times: they ridiculed those, "who would rather be right than in power." This is the profound cynicism of the professional politician for whom getting elected and then re-elected is always job priority one; who tells voters what they want to hear, who is not a leader but is a leader of the followers; who avoids hard issues; who never admits an error; who is always ready with standard excuses for doing something different than they said ("circumstances have changed," and "unforeseen problems have arisen," and "the promise I made was not understood properly.") If that is the choice, I have no problem in plumping for being in the right rather than in power. But it is not the choice. We can be both. The legacy we now have is of a squandering of the good will that had been built up by hard work through long years by many people. But it is not an irreversible situation.

Still, there will be difficulties in reestablishing credibility. As Opposition, we used to chant at the government, "Why should we believe you now?" This was always a good point. When credibility has been eroded it is hard to reestablish. Not impossible, but it requires a serious objective demonstration of why voters should believe that we are now different from the Liberals or Tories. For example, how can the NDP opposition members now criticize any P-3 (Public-Private Partnership) proposals that might come from the Liberals, having so prominently, while in government, put money into the P-3 Convention Center? How can we criticize proposals for contracting out government services, having been the initiator of contracting out the SAP (Systems, Applications, and Products in Data Processing) function of the Department of Finance? What credibility did the caucus have when speaking against the Liberals' bill to step into health sector bargaining at Northwood, when the Dexter government had legislated paramedics into binding arbitration just eight months before? The seven NDP MLAs who form the current caucus are dominated by former members of cabinet (five of seven). It will be hard for them to indicate a change in direction. This must be the task of the next leader.

Ultimately what should inspire internal party change is that the province's voters are, in fact, largely of the traditional left values the NDP had previously stood for. It was a very good thing that the voters were so profoundly skeptical about pushing so much public money at big businesses. It was a good thing that the voters displayed a distaste for a government that saw itself as a spokesperson for Nova Scotia Power. It was a good thing that the voters took offense against the abuse of expenses. It was a good thing that the public had little problem with the increase of the HST (the social contract – broken – being that services be improved.) And it was a good thing that canvassers in low-income areas found resentment about social inequality. The public is a traditional NDP values public. One of the great missed opportunities of the Dexter government was in not setting out those old values in clear terms, and not giving the voters something to support.

One important segment of the population, those under thirty, have really never experienced an NDP that is anything other than middle-of-the-road, or quasi-Liberals. This is unfortunate. When those of us of an older generation talk about 'old values' the language baffles them. Not having been involved in the years when the Nova Scotia NDP was an activist opposition, hearing Dexterities refer to hardworking progressive NGOs as 'frenemies,' or being on the receiving end of tight-fisted education policies, the next generation feel profoundly skeptical about the NDP. It will take a lot of work to win them over.

I find it hard to see any member of the Dexter cabinet as a credible candidate for the next party leader. This is especially so after their post-election decision to increase severance payments for Premier's Office staff. This was an offensive decision, widely noted with repulsion both inside the party and by the public generally. If the NDP becomes Dexter version 2.0, through selecting someone like Dave A. Wilson or Maureen MacDonald as leader, what will be their electoral strategy? They are convinced that the party came to power in 2009 through moderation, through distancing itself from traditional NDP policies. Their view is that the party attracted disaffected Red Tories and soft Liberals, and added their votes to those of reliable NDP voters, so as to attain 45 per cent of the vote. I do not believe that is what happened, but suppose it was; will it be possible to repeat this? I think not. Those swing voters will not be fooled twice. For the party to rebuild, it will have to appeal to a different segment of voters (and those who have tended not to vote). Building on the 27 per cent who stayed with the party in 2013 will require attracting women, youth, the poor, labour, environmentalists, and new economy entrepreneurs. An NDP of Dexterite version 2.0 has no chance of doing that. The party has been put into serious debt, virtually to the point of bankruptcy, and has been shedding members at an unprecedented rate, reaching an historic low of circa 1800. Little wonder.

In Ontario in the 1990s, the one-term Bob Rae NDP government became so problematic for voters that the result has been an unbroken run of twenty years of exclusion from power. That might be Darrell's legacy, but I do not think so. That legacy can be overcome. In recent Nova Scotia history there have tended not to be two terms of Tories followed by two terms of Liberals; the voters switching periodically so as to minimize arrogance and corruption. The voters have been even crankier than that, and a three-party presence has added possible scenarios. The recent pattern (until we broke it) had been a term as a majority followed by a term as a minority. That is likely what the Liberals face. The party's job over the coming years will be to rebuild. We need to rebuild our party internally (membership, constituency associations, engagement, and finances) and to rebuild public credibility. If we do have a future, profound change, starting with new and progressive leadership, is required. If.

Inside the party we are certainly focused on the future. But there can be no useful planning for the future absent a frank assessment of the past. In fact, the 2013 numbers are not entirely discouraging. Press exaggeration used terms like "rout" and, "the province turned its back," on the Dexter NDP. But the party ran second. In the popular vote we edged out the PCs (although very slightly) and held 27 per cent of the vote. That is not a wipeout. What it shows is that a three-party system remains in Nova Scotia. All three parties remain viable. It is certainly the case that working with a seven-member caucus will be difficult, and it is certainly the case that for every one of those seven seats the plurality was not large: for six the difference was 500 votes or less and in the other the difference was just 600 votes. We won seven seats; ran second in 27 seats; and ran third in seventeen seats. Ten seats certainly *were* routs with total NDP votes of 1,000 or less: Annapolis, Argyle, Clare-Digby, Colchester North, Cumberland South, Glace Bay, Hants West, Inverness, Kings West, and Yarmouth.

The election numbers illustrate additional points. For the NDP the Greens were a factor in only one seat, Kings North, lost by Jim Morton by some 37 votes, in which the Green candidate, Mary Lou Harley, took 362 votes. Losing Jim Morton from caucus was a great loss: he has always been a sensible, thoughtful, and progressive colleague. This was a standout constituency for the Greens, who ran only sixteen candidates in total, taking 3,698 votes in all, down greatly from 9,636 in 2009. Despite the very fine work in Parliament of national Green Party leader Elizabeth May, and her personal popularity in Nova Scotia, support for the provincial Green Party remains miniscule. With a better record on sustainability, Green votes could go to the NDP.

Importantly with respect to the PCs, they won no seats in HRM, taking only about 13 per cent of the vote in the province's main urban area. The NDP holds seats or remains competitive in all parts of the province except for southern-most portion (Yarmouth, Argyle, Clare-Digby, Annapolis and the Shelburne portion of Queens-Shelburne). The main opportunity for the NDP to re-win seats will probably be in HRM, where we will have to go head-to-head with the Liberals.

All things being equal, the odds would favor NDP gains in the next election, gains likely to be in excess of those of the PCs but leaving the Liberals in power. Whether it is possible for the NDP to win the next election or even take second place, depends most crucially on whether we can build our general positioning through countering what the voters found objectionable in our first term, and then rejected in the 2013 election. This means change. To me this means not only new leadership, new staff, and finally coming to grips with organizational basics, but also a clear progressive agenda anchored in traditional NDP values. Nothing else will do.

It is not difficult to speculate over probable candidates, or people who would be asked by others to consider running for leader. The task is likely to be a long-range one. A new leader will have to be there during the rest of the Liberal term, run in the 2017 election, likely remain in the Oppo-sition for some years after that, and

Lenore Zann, MLA for Truro-Bible-Hill.

then go into a subsequent election hoping to form a government. It would be at least a seven- to ten-year commitment.

In addition to Dave A. Wilson and Lenore Zann, both in the caucus, former MLAs Jim Morton and Gary Burrill will be asked to consider running. Kevin Deveaux would have been in this category, even though he has been out of the caucus for a long time, but in the 2013 election he campaigned for the Liberal candidate in Eastern Passage, against NDP incumbent Becky Kent, thus effectively switching parties. Halifax MP Megan Les-lie would be the most attractive candidate, being best able to bring some internal harmony to the party, having promi-nence and skills, and also well-placed to step into a seat since she lives in North End Halifax

Former MLA, Gary Burrill.

where Maureen could step aside to allow her to become an MLA in a by-election. But she has said she is not interested. Beyond these, there is a slender list. Former party president David Wallbridge has skills, but is deeply involved in his law practice and shows little interest in being a candidate. Graham Steele showed every sign for years of being interested, but not of late; he has enrolled in graduate legal studies and seems to be looking to head off in another direction. With the publication of his book and its message of profound skepticism about politics, it is not at all clear he wants to continue to be involved at all. It is one of the consequences of the party failing to foster municipal-level NDP candidates that we have no real Dippers of prominence holding office at that level; likewise, policies that have generally alienated the most tal-

Megan Leslie as a volunteer on my 2003 re-election campaign.

ented of the young have meant that we have a weak youth wing. The labour movement leadership has been stagnant for years and offers no candidates.

One exception might be Susanna Fuller, a fisheries PhD who has worked at the Ecology Action Centre and is a successful community organizer in Maureen's constituency, Halifax Needham. Susanna has been the force behind the redevelopment of the old Bloomfield School lands; she also went out on a long financial limb to purchase seven houses put on the market by one neighborhood landlord, and found individual purchasers for them, resulting in saving a nice North End Halifax street and improving the housing stock. She has been a member of the group headed by Acadia University president (and NS Power board member) Ray Ivany, appointed to study the Nova Scotia economy. Regardless of whether she seeks the leadership, if Maureen decides to retire before her term is up, Susanna could probably hold Needham for the NDP and could be a solid addition to the caucus.

Susanna Fuller

Among the candidates who ran for the first time in 2013 but were not elected, both Tanis Crosby and Abad Khan might think seriously about party leadership, though the disadvantage of taking on that role fresh from an election loss is daunting. Tanis has now

Tanis Crosby and Abad Khan.

chosen to take a position with the YWCA in San Francisco, a real loss for our province.

The future of the NDP all across Canada is in doubt. In most places the party membership is ageing and disappointed. Transition to a new and progressive generation has to occur for the party to continue as a robust organization. There is relatively little to attract a youth that admires Occupy, that is concerned for its economic future, that has educated itself at great expense, that is concerned for its environmental future, that has ideas, that has energy. My title, *Rise Again*, echos the haunting 1985 Leon Dubinsky song written for *The Rise and Follies of Cape Breton*:

> *As sure as the sunrise, as sure as the sea;*
> *As sure as the wind in the trees.*
> *We rise again in the faces of our children.*

But there is nothing sure about it. Profound change has to happen in our party. What we have here is contingency, in all its meanings. Good luck to us all.

Endnotes

Chapter 1 - Foreword

1   Graham Steele. 2014. What I learned about politics: Inside the rise – and collapse – of Nova Scotia's NDP government. Nimbus Publishing, Halifax, Nova Scotia.

2   P.J. O'Rourke. 1991. Parliament of whores. Atlantic Monthly Press, New York, NY.

3   Jeffrey Simpson. 2014. Ontario's NDP sound awfully conservative. The Globe and Mail, May 28, 2014. Available from: http://www.theglobeandmail.com/globe-debate/meet-ontarios-ndp-conservative-wannabes/article18865860/

4   James Laxer. 1997. In search of a new left: Canadian politics after the neoconservative assault. Penguin Canada, Toronto, Ontario.

5   See: Hansard for second reading debates on the *HRM By Design Act*, May 27, November 3, November 4, 2008. This was an issue to reappear in 2012–2013 as "density bonusing" as an instrument of legal control of development in the HRM Regional Centre.

Chapter 2 - Why We Lost in 2013

1   Jeffrey Simpson. 1988. Spoils of power: The politics of patronage. HarperCollins Canada, Toronto, Ontario.

2   Elizabeth Beale, Tim O'Neill, Lars Osberg, and Donald J. Savoie. 2009. Addressing Nova Scotia's fiscal challenge: A report prepared by the Nova Scotia Economic Advisory Panel. Available from: https://www.novascotia.ca/ppo/PDFs/EAP_FinalReport_Nov12_rev.pdf

3   Frank Magazine. 1998. NDP fashion police continue manhunt for Dartmouth man. April 21, 1998.

4   Minority governments have been relatively rare at the provincial level, and as Graham Steele observes, "In order for there to be a minority government, there have to be at least three parties capable of winning seats." Also, "Because there is no tradition of minority governments, and therefore no tradition of coalitions ... our politicians are generally ill-equipped to handle minorities when they happen." See: Graham Steele. 2010. Minority government in Nova Scotia, 1998–2009: What lessons can we learn? Journal of Parliamentary and Political Law 4(2): 55–60.

5   See: Christopher G. Majka. Election Nova Scotia: Orange crush to red tide. Rabble.ca, October 12, 2013. Available from: http://rabble.ca/blogs/

bloggers/christophermajka/2013/10/election-nova-scotia-orange-crush-to-red-tide
6   Juha Mikkonen, and Dennis Raphael. 2010. Social determinants of health: The Canadian facts. York University School of Health Policy and Management, Toronto, Ontario. Available from: http://www.thecanadianfacts.org/the_canadian_facts.pdf
7   The Contrarian. Available from: http://contrarian.ca/tag/parker-donham/
8   Claire McIlveen. 2013. When it comes to politics, negative spin obscures reality. The Chronicle Herald, October 2, 2013. Available from: http://thechronicleherald.ca/opinion/1158073-mcilveen-when-it-comes-to-politics-negative-spin-obscures-reality
9   The Contrarian. Available from: http://contrarian.ca/tag/parker-donham/
10   *See:* NDP stays silent on loan tinkering, September 12, 2013; and; New ferry collides with small NDP surplus, September 6, 2013. AllNovaScotia.com. Available from: http://www.allnovascotia.com/
11   Tim Bousquet. 2013. The politics of bullshit. The Coast, October 90, 2013. Available from: http://www.thecoast.ca/halifax/the-politics-of-bullshit/Content?oid=4091547
12   *See:* Larry Hughes offers liberals energy advice, October 18, 2013. AllNovaScotia.com. Available from: http://www.allnovascotia.com/

Chapter 3 – Seems Like Old Times
1   Paul MacEwan. 1980. The Akerman years: Jeremy Akerman and the Nova Scotia NDP, 1965–1980. Formac Publishing, Halifax, Nova Scotia.
2   J. Murray Beck. 1985. Politics of Nova Scotia, volume 2: Murray–Buchanan, 1896–1968. Four East Publications, Tantallon, Nova Scotia. p. 343.
3   Nova Scotia Legislature, Hansard. February 25, 1982. p. 244.
4   The Shaw Group of Companies. Available from: http://shawgroupltd.com/
5   Frank Magazine. 1988. Cover. August 29, 1988.
6   Murray Brewster. 2001. Take prayer out of House – Epstein. The Chronicle Herald, February 12, 2001.
7   David Rodenhiser. 2001. Secular argument : Government is no place for daily prayer. The Daily News, February 18, 2001.
8   A.W. Johnson. 2004. Dream no little dreams: A biography of the Douglas government of Saskatchewan, 1944–191. University of Toronto Press, Toronto, Ontario.
9   Jane Purves. 1999. Statement released by Education Minister Jane Purves. Nova Scotia Department of Education. September 22, 1999. Available from: http://novascotia.ca/news/release/?id=19990922002
10   Lori Errington. 2011. The experiences of female members in the Legislative Assembly in Nova Scotia. MA thesis, Mount Saint Vincent University, Halifax, Nova Scotia. Available from: http://dc.msvu.ca:8080/xmlui/bitstream/handle/10587/1155/LoriErringtonMAPRThesis2011.pdf

11 Robert Everett-Green. 2006. Music to the ears of Nova Scotia. The Globe and Mail, April 18, 2006. Available from: http://www.theglobeandmail. com/arts/music-to-the-ears-of-nova-scotia/article18160359/

12 Jeremy Paxman. 2003. The political animal. Penguin Books, London, UK. [*See:* pages 89 and 91.]

Chapter 4 – That was Then, This is Now

1 Nova Scotia Legislature, Hansard. November 16, 1999. Available from: http://nslegislature.ca/index.php/proceedings/hansard/C52/58_1_h99nov16/#[Page%202064]

2 Nova Scotia Legislature, Hansard. December 7, 1979.

3 Nova Scotia Legislature, Hansard. December 11, 1979, p. 3343.

4 NDP Policy Book. [F 2.1, 1980.]

5 Amy Smith. 2009. NDP wouldn't kill Michelin Bill. The Chronicle Herald, May 12, 2009.

6 John Reid. 1993. The 1970s: Sharpening the skeptical edge. In: The Atlantic Provinces in Confederation. Edited by: E.R. Forbes and D.A. Muise. University of Toronto Press, Toronto, Ontario. pp. 469 – 470.

7 Michelin's Speaking Points, November 30, 2011.

8 Province of Nova Scotia. 1989. Labour Standards Code. Available from: http://nslegislature.ca/legc/statutes/labour%20standards%20code.pdf

9 Darrell Dexter. 2001. The Chronicle Herald, September 4, 2001.

10 Kyle Buott, Larry Haiven, and Judy Haiven. 2012. Labour standards in Nova Scotia: Reversing the war against workers. The Canadian Centre for Policy Alternatives – Nova Scotia. Available from: https://www.policyalternatives. ca/publications/reports/labour-standards-reform-nova-scotia

11 Nova Scotia Occupational Health and Safety. 2013. Annual Report 2012/13. Available from: http://novascotia.ca/lae/healthandsafety/documents/2012-2013OHSAnnualReport.pdf

12 Province of Nova Scotia. 2013. Nova Scotia Annual Gaming Report, 2012–2013. Available from: https://www.novascotia.ca/snsmr/pdf/agd-nova-scotia-annual-gaming-report-2012-13.pdf

13 Nova Scotia Legislature, Hansard. November 4, 1998, p. 3298. Available from: http://nslegislature.ca/index.php/proceedings/hansard/C56/57_1_h98nov04/#[Page%203298]

14 Nova Scotia Legislature, Hansard. October 25, 1999. Available from: http://nslegislature.ca/index.php/proceedings/hansard/C52/58_1_h99oct25/#[Page%20709]

15 Nova Scotia Legislature, Hansard. October 26, 1999. Available from: http://nslegislature.ca/index.php/proceedings/hansard/C52/58_1_h99oct26/#[Page%20906]

16 Editorial: The Globe and Mail. 2003. Car insurance rates and how to tame them. The Globe and Mail, June 20, 2003. Available from: http://www.

theglobeandmail.com/globe-debate/car-insurance-ratesand-how-to-tame-them/article751286/

17   Nova Scotia Legislature. 2010. *Insurance Act* (amended). Available from: http://nslegislature.ca/legc/bills/61st_2nd/3rd_read/b052.htm

18   Automobile Accident Minor Injury Regulations. Nova Scotia Regulations 94/2010. Available from: http://www.novascotia.ca/just/regulations/regs/iminor.htm

19   *See:* Nova Scotia Public Interest Research Group, Ecology Action Centre, and Concerned Citizens of Lincolnville. 2011. Lincolnville protest against environmental racism. Halifax Media Co-op, May 10, 2011. Available from: http://halifax.mediacoop.ca/newsrelease/7215

20   Paul MacEwan. 2001. Howard Epstein, environmental critic. New Waterford Press, October 9, 2001.

21   The health and environmental dangers of coal as a substanceto burn are well-documented. Coal as a source for simple carbon, for example in nanotechnology, may have some limited future, but this is dependent on various technological advances and also might not require large quantities of coal. *See:* John Colapinto. 2014. Material Question. The New Yorker, December 22, 2014. Available from: http://www.newyorker.com/magazine/2014/12/22/material-question

22   Cpl. D. Hubley, Public Complaints Reviewer, "H" Division. 2004. Letter, March 17, 2004.

23   Demonstrations and police actions in Canada have been studied, and been the subject of formal inquiries. One legal survey published in 2002 just after the Halifax events but not including them, said: "The last several years have witnessed an upsurge in the size and level of militant protest, in a way not seen in Canada for some time. Organized broadly around themes of 'anti-globalization' or 'global justice,' this resistance has become an international movement, with mass demonstrations occurring in various countries around the world. The Canadian segment of the global justice movement has been quite active, holding large demonstrations at meetings of international economic and political leaders in Vancouver (1997), Windsor (2000), Quebec City (2001), Toronto (2001), Ottawa (2002), and Calgary (2002). However, the protests are usually remembered more for tear gas, plastic bullets, and clashes with the police than they are for the issues that brought the protesters there in the first place. Global justice protests in Vancouver in 1997 and Quebec in 2001 were followed by highly critical reports documenting serious Charter violations by police and allegations of political interference by highly placed government representatives." – Jackie Esmonde. 2002. The policing of dissent: The use of breach of the peace arrests at political demonstrations. Journal of Law and Equality 1(2): 246–263.

24   Jeremy Paxman. 2003. The political animal, Penguin Books, Great Britain. [p. 113]

Chapter 5 – Off to a Bad Start: Three Conversations

1 Pierre Bayard. 2009. How to talk about books you haven't read. Bloomsbury, New York, NY.

2 Elizabeth Beale, Tim O'Neill, Lars Osberg, and Donald J. Savoie. 2009. Addressing Nova Scotia's fiscal challenge. November, 2009. Available from: http://www.novascotia.ca/ppo/PDFs/EAP_FinalReport_Nov12_rev.pdf

3 • Martin Turcotte. 2012. Charitable giving by Canadians. Statistics Canada. Canadian Social Trends, April 16, 2012, No.93, Table 5. Available from: http://www.statcan.gc.ca/pub/11-008-x/2012001/article/11637-eng.pdf • Statistics Canada. 2012. Charitable donors, 2012. The Daily, March 27, 2014, Table 1. Available from: http://www.statcan.gc.ca/daily-quotidien/140327/dq140327c-eng.htm

Chapter 6 – Whack–a–Mole

1 Province of Nova Scotia. 2010. Better care sooner: The plan to improve emergency care. Available from: http://novascotia.ca/dhw/publications/Better-Care-Sooner-plan.pdf

2 Province of Nova Scotia. 2011. The path we share: A natural resources strategy for Nova Scotia, 2011–2020. Available from: http://novascotia.ca/natr/strategy/pdf/Strategy_Strategy.pdf

3 John Ross. 2010. The patient journey through emergency care in Nova Scotia: A prescription for new medicine. Available from: http://novascotia.ca/dhw/publications/Dr-Ross-The-Patient-Journey-Through-Emergency-Care-in-Nova-Scotia.pdf

4 Ralph S. Johnson. 1986. Forests of Nova Scotia: A history. Four East Publications, Tantallon, Nova Scotia.

5 L. Anders Sandberg (Editor). 1992. Trouble in the woods: Forest policy and social conflict in Nova Scotia and New Brunswick. Acadiensis, Fredericton, New Brunswick.

6 Sara Wilson, Ronald Coleman, Minga O'Brien, and Linda Pannozzo. 2001. The Nova Scotia Genuine Progress Index forest accounts, volume 1: Indicators of ecological, economic & social values of forests in Nova Scotia. GPI Atlantic, Halifax, NS. Available from: http://www.gpiatlantic.org/pdf/forest/forest1.pdf

7 Linda Pannozzo and Ronald Coleman. 2008. Genuine Progress Index forest headline indicators for Nova Scotia. GPI Atlantic, Halifax, Nova Scotia. Available from: http://www.gpiatlantic.org/pdf/forest/forestupdate.pdf

8 David Jackson. 2012. Bowater bailout bucks could be used better, small business group says. The Chronicle Herald, February 28, 2012. Available from: http://thechronicleherald.ca/business/68159-bowater-bailout-bucks-could-be-used-better-small-business-group-says

9 Parker Donham. 2013. Six things the NDP did wrong, part 2. The Contrarian. September 15, 2013. Available from: http://contrarian.ca/

10 Barrie McKenna. 2012. For government subsidies, what price is too high to save a job? The Globe and Mail, Report on Business. September 30, 2012. Available from: http://www.theglobeandmail.com/report-on-business/economy/for-government-subsidies-what-price-is-too-high-to-save-a-job/article4577935/

11 Michael Porter. 1990. The competitive advantage of nations. The Free Press, New York, NY.

12 Tim Bousquet. 2010. First look at convention centre costs: City will be asked to pay $57 million. The Coast, September 27, 2010. Available from: http://www.thecoast.ca/RealityBites/archives/2010/09/27/first-look-at-convention-centre-costs-city-will-be-asked-to-pay-57-million

13 See: Christopher Majka. 2010. Convention Centre in Nova Scotia: Economic wellspring or bottomless pit? The Canadian Centre for Policy Alternatives – Nova Scotia. Available from: https://www.policyalternatives.ca/publications/reports/convention-centre-nova-scotia

14 Chronicle Herald editorial. 2012. Convention centre deal: Let's move on. The Chronicle Herald, July 11, 2012. Available from: http://thechronicleherald.ca/editorials/115895-convention-centre-deal-let-s-move-on

15 Laura Penny. 2010. New party in power: Same old politics. The NovaScotian, October 17, 2010.

16 Nova Scotia Reg. 101/2001: Statement of Provincial Interest. Available from: http://www.novascotia.ca/just/regulations/regs/mgstmt.htm
Nova Scotia Reg. 310/2013. Interim Planning Area Order. Available from: http://www.novascotia.ca/just/regulations/regs/hrmplanorder.htm

17 BM Halifax Holdings Ltd v Nova Scotia. 2014. Supreme Court of Nova Scotia. December 17, 2014, NSSC 430. Available from: http://www.courts.ns.ca/Decisions_Of_Courts/documents/2014nssc430.pdf

18 See: Christopher Majka. 2012. Down our throats: Fed up with salmon feedlots. http://rabble.ca/blogs/bloggers/christophermajka/2012/12/down-our-throats-fed-salmon-feedlots

19 Silver Donald Cameron. 2012. Salmon Wars. Available from: http://www.salmonwars.com/

20 Remo Zaccagna. 2012. Cooke Aquaculture says expansion 'makes sense'. The Chronicle Herald, June 20, 2012. Available from: http://thechronicleherald.ca/business/109242-cooke-aquaculture-says-nova-scotia-expansion-makes-sense

21 Bruce I. Cohen. 2012. The uncertain future of Fraser River Sockeye, volume 1: The Sockeye fisher. Report of the Commission of Inquiry into the Decline of Sockeye Salmon in the Fraser River, Government of Canada, November, 2012. Available from: http://www.watershed-watch.org/wordpress/wp-content/uploads/2013/02/CohenCommissionFinalReport_Vol01_Full.pdf

22 Meinhard Doelle and Bill Lahey. 2014. Independent Aquaculture Regulatory Review for Nova Scotia: Draft version for public comment. July 3, 2014. Available from: http://www.aquaculturereview.ca/sites/default/files/Draft%20Report%20July%203.pdf

Chapter 7 – Expenses Scandal

1 This appears to be the core issue in the U.K. Parliament as well. *See:* Michael Carpenter. 2011. The accountability of Members for their expenses: legal and jurisdictional issues. Journal of Parliamentary and Political Law 5(2): 323–336.
2 Graham Steele. 2014. What I learned about politics: Inside the rise – and collapse – of Nova Scotia's NDP government. Nimbus Publishing, Halifax, Nova Scotia: p. 60.
3 Paul Pross. 2010. Contrarian. February 18, 2010. Available from: http://contrarian.ca/
4 Parker Donham. Contrarian. February 15, 2010. Available from: http://contrarian.ca/

Chapter 8 – Ships Sink Here

1 Tom Traves. 1979. The state and enterprise: Canadian manufacturers and the federal government, 1917–1931. University of Toronto Press, Toronto, Ontario.
2 Frank Magazine. 2013. July 23, 2013, p. 26.
3 CBC News. 2012. Irving gets $304M from N.S. for shipbuilding. March 30, 2012. Available from: http://www.cbc.ca/news/canada/nova-scotia/irving-gets-304m-from-n-s-for-shipbuilding-1.1236105
4 Ships Start Here. Available from: http://shipsstarthere.ca/
5 David Jackson. 2012. 'There's not enough lipstick you can put on that pig.' The Chronicle Herald, January 8, 2012. Available from: https://thechronicleherald.ca/opinion/49855-there-not-enough-lipstick-you-can-put-pig
6 Jane Taber. 2013. Dexter doles out the blame after stunning N.S. election loss. The Globe and Mail, October 20, 2013. Available from: http://www.theglobeandmail.com/news/politics/dexter-doles-out-blame-after-stunning-ns-election-loss/article14956112/
7 Graham Steele. 2014. What I learned in politics: Inside the rise and – and collapse – of Nova Scotia's NDP government. Nimbus Publishing, Halifax, Nova Scotia.
8 National Shipbuilding Procurement Strategy. Available from: http://www.tpsgc-pwgsc.gc.ca/app-acq/sam-mps/snacn-nsps-eng.html
9 Rick Williams. 1993. Hard times: In another land: Hope tinged by despair. New Maritimes, March/April 1993. p. 33.
10 Rick Williams. 1993. Hard times: NAFTA: Full speed ahead, backwards. New Maritimes, January/February 1993. p. 29.

11 Rick Williams. 1988. Hard times: Rethinking the welfare state. New Maritimes, September/October 1988.

12 Rick Williams. 1989. Hard times: Planning not to plan. New Maritimes, November/December 1989.

13 Royal Commission on Post-secondary Education. 1983–1985. Available from: https://memoryns.ca/nova-scotia-royal-commission-on-post-secondary-education-fonds

14 Ronald L. Watts, J. Fraser Mustard, and Edmund C. Bovey. 1984. Ontario universities: Options and futures. Commission on the Future Development of the Universities of Ontario. Toronto, Ontario.

15 Tim O'Neill. 2010. Report on the university system in Nova Scotia. Prepared for Premier Darrell Dexter, Province of Nova Scotia. Available from: https://www.novascotia.ca/lae/HigherEducation/documents/Report_on_the_Higher_Education_System_in_Nova_Scotia.pdf

16 Nova Scotia Legislature, Hansard, February 4, 2004. Standing Committee on Public Accounts. Available from: http://nslegislature.ca/index.php/committees/committee_hansard/C7/pa_2004feb04

17 Chronicle Herald Editorial. 2004. In defence of NSCAD. The Chronicle Herald, February 23, 2004.

18 Nova Scotia Post-secondary Education Coalition. 2014. Building for the future: Public opinion on post-secondary education in Nova Scotia. Available from: http://fileserver.cfsadmin.org/file/cfsns/44716a29655e79875bc3f1f4ee889c76e0299a6f.pdf

19 jobsHere. Nova Scotia's Workforce Strategy. Available from: http://careers.novascotia.ca/sites/default/files/WorkforceStrategy.pdf

20 Michael E. Porter. 1990. The competitive advantage of nations. The Harvard Business Review, March/April 1990: 73–91.

21 Michael E. Porter. 1991. Canada at the crossroads: The reality of a new competitive environment. The Business Council on National Issues and the Government of Canada. Available from: http://www.ceocouncil.ca/wp-content/uploads/archives/OCT_1991_ENG_Canada_at_the_Crossroads.pdf

22 See: Richard A Posner. 2009. A failure of capitalism. Harvard University Press, Cambridge, Massachusetts, USA.

23 Jacques R. Lapointe. 2012. Message from the Auditor General: Report of the Auditor General. January, 2012. Available from: http://oag-ns.ca/index.php/publications?task=document.viewdoc&id=703

24 Statistics Canada. 2009. Labour force characteristics by province, August 2009. Available from: http://www.statcan.gc.ca/daily-quotidien/090904/t090904a3-eng.htm
Statistics Canada. 2013. Labour force characteristics by province, October 2013. Available from: http://www.statcan.gc.ca/daily-quotidien/131108/t131108a003-eng.htm

Chapter 9 – Carbon, Climate Change, Nova Scotia Power

1   Richard Starr. 2011. Power Failure? Formac Publishing, Halifax, Nova Scotia.

2   J. Murray Beck. 1985. Politics of Nova Scotia, Volume 2: Murray–Buchanan, 1896–1968. Four East Publications, Tantallon, Nova Scotia.

3   Probably this phrase was meant to indicate "carbon capture and storage" (CSS), a very expensive and still unproven technology.

4   Nova Scotia Legislature, Hansard, May 16, 2012. p 2320. Available from: http://nslegislature.ca/index.php/proceedings/hansard/C89/house_12may16/#HPage2320

5   Nova Scotia Utility and Review Board. 2014. In the matter of an application by Nova Scotia Power Inc. for approval of a deferral of fuel costs. November 25, 2014. Available from: http://nsuarb.novascotia.ca/sites/default/files/decisions/m06475_decision.pdf

6   Catherine Abreau. 2013. Electricity and Nova Scotia's future: Hurdles and opportunities. Ecology Action Centre, August, 2013

7   See: Christopher G. Majka. 2012. Power to the people? Canadian Centre for Policy Alternatives. Available from: https://www.policyalternatives.ca/publications/commentary/fast-facts-power-people

8   Nova Scotia Utility and Review Board. 2013. Decision: In the matter of the Maritime Link Act. July 22, 2013. Available from: http://nsuarb.novascotia.ca/sites/default/files/documents/electricityarchive/decision_maritime_link_project.pdf

9   Canadian Steel Producers Association. Available from: http://canadiansteel.ca/

10 Robert Devet. 2014. Donkin coal mine may reopen. Halifax Media Co-op. Available from: http://halifax.mediacoop.ca/story/donkin-coal-mine-may-reopen/32508

11 Environmental Goals and Sustainability Act. 2007. Available from: http://www.novascotia.ca/nse/egspa/

12 Efficiency Nova Scotia. Available from: http://www.efficiencyns.ca/

13 Shawn McCarthy. 2010. Shale: The next energy game changer. The Globe and Mail, May 14, 2010. Available from: http://www.theglobeandmail.com/report-on-business/industry-news/energy-and-resources/shale-the-next-energy-game-changer/article4353125/

14 See: Christopher G. Majka. 2012. Down our throats: Fed-up with salmon feedlots. Rabble.ca. Available from: http://rabble.ca/blogs/bloggers/christophermajka/2012/12/down-our-throats-fed-salmon-feedlots

15 United Nations General Assembly. 1992. Rio declaration on environment and development. Available from: http://www.un.org/documents/ga/conf151/aconf15126-1annex1.htm

16 Frank Atherton, Michael Bradfield, Kevin Christmas, Shawn Dalton, Maurice Dusseault, Graham Gagnon, Brian Hayes, Constance MacIntosh,

Ian Mauro, Ray Ritcey, and David Wheeler. 2014. Report of the Nova Scotia Independent Review panel on Hydraulic Fracturing. August 28, 2014. Available from: http://energy.novascotia.ca/sites/default/files/Report%20 of%20the%20Nova%20Scotia%20Independent%20Panel%20on%20 Hydraulic%20Fracturing.pdf

17   Michael Bradfield. 2014. Fracking – Dollars and Sense. Canadian Centre for Policy Alternatives – Nova Scotia, InFocus. October 20, 2014. Available from: https://www.policyalternatives.ca/publications/commentary/ fracking—dollars-and-sense

18   Michael Gorman. 2014. Nova Scotia fracking ban bill allows testing and research. The Chronicle Herald, September 30, 2014. Available from: http://thechronicleherald.ca/novascotia/1240152-nova-scotia-fracking-ban-bill-allows-testing-and-research

Chapter 10 – Poverty and Housing

1   Lesley Frank. 2013. The Nova Scotia Child Poverty Report Card, 2013. Canadian Center for Policy Alternatives, November 26, 2013. Available from: https://www.policyalternatives.ca/publications/reports/nova-scotia-child-poverty-report-card-2013

2   Province of Ontario. 2008. Breaking the cycle: Ontario's poverty reduction strategy. Available from: https://dr6j45jk9xcmk.cloudfront.net/.../3367/ breaking-the-cycle.pdf

3   Province of Newfoundland and Labrador. 2006. Reducing poverty: An action plan for Newfoundland and Labrador. Available from: http:// monctonhomelessness.org/documents/NL_poverty-reduction-strategy.pdf

4   Province of Nova Scotia. 2009. Speech from the throne. Delivered by the Hounourable Mayann E. Francis. Sept.17, 2009. Available from: http://0-fs01.cito.gov.ns.ca.legcat.gov.ns.ca/deposit/b10451638_Sep2009.pdf

5   Province of Nova Scotia. 2013. A housing strategy for Nova Scotia. Available from: https://novascotia.ca/coms/hs/Housing_Strategy.pdf

6   Province of Nova Scotia. 2009. Premier appoints ministerial assistants. News Release, June 29, 2009. Available from: http://novascotia.ca/news/ release/?id=20090629003

7   United Nations High Commission for Human Rights. 1966. International Convention on Economics, Social and Cultural Rights. Available from: http://www.ohchr.org/en/professionalinterest/pages/cescr.aspx

8   For background on affordable housing, especially co-ops see:
• Leslie Cole. 2008. Under construction: A history of co-operative housing in Canada. Borealis Press, Nepean, Ontario.
• Anthony Pitt. 1994. Co-operative housing: The social imperative. MA Thesis, Saint Mary's University, Halifax, Nova Scotia. Available from: http://www.library2.smu.ca/handle/01/22199
• Sharon Chisholm. 2003. Affordable housing in Canada's urban communities: A literature review. Canada Mortgage and Housing

Corporation Research Report. Available from: http://publications.gc.ca/
collections/collection_2011/schl-cmhc/nh18-1/NH18-1-2-2003-eng.pdf

9   Province of Nova Scotia. 2013. A housing strategy for Nova Scotia.
Available from: https://novascotia.ca/coms/hs/Housing_Strategy.pdf

10   What our government was supporting was exactly the discredited high-
rise housing projects of the 1960s that have been so problematic in other
cities, especially Toronto. *See:* Laurie Monsebraaten. 2014. Highrise
hell for lower income families in Toronto. Toronto Star, March 14, 2014.
Available from: http://www.thestar.com/news/gta/2014/03/12/
highrise_hell_for_lowincome_families_in_toronto.html

Chapter 11 – Legislation: It's What We Do

1   Charles Dickens. 1842. American notes. Chapman & Hall, London, UK.

2   Hay Island is designated a wilderness area under the *Wilderness Areas
Protection Act*, SNS 1998, c. 27. Available from: http://nslegislature.ca/
legc/statutes/wildarea.htm

3   *See:* The Canadian Press. 2013. Nova Scotia does U-turn on in-store
U-Vint operators. January 31, 2013. Available from: http://www.cbc.ca/
news/canada/nova-scotia/nova-scotia-does-u-turn-on-in-store-u-vint-
operators-1.1352134

4   Nova Scotia Legislature. 2010. *Internal Trade Agreement Implementation
Act.* Available from: http://nslegislature.ca/index.php/proceedings/bills/
internal_trade_agreement_implementation_act_amended_bill_55

5   *See:* Brian Flinn. 2007. Bid collapses. Daily News, March 9, 2007.

6   Canada's Atlantic Gateway. Available from: http://atlanticgateway.gc.ca/

7   Nova Scotia Legislature, Hansard. November 24, 2008. p. 6324 ff. Available
from: http://nslegislature.ca/index.php/proceedings/hansard/C49/60_2_
house_08nov24/#H[Page%206324]

Chapter 12 – Putting Neighbourhoods at Risk

1   Province of Nova Scotia. 1998. *Municipal Government Act.* Available from:
http://nslegislature.ca/legc/statutes/municipal%20government.pdf

2   Province of Nova Scotia. 2008. Halifax Regional Municipality Charter.
Available from: http://nslegislature.ca/legc/statutes/halifax%20
regional%20municipality%20charter.pdf

3   *See*: Elizabeth Pacey. 1979. The battle of Citadel Hill. Lancelot Press,
Hantsport, Nova Scotia.

4   *See*: Peter Clancey, James Bickerton, Rodney Haddow, and Ian Stewart.
2000. The Savage years: The perils of reinventing government in Nova
Scotia. Formac Publishing, Halifax, Nova Scotia; particularly Chapter 8: The
dangers of municipal reform in Nova Scotia.

5   Nova Scotia Legislature. 2008. Bill 138: *Municipal Government Act.*
Available from: http://nslegislature.ca/legc/bills/60th_2nd/1st_read/
b138.htm

6   *See*: Halifax Regional Municipality. RP+5. Available from: http://www. halifax.ca/planhrm/RP5.php

7   An R-1 zone is a "single family dwelling zone," intended for such residences and related facilities.

8   An R-2 zone is a "two-family dwelling zone," in which duplexes and three-unit dwellings are permitted in addition to all R-1 buildings.

9   Nova Scotia Legislature. 2008. Bill 179: *An Act Respecting the Halifax Regional Municipality.* Available from: http://nslegislature.ca/legc/PDFs/bills/2008/b179.pdf

10 Nova Scotia Legislature. 2008. Bill 181: HRM by Design. Available from: http://nslegislature.ca/legc/bills/60th_2nd/1st_read/b181.htm

11 Nova Scotia Legislature, Hansard. November 24, 2008. p. 6324–6332. Available from: http://nslegislature.ca/index.php/proceedings/hansard/C49/60_2_house_08nov24/#H[Page%206324]

12 Roger Taylor. 2014. Architect builds case for growth. The Chronicle Herald, June 13, 2014. Available from: http://thechronicleherald.ca/business/1214656-taylor-architect-builds-case-for-growth

13 Originally introduced as Bill 160 in the fall of 2012, the legislation was reintroduced in the spring of 2013 as Bill 83, which amends Chapter 39 of the Halifax Regional Municipality Charter. Available from: http://nslegislature.ca/index.php/proceedings/bills/halifax_regional_municipality_charter_amended_-_bill_83

14 *See*: Halifax Regional Municipality. 2012. Proposed built form and land use, Young Street. Available from: http://www.halifax.ca/PlanHRM/documents/Youngrobieboards_000.pdf

15 Elderkin v Nova Scotia (Service and Municipal Affairs), 2012 NSSC 61. Available from: http://caselaw.canada.globe24h.com/0/0/nova-scotia/supreme-court-of-nova-scotia/2012/02/09/elderkin-v-nova-scotia-service-and-municipal-relations-2012-nssc-61.shtml

Chapter 13 – Electoral Boundaries

1   J. Colin Dodds. 2002. Just boundaries: Recommendations for effective representation for the people of Nova Scotia. The final report of the Nova Scotia Electoral Boundaries Commission. Available from: http://0-fs01.cito.gov.ns.ca.legcat.gov.ns.ca/deposit/b10097223.pdf

2   *See:* Table 1 in Appendix 5.

3   Teresa MacNeil. 2012. Revised Interim Report, July 20, 2012. Nova Scotia Electoral Boundaries Commission. Available from: http://0-fs01.cito.gov.ns.ca.legcat.gov.ns.ca/deposit/b10651111.pdf

4   Teresa MacNeil. 2012. Toward fair and effective representation, September 24, 2012. Nova Scotia Electoral Boundaries Commission. Available from: http://0-fs01.cito.gov.ns.ca.legcat.gov.ns.ca/deposit/b10653107.pdf

Chapter 14 – Real Accomplishments

1   Nova Scotia Legislature, Hansard. December 5, 2012. p. 4871. Available from: http://nslegislature.ca/index.php/proceedings/hansard/C89/house_12dec05/#HPage4871

2   D.G. McNeil, Jr. 2013. New tools to hunt new viruses. New York Times. May 27, 2013. Available from: http://www.nytimes.com/2013/05/28/health/new-tools-to-hunt-new-viruses.html

3   Jacques R. Lapointe. 2009. Pandemic preparedness. Office of the Auditor General of Nova Scotia, Halifax, Nova Scotia. Available from: http://oag-ns.ca/index.php/reports-by-department?task=document.viewdoc&id=938

4   Corpus Sanchez International Consultancy. 2007. Changing Nova Scotia's healthcare system: Creating sustainability through transformation. Available from: https://novascotia.ca/health/reports/pubs/Provincial_Health_Services_Operational_Review_Report.pdf

5   John Ross. 2010. The patient journey through emergency care in Nova Scotia: A prescription for new medicine. Available from: http://novascotia.ca/dhw/publications/Dr-Ross-The-Patient-Journey-Through-Emergency-Care-in-Nova-Scotia.pdf

6   Province of Nova Scotia. 2010. Better care sooner: The plan to improve emergency care. Available from: http://novascotia.ca/dhw/publications/Better-Care-Sooner-plan.pdf

7   See: Bob Rae. 2006. From protest to power: Personal reflections on a life in politics. McClelland and Stewart, Toronto, Ontario.

8   Graham Steele. 2014. What I learned about politics: Inside the rise – and collapse – of Nova Scotia's NDP government. Nimbus Publishing, Halifax, NS.

9   Bill Black. 2014. Steele's book illuminating, but NDP had other flaws. The Chronicle Herald, September 12, 2014. Available from: http://thechronicleherald.ca/opinion/1236080-black-steele-s-book-illuminating-but-ndp-had-other-flaws

10   Nova Scotia Legislature. 2012. *Environmental Goals and Sustainability Act.* Available from: http://nslegislature.ca/legc/statutes/environmental%20goals%20and%20sustainable%20prosperity.pdf

11   United Nations. 1992. Rio Declaration on environment and development. Available from: http://www.jus.uio.no/lm/environmental.development.rio.declaration.1992/portrait.a4.pdf

12   Province of Nova Scotia. 2012. Marine renewable energy strategy. Available from: http://energy.novascotia.ca/sites/default/files/Nova-Scotia-Marine-Renewable-Energy-Strategy-May-2012.pdf

13   See: Province of Nova Scotia. 2013. Nova Scotia's jobs and building plan: 2013–2014 Capital Plan. Available from: http://www.novascotia.ca/finance/docs/Capital_Plan_2013-14.pdf

14   Nova Scotia Department of Mines and Energy. 1982. Uranium in Nova
     Scotia: A background summary for the uranium inquiry. Nova Scotia.
     Report 82-7. Available from: http://novascotia.ca/natr/meb/data/
     pubs/82re07/report_me_1982-7.pdf

15   *See*: Donna E. Smyth. 1986. Subversive elements. Women's Press, Toronto,
     Ontario.

16   Robert J. McCleave. 1985. Report of the Commission of Inquiry on Uranium.
     Province of Nova Scotia, Open File Report ME 612. Available from: https://
     www.novascotia.ca/natr/meb/data/pubs/ofr/ofr_me_612.pdf

17   Nova Scotia Legislature. 1994–1995. *Environment Act.* Available from:
     http://nslegislature.ca/legc/statutes/environment.pdf

18   Spraytech v. Town of Hudson. 2001. 19 MPLR (3d) 1. Available from:
     http://www.canlii.org/en/ca/scc/doc/2001/2001scc40/2001scc40.pdf

Chapter 15 – A Taste of Bitterness: Internal Dissent

1   Paola Loriggio. 2014. Andrea Horwath blasted in letter from 'deeply
     distressed' NDP stalwarts for party's 'moderate right-wing program.'
     National Post, May 23, 2014. Available from: http://news.nationalpost.
     com/2014/05/23/andrea-horwath-blasted-in-letter-from-deeply-
     distressed-ndp-stalwarts/

2   Graham Steele. 2014. What I learned about politics: Inside the rise – and
     collapse – of Nova Scotia's NDP government. Nimbus Publishing, Halifax,
     Nova Scotia. p. 177.

Chapter 16 – Air War, Ground War: Year Four – Into the Election

1   Lysiane Gagnon. 2013. Quebec's Liberal 'rebirth' is just a PQ fade. The
     Globe and Mail, May 15, 2013. Available from: http://www.vigile.net/
     Quebec-s-Liberal-rebirth-is-just-a

2   Paul MacEwan. 1976. Miners and steelworkers: Labour in Cape Breton.
     Samuel Stevens Hakkert and Company, Toronto, Ontario.

3   CBC News. 2013. N.S. cabinet minister resigns after bathroom fight. May
     10, 2013. Available from: http://www.cbc.ca/news/canada/nova-scotia/n-
     s-cabinet-minister-resigns-after-bathroom-fight-1.1344073

4   *See*: Eva Hoare. 2013. Earle leaves NDP over handling of Home case. May 9,
     2013. The Chronicle Herald. Available from: http://thechronicleherald.ca/
     novascotia/1128701-earle-leaves-ndp-over-handling-of-home-case

5   Corporate Research Associates. 2013. NS Liberals widen lead although
     many voters still undecided. June 10, 2013. http://cra.ca/wp-content/
     uploads/2013/06/13-2-NS-Press-Release.pdf

6   Electricity Marketplace Governance Committee. 2002. Final Report.
     Province of Nova Scotia. Available from: http://www.scotianwindfields.ca/
     sites/default/files/publications/emgcfinalreport.pdf

7   Sara Wuite, Christine Saulnier, and Stella Lord. 2013. Cornerstone compromised: A critical analysis of changes to special needs assistance in Nova Scotia. Canadian Centre for Policy Alternatives, July 17, 2013. Available from: https://www.policyalternatives.ca/publications/reports/cornerstone-compromised

8   John Hugh Edwards. 2012. Provincial department treated Talbot House shamefully. Letter to the Editor, Cape Breton Post. Available from: http://www.capebretonpost.com/Opinion/Letters-to-the-Editor/2012-07-20/article-3035268/Provincial-department-treated-Talbot-House-shamefully/1

9   Public Accounts Committee. 2012. Hansard for January 18, 2012. Available from: http://nslegislature.ca/index.php/committees/committee_hansard/C7/pa2012jan18

10   The Canadian Press. 2012. Dexter shrugs off Epstein's criticism of auditor general. The Chronicle Herald, January 19, 2012. Available from: http://thechronicleherald.ca/novascotia/53741-dexter-shrugs-epsteins-criticism-auditor-general

11   Frances Willick. 2013. N.S. requests halt to school closures, reviews. The Chronicle Herald, April 3, 2013. Available from: http://thechronicleherald.ca/novascotia/1120888-ns-requests-halt-to-school-closures-reviews

12   CBC News. 2013. Nova Scotia to fund sex-reassignment surgery: Reversal of government's previous stand on the issue. June 12, 2013. Available from: http://www.cbc.ca/news/canada/nova-scotia/nova-scotia-to-fund-sex-reassignment-surgery-1.1399700

13   Haley Ryan. 2013. 'Big surprise' for advocates as province to start funding gender reassignment surgery. Metro, June 12, 2013. Available from: http://metronews.ca/news/halifax/703972/province-announces-they-will-start-funding-gender-reassignment-surgery/

14   David Jackson. 2013. Four more years? Pundits agree NDP struggled in areas of economic development, environment. The Chronicle Herald, June 7, 2013. Available from: http://thechronicleherald.ca/novascotia/1134478-four-more-years

15   Marilla Stephenson. 2013. NDP woes raise Dexter question. The Chronicle Herald, June 11, 2013. Available from: http://thechronicleherald.ca/opinion/1134863-stephenson-ndp-woes-raise-dexter-question

16   Michael Gorman. 2013. Steele: N.S. finances on track, surplus hits $18.3 m. The Chronicle Herald, August 19, 2013. Available from: http://thechronicleherald.ca/novascotia/1148519-steele-ns-finances-on-track-surplus-hits-183m

17   ThreeHundredEight.com. Available from: http://www.threehundredeight.com/

18   Nova Scotia Legislature, Hansard. November 8, 2011, p. 3329. Available from: http://nslegislature.ca/index.php/proceedings/hansard/C81/house_11nov08/#HPage3329

19   Nova Scotia Legislature, Hansard. April 24, 2013, p. 1320. Available from: http://nslegislature.ca/index.php/proceedings/hansard/C90/house_13apr24/#HPage1320

20   Nova Scotia Legislature, Hansard. November 14, 2012, p. 3734, Available from: http://nslegislature.ca/index.php/proceedings/hansard/C89/house_12nov14/#HPage3734; and
December 5, 2012, p. 4952. Available from: http://nslegislature.ca/index.php/proceedings/hansard/C89/house_12dec05/#HPage4952

21   J.J. Grant. 2013. Turning the corner to a better future: Speech from the Throne, 2013. March 26, 2013. Available from: http://0-fs01.cito.gov.ns.ca.legcat.gov.ns.ca/deposit/b10451638_Mar2013.pdf

22   Parker Donham. 2013. The Contrarian, October 1, 2013. Available from: http://contrarian.ca/

Chapter 17 – Picking Up The Pieces

1   Michael Gorman. 2013. Now what? Dexter takes full blame. The Chronicle Herald, October 9, 2013.

2   Jane Taber. 2013. Dexter doles out blame after stunning N.S. election loss. The Globe and Mail, October 20, 2013. Available from: http://www.theglobeandmail.com/news/politics/dexter-doles-out-blame-after-stunning-ns-election-loss/article14956112/

3   Adrian Dix. 2013. Full text of Adrian Dix resignation statement. The Globe and Mail, September 18, 2013. Available from: http://www.theglobeandmail.com/news/british-columbia/full-text-of-adrian-dix-resignation-statement/article14403888/

List of Appendicies

Photo and Illustration Credits

Stephen Archibald: p. 46
Communications Nova Scotia: pp. 63, 127, 256, 265, 303
Paul Darrow: p. 73
Elections Nova Scotia: pp. 248, 249
Howard Epstein (contributed): pp. 4, 9, 18, 20, 53, 55, 79, 80, 134, 218, 254, 320
Verne Equinox: p. 244
Mary Evans: back cover
Kathleen Flanagan: p. 120
David Hardie: p. 159
Joan Jessome (contributed): p. 261
Bruce MacKinnon: pp. 16, 58, 105
Christopher Majka: pp. 7, 35, 37, 39, 46, 60, 112, 122, 136, 141, 154, 155, 161, 162, 210, 253, 259, 270, 281, 305, 310, 312, 321
Dan Morton: p. 319
Nova Scotia Legislature: pp. 51, 219, 234
Nova Scotia NDP: pp. 124, 229, 132, 172
Cheryl Ozon: p. 149
Chris Reardon: p. 49
Alice Reed: front cover
Douglas Ruck (contributed): p. 262
Jamie Simpson: p. 139
Lenore Zann (contributed): p. 319

Index